SPORT AND THE LAW

THE SCOTS PERSPECTIVE

SPORT AND THE LAW

THE SCOTS PERSPECTIVE

Edited by William J Stewart

T&T CLARK
EDINBURGH
2000

T&T CLARK LTD
59 GEORGE STREET
EDINBURGH EH2 2LQ
SCOTLAND

First published 2000

ISBN 0 567 00563 1

British Library Cataloguing-in-Publication Data.
A catalogue record for this book is available from the British Library.

Typeset by STM Typesetting, Glasgow
Printed and bound by MPG Books, Bodmin

PREFACE

Compile a list of things which do not sit well together. Readily would spring to mind oil and water, chalk and cheese, cats and dogs, malt whisky and lemonade. Add to that, sport and law. And yet, ever increasingly, these two apparently unsuitable bedfellows, are finding themselves locked in an uneasy embrace. Today, in our society, sport commands such a prominent profile, and is so integrally linked with high finance and big business, that I suppose it was inevitable that the lawyers would get their hands on it. And rightly so, in my view. As an example, in football, the *Bosman* decision (discussed in detail in Chapter 5) has had a major impact on all levels of the game not only in the United Kingdom but also throughout Europe.

So, be it football, tennis, golf, athletics, to name but a few, we must recognise that the leading participants command such enormous salaries and have such earning potential that contract disputes, tax problems and investment management are now more widely discussed than the performance of the referee. (I never thought I would see the day when I would witness two professional football players discussing the Budget implications with a degree of comprehension and acuity, which would make the average accountant blush!) However, there is another side of the coin and it is that with success and public image, comes responsibility. Of course we expect our sportsmen and women to set the right example: to play by the rules, not to cheat, not to take performance-enhancing drugs. I do not suggest that we demand they live by some theoretical moral code. Sportsmen and women are human, after all. They make mistakes. They have failings. But young people seek role models, need role models. They are entitled to be encouraged and inspired, not let down or betrayed.

And the players must also comply with the law. This is especially important in our two leading team sports, football and rugby. We have seen examples of sportsmen from each code falling foul of the law as a result of acts of violence. This led to suggestions that the law had no place in sport as if it was somehow divorced from the rest of society and entitled to special treatment. This view is unjustified and unsupportable. In the nature of contact sports, acts are committed which would be illegal if they took place on the street. But there is, and must be, a boundary between the rules of the game and the rule of the law. Let me give you an obvious example. If a football player grabs the corner flag and pursues an opponent across the pitch in order to whack him with it, that would clearly be an assault. It would be ridiculous to suggest that this should be ignored just because it occurred during a game. But the difference between a bad tackle and something which amounts to an attack, is much harder to define. The relevant sporting authorities must of course be seen to deal firmly and effectively with acts which are clearly outwith the scope of the rules.

However, these disciplinary procedures must themselves be conducted in a way which are consistent with the basic principles of justice. Proper notice of the allegation, time to prepare a defence if so advised, legal or other representation if appropriate and a hearing before an independent tribunal. Too often such matters have been conducted behind closed doors in a "Star Chamber" where contrition is the only permissible defence. Governing bodies, all too often, do not like the lawyers to interfere. It upsets their cosy world. They must now accept the law will intervene where there has been an apparent injustice and any body which ignores the concept of review by the courts, will do so at its peril. Accordingly, disciplinary procedures must be properly conducted and must be effective. Sanctions must be appropriate, must fit the offence and must be enforced. If this is done fairly, there is nothing to fear. Otherwise, the law will and should intervene. However, it is imperative that the law must be seen to act even handedly. I am of the view that too often it fails to do so. The law must be applied to all sports. Regularly at rugby matches, including internationals, players indulge in what could only be described as a brawl. Undoubtedly if this happened outside the ground the local constabulary would have no hesitation in arresting all concerned. However, the game's most eminent commentator has regularly dismissed this as the fellows "letting off a bit of steam"? I pose the question: "if this occurred in a Premier League football match, would the prosecuting authorities regard this as "letting off a bit of steam"?

The civil law has an ever increasing role to play in sport. Professional players are valuable commodities in their own right and if not fit for the job for which they were contracted, are a considerable drain on a club's resources. Let me illustrate. You sign a player for £3 million on a four year contract. He will be guaranteed a certain basic salary, bonus payments for a win or a draw, and further bonuses if the club wins a cup or league. There may be extra payments if he plays a certain number of matches. In his first game he is the victim of a vicious tackle which damages his cruciate ligament. He is unable to play for a year. The club loses out. It has to pay his wages, for no return, pay his share of team bonuses, and bear the cost of medical treatment. Insurance is not the answer. The cost of "comprehensive" insurance for a professional sportsman, let alone a team, is so astronomical as to be prohibitive. The player loses out. He has the pain of the injury and the recovery period and will be deprived of some of the bonuses to which he might have expected to be entitled. So who is to pay? I believe that it is inevitable that there will be an increase in civil cases where damages are sought for injury resulting from, for example, illegal challenges. The problem for the courts will be to define in some clear way the difference between a challenge which is merely bad as opposed to one which is reckless. To what extent is there a voluntary acceptance of the risks involved in a contact sport? On a view, bad challenges are part of the game. The classic player's response to being cautioned for a late tackle is, "I got there as soon as I could". To what extent can or should allowance be made for the heat of battle? If players do not show passion and total commitment, they are accused of taking the money and failing to play for the jerseys. These are all areas in which lawyers are going to play a vital role in the development and application of the law.

Traditionally, any doctor who finds himself, or herself, watching sport, runs the risk of becoming involved with the team. These professionals give their services freely and voluntarily, out of a desire to help and be involved. If they are wise, they will look at an injury, and if there is any doubt about the matter, take the player from the field and send him or her to hospital. These volunteers are vital to sport. They provide a service to the welfare of the players. They lend expertise to clubs and bodies who could not otherwise afford it. Sometimes this produces strange situations. I know, for example, of one eminent gynaecologist who regularly treats hulking great rugby players. For what, I have never dared ask. But then again, I suspect neither have they. With the advent of professionalism at all levels of sport, this will and, indeed, must change. The law, and the medical authorities, will always protect the Good Samaritan who renders first aid to an injured player. Sports medicine has greatly advanced in recent years. The days of the magic sponge are long gone. (Incidentally, for the benefits of anyone who has never played sport, there was nothing magic about it at all. The water was so freezing cold that it was preferable to get up and run around, rather than have it poured over you! The alternative was to lie there wet and shivering, while the trainer pushed and pulled your knee into weird and wonderful shapes. You were then invited to continue with the advice, "You'll be fine".) A doctor who makes a misdiagnosis, or fails to identify an injury or fails to recognise a potential injury, could cost his employer a considerable sum of money. Not just in the loss of one player, but because the absence of that individual could make all the difference between winning and losing a championship with all the financial rewards which that may involve.

Legal advisers to clubs and individuals must make the medical advisers aware of the responsibility placed upon them and their duty to advise the club of any potential problems. It is vital, nowadays, to keep detailed records of all medical and legal matters relating to players. This gives rise to another problem. What is the position with regard to confidentiality?

Here is a scenario. A player is contracted to the club. The doctor is employed by the club. The player is injured but fears that he may lose his place in the team if does not play. The doctor advises a two-week break. The player directly tells the doctor that he intends to play and that the doctor must not tell the manager. The doctor seeks legal advice.

He has duty to his employer but also has a duty to the player who is his patient. A half-fit player could cost the team dear. In these circumstances, I venture the opinion that the doctor's primary duty is to his employer.

What if the player is found to be HIV during a routine blood test? Leaving aside the effects on his own health there is also potential danger to others from a bleeding injury.

What if a player is injured, recovers, but there is a risk of permanent damage if he continues to play? Yes he will harm himself, but there is also a possibility that he will, in the future, seek to recover some form of compensation from his employers.

A related scenario, is the player who is injured but who is required to play for the sake of the team before he is fully recovered. Player A is 30, probably past his best, but Athletic Gorbals come in to the transfer market and offer £5 million for him. They also ask for his medical records, which will disclose that he has a damaged knee which could end his career at any moment. Neither player nor club wants to lose out.

These are but examples of types of problems which face those who act as legal advisers for clubs. There is no easy answer as to how to deal with them, but it is essential that the lawyer devises a set of clear procedures to be followed and ensures that the most accurate records are maintained. If medical advice is given to a player this must be detailed in his records and a copy given to the player. If there is any dispute as to the medical advice to be given, the doctor must be told to advise the player to seek independent advice and, if need be, the club should pay for it. Medical records are the property of the club and should not be released without specific written consent of the player. The player should be told that the records will be sent in their entirety. A photocopy should be kept for reference purposes. If a player wishes to continue his career with an injury which could lead to degenerative changes such as arthritis, the whole position should be set out for him in writing, he should be advised to seek independent legal and medical advice, and he should be asked to sign the appropriate discharge indicating that he understands what has been explained to him and that he accepts the future risks as being his.

The same must apply to a new player who has been identified as having a potential problem. This must be dealt with at the time and fully documented. The player should agree to accept the risk and this should be incorporated into his contract. If he refuses, let him go elsewhere.

Problems with work permits, visas, taxation, freedom to ply one's trade and play one's sport, are but the merest selection of the areas in which the "sports lawyer" will require expertise.

I have merely tried to highlight some of the many ways in which sport and the law have become mixed. It is a branch of the law which continues to grow and merely keeping pace with it takes an ever increasing part of my time. Sports law is new, growing and fascinating and I have no doubt that this book will serve as a most useful aid to those already involved with it. I hope that it will also serve to encourage other lawyers to take an active interest in a branch to our law which is as exciting as it is rewarding.

Donald R Findlay, QC
February 2000

CONTENTS

THE AUTHORS

Heather-Anne Barton graduated from the University of Dundee in 1988. After qualification she moved to London and whilst working as an in-house litigation solicitor she qualified as a solicitor in England and Wales. On her return to Glasgow she worked for 3 years with Scottish Media Group. Heather then joined Celtic plc and was subsequently appointed Company Secretary of Celtic plc and Club Secretary of Celtic Football Club in July 1998. She left Celtic in 1999 to join the SFA as Head of Legal/Special Projects.

Professor Lorne Crerar is the managing partner of Harper Macleod solicitors, Glasgow. He graduated as top private law student from the University of Glasgow in 1976. Lorne is listed in *Chambers Guide to the Legal Profession* as one of Scotland's very few "Sports Law Experts", and his firm's sports law practice group is recognised as the leading group in Scotland. He advises the Scottish Rugby Union on all matters to do with club management and sports discipline, and was recently appointed the first President of the Scottish Sports Law Forum at Napier University. He was one of four Legal Chairmen of the Rugby World Cup 1999 and is Chairman of the European Cup Discipline Appeals Committee.

Alistair Duff won a scholarship to the USA on academic and sporting grounds, and graduated from the University of Aberdeen. He has completed 13 marathons and has recently climbed Mount Everest. He is currently litigation/sports partner in Henderson Boyd Jackson. He has published over 27 articles which include the regular Scottish update to the *Sports and Law Journal*. He is a member, a Committee Member, and a member of the Advisory Board of the British Association for Sport and the Law. He is also one of the Scottish Arbiters for The Sports Dispute Resolution Panel Ltd.

Robin Fletcher is a solicitor at Ledingham Chalmers. He was educated at the University of Glasgow and Balliol College, University of Oxford. He is a member of the Forum for Sports Law at Napier University and his special professional interests include sports law.

Alan Grosset is the head of the sports law team of Morison Bishop & Co, where he is a partner. He is currently the vice chairman of the Scottish Sports Council; the vice chairman of the Confederation of British Sport; the Scottish director of the Sports Dispute Resolution Panel Limited; and a former chairman of the Scottish Sports Association.

Stephen Miller has been a partner in Harper MacLeod since 1994 and represents, amongst others, the Scottish Premier League. He is a member of the British Association of Sport and the Law and a Committee Member of the Employment Law Group. He is a member of the Forum for Sports Law at Napier University.

Philip Morris is a senior lecturer in business law and Head of the Business Law Group at the University of Stirling. His main academic interests are in the fields of Financial Regulations and Alternative Dispute Resolution. Philip is an Associate Member of the British and Irish Ombudsman Association, a member of the British Association of Sport and the Law and was recently elected onto the Society of Public Teachers of Law Consumer Law Panel. He is also a member of the Forum for Sports Law at Napier University.

Paul Spink is a lecturer in business law at the University of Stirling. His principal academic interests are in the broad fields of European Union Competition Law and legal regulation of sport. He has published widely in both fields.

William Stewart was formerly a senior lecturer at the University of Strathclyde. He is presently a partner in MacMillans, solicitors. He is a Scottish Premier League Commissioner; a member of the British Association for Sport and the Law; and a member of the Forum of Sports Law at Napier University. He is also the author of several legal texts, including *Skiing and the Law*. He has recently been appointed Appeals Chairman of the SFA.

David Williamson is a Solicitor-Advocate and a Fellow of the Chartered Institute of Arbitrators. He has been a litigation partner in Brodies, W.S. since 1976. He has regularly contributed to, and has convened, conferences on reparation topics, and was a tutor, and thereafter lecturer, in Civil Court Practice in Edinburgh University. He is a part-time Chairman of Employment Tribunals, and a member of the Criminal Injuries Compensation Board.

" Kirsty G Middleton, LLB (Hons), LLM, is a solicitor and lecturer in law at the University of Dundee where she teaches competition law and European law. Kirsty has published widely in the field of competition law and is currently writing a text on competition law and policy. She is a member of the Scottish Competition Law Group, the Scottish Lawyers European Group and Law Society of Scotland's International Relations Committee."

TABLE OF CASES

TABLE OF STATUTES

TABLE OF STATUTORY INSTRUMENTS

TABLE OF EUROPEAN LEGISLATION

INTRODUCTION

There is money in sport and those who are deprived of the money they expect are potential litigants—potential litigants who did not exist in an amateur era. It is a fact now that everyone has shown a need for legal advice: the player, the spectator, the fan, the club, the manager, the league, the association, the international association and the IOC. The contributors to this book have in some capacity or other been called upon to answer legal questions like these in the past, either in theory or practice. This book is a tangible attempt to bring together these efforts to produce a whole as great as its parts of value to all lawyers who are already involved in giving advice to sportsmen and sportswomen—or those who intend to start.

Unusually for a book written by a lawyer for lawyers, this book at least tries to be open to sportspeople who are starting to see the potential importance of law in the day to day conduct of sporting activities—even if only in the negative sense of trying not to get into expensive trouble. The more advanced sportspeople—the football club chairman is a good example—already know that advanced ability in sports law is good for the bank balance and have themselves created all sorts of exciting mechanisms in practical business contracting. The first two chapters hope to initiate those for whom law is as obscure as is the offside-rule in football to the non-footballer before they embark upon the other more detailed chapters which are written primarily for the lawyer (although written as clearly as possible so that they may well alert a club administrator or sportsman to his or her legal rights and duties).

While I discovered on publication of my *Skiing and the Law* (W. Green, 1986) that there were lawyers interested in sport about, this book grew out of the demand which appeared among lawyers interested in sport in Scotland which manifested itself in two conferences which I was privileged to convene at the request of the Law Society of Scotland in Stirling in 1994 and at Ibrox Park in 1999. At the first in 1994 it was clear there were a number of active sports lawyers and a number of people interested in pursuing this area of work. The "is there such a thing as sports law" debate had rather been treated as academic after JB Stewart of Heriott Watt had published his extremely helpful contribution to the *Stair Memorial Encyclopaedia*. By the 1999 Ibrox conference there were many more interested, many more with some active involvement and much more interest in the Universities. December 1999 saw the inaugural meeting of the Forum for Sports Law at the Law Department, Napier University. Its members include many (but not all!) of the leading practitioners from the solicitors branch and the bar and some active academics. It may well become the focus for more sustained development in the research, teaching and practice of sports law in Scotland in the next decade. Some of its members have contributed to this volume as have other lawyers from the pre-eminent sports law firms in Scotland. Leading Scots sports lawyers continue to agitate for a Scottish perspective within the British Association for Sport and the Law which itself has done so much for sports law in the UK and hence in Scotland.

I am grateful to Donald Findlay QC for supporting the Ibrox Conference and for revising his speech for inclusion as a preface to this volume.

It is a happy feature of this book (and contrary to the image that some of the public have of some lawyers) that all of the authors have donated all of their royalties to educational, sporting or charitable causes. Amateurs all—in the best sense.

The contributors did not have the benefit of the publication of Edward Grayson's third edition of *Sport and the Law* (Butterworths, 2000) nor the interesting new work by Lord Beloff and others, *Sport and the Law* (Hart, 1999). The law is intended to be stated as at January 2000. In that it is hoped that the book may fall into the hands of laymen, it must be made clear that this book does not seek to give legal advice as such and that it should not be relied upon in that way, the writers not assuming responsibility for any such reliance. I probably speak for all when I say that the proper course is to seek legal advice from a Scots lawyer, albeit it is hoped that a lay person having read this book will be much better placed to obtain good value legal services.

William J Stewart
Anderston, February 2000

1   LAW FOR THE SPORTSPERSON

William J Stewart*

The purpose of this chapter is to set out the basic matters which a non- **1-1**
legally qualified reader should know in order to understand the following
chapters. It should make sense to the ordinary sportsperson and the
administrator of a club or association. Its purpose is also to explain to the
sportsperson why a legal adviser cannot always just look up a book (even
this one) and say what the law decides on any particular question. Of
course, in the present age many people who are not lawyers know the basic
essentials of law as a result of universities teaching business law, and such
graduates will find much of this chapter "old hat".[1] The second chapter,
"Law for the Club", takes that rudimentary treatment one step further by
dealing with actual legal rules. Thereafter, the chapters assume a basic legal
knowledge and, while the text may be in places beyond the lay reader, it
should be of interest to those who have understood the first two chapters.

WHAT IS LAW?

Most people think that the law is what the Queen in Parliament says it is. **1-2**
This is not wrong—it is simply not the whole story. Another, most important, source of legal rules is the customary law and that, for practical purposes, is the body of decisions of the courts of law. Yet another source is the
legislation of the European Union. Finally, Scotland has an unusual
source—the writing of certain recognised legal writers from previous cen-
turies—called the institutional writers. Ordinary law books and legal
articles are very helpful to lawyers and often to judges but they are not the
law itself.

---

* The writer is grateful to Rod McKenzie, Harper McLeod, for commenting on an earlier draft
(the usual disclaimer applying) and to Kirsty Middleton for the short section on European Law.

[1] A good single source for a detailed treatment introducing the law of Scotland is Mays *et al*,
Scots Law—A Student Guide (T&T Clark, 2000). For an overview of Scots law and its position in
history and in the world, see Meston, Sellar and Cooper, *The Scottish Legal Tradition* (2nd edn:
Styles, SC; Saltire Society, 1991). A condensed statement of the bulk of the law of Scotland,
sufficient for practical daily use by lawyers, is available in one authoritative volume: Gloag &
Henderson, *Introduction to the Law of Scotland* (10th edn, 1995). Finally, lawyers and citizens
alike have access to a comprehensive and authoritative statement of all the law in the updated
multi-volume *Stair Memorial Encyclopaedia of the Laws of Scotland*.

Legislation

1-3   The basic form of law making, or legislation, is the Act of Parliament.[2] Normally Parliament is really changing the judge-made law or fixing a defect in it. Often, the need for legislation arises from political or economic or social pressure—that is what Parliament is there to respond to. A sporting example is the Fire Safety and Safety of Places of Sports Act 1987 by which Parliament amended the Safety of Sports Grounds Act 1975 as a result of the publication of reports following the Bradford fire disaster and the Heysell Stadium disaster.[3] As can be seen from the Table of Statutes, which is produced for the benefit of lawyers, there are a number of Acts of Parliament which relate to sport and are discussed in this book. The precise details of what it is that people must do are often set out in what is called "delegated legislation" which has the same force as an Act of Parliament. The most common type of delegated legislation is the statutory instrument.[4]

Case law

1-4   The way in which decisions of the court are the law of the land is a detailed and technical topic, but the essence of it is easily expressed. The law has always been there because it represents right conduct of the community. The judges declare what the law is on any particular case that comes before them because the parties to a case ask them to. Rather than consider every legal problem again and again, it is accepted that the records of previous decisions can rule on the law for later cases. The decision on a point of law (but not who was telling the truth or telling lies) is thus every bit as much law as what Parliament lays down in statute. There is another layer of complexity. Judges are human and make mistakes, so there is a right of appeal against most judicial decisions. It makes sense, then, to hold that decisions of appeal courts should be followed rather than lower courts. The extent to which a decision is followed by a later court in a new case depends on the place in the appeal structure of the court in question, so a previous decision of the sheriff court is trumped by a decision of the Inner House of the Court of Session (the Scottish Court of Appeal) and that in turn is trumped by a decision of the House of Lords in a Scottish appeal. This evaluation of previous decisions (or precedents) is very much part of the lawyer's art. It is reflected in legal writing (such as the following chapters of this book) where, in stating the law, the legal writer is trying to assess, in advance, the attitude a court would take when confronted with a number of previous decisions on slightly different points and from courts at different levels. So, if the question is asked of a lawyer by a footballer, "Can I make a gesture at the other side's fans if I score a goal?" the lawyer will have to scrutinise the decision of the court in *Jessop v Butcher*.[5] He is then likely to ask the footballer what kind of gesture he intends, how many fans will be there and

---

[2] Including, now, Acts of the devolved Parliaments in Scotland, Wales and Northern Ireland.

[3] The Popplewell Reports: Cmnd 9588 (1985); Cmnd 9710 (1985).

[4] *eg* Safety of Sports Grounds Regulations 1976 (SI 1976/1263).

[5] 1989 SLT 593.

whether the game is of the nature of a local derby where tempers are likely to be running high and fans easily incited. The layman must understand that there are sound reasons for a very good lawyer to say that the law is not clear—it may well depend upon a skilful interpretation of various levels of precedent from various jurisdictions. It is impossible for the layman fully to grasp that skill and so this topic is not explored further here. It is, of course, assumed that legal readers are in the same position as the "very good lawyer"!

The rule book

It should be mentioned that "the law" for many sports administrators will **1-5** be the rulebooks of their governing bodies. This for many practical purposes is the law. It might also be unknown to a legal adviser who is not active in sports law. The internal law should usually be brought to the attention of any lawyer consulted. Often the rule book will have the effect, by virtue of the law of contract, of creating a mini-legal system for those subscribing to it. The power of governing bodies to fine or expel members means that courses of action available in strict law to other commercial bodies may not be open to a sporting club for fear of infringing this "internal" law.

European law

European law is in its own sphere, superior to Scots law and the law of the **1-6** UK Parliament. The most famous sporting example is the case *ASBL Union Royale de Sociétés de Football Association and Others v Jean-Marc Bosman*,[6] which is discussed in detail in Chapter 5. Not only do the European Treaties rule over UK law in appropriate circumstances but the legislation of the European institutions can do so too.

European Community law is the body of law created by the three founding Treaties of the European Community. The Treaty of Paris (1951) established the European Coal and Steel Community (ECSC); and the two Treaties of Rome (1957) established the European Economic Community (EEC) and the European Atomic Energy Community (EAEC or Euratom). These three Communities are legally distinct. The terms "the Community" and "Community law" refer to any one of these Communities or the whole legal structure. "Community law", however, generally means the law of the EEC. This legal structure was amended by the Treaty of European Union (TEU) on 1 November 1993.[7] The TEU retitled the EEC the "EC". It also created a new constitutional legal order, the "European Union" (EU), which came into being in November 1993, is made up of 15 member states

---

[6] [1996] CMLR 645 (Case C-415/93).

[7] The Treaty of Amsterdam, which was concluded in 1997 and came into force on 1 May 1999, was supposed to have made radical changes to the institutional framework of the EC to prepare for enlargement. Instead, the Treaty will best be remembered for its changes to the numbering of the articles of the TEU and the EC Treaty. The chapter on European Community Law and Sport refers to the new numbering and indicates in parentheses the pre-Amsterdam numbering to avoid unnecessary confusion.

and consists essentially of three so-called pillars: the central pillar is existing Communities and their law, whereas the other two pillars comprise provisions on common foreign and security policy and provisions on co-operation in the fields of justice and home affairs. These three pillars form the foundations of the constitutional order of the EU. The latter two pillars do not form part of Community law. This means that they do not fall within the jurisdiction of the European Court of Justice. Moreover, although the Community institutions are the same for the EU, their powers are distinct depending upon whether they are acting under the non-Community pillars of the Union or the EC Treaties. Community law is part of the law of the United Kingdom and may be enforced in the domestic courts.

1-7   There are five Community institutions: the European Parliament, the Council of Ministers, the European Commission, the European Court of Justice and the Court of Auditors. The principal EC institutions responsible for the adoption of legislation in the Community are the Commission, the Council and the Parliament. Of these, the Commission is the most powerful, with responsibility for initiation and enforcement of Community legislation. The European Court of Justice (ECJ), to which the Court of First Instance is attached, is the judicial arm of the EC. Decisions of the ECJ are binding on the national courts. The ECJ consists of 15 judges assisted by nine Advocates General. The function of the Advocate General in each case is to assist the Court by providing an impartial and independent opinion. The opinion is not binding on the Court but is usually highly persuasive.

The founding treaties provide the overall framework to achieve the objectives of the EC and are regarded as primary legislation. The Treaties are, however, amplified by secondary legislation which is passed by the institutions of the Community. There are various forms of Community legislation. A regulation is equivalent to an Act of the UK Parliament in effect. Thus a Community regulation is binding in its entirety and is directly applicable in the member states. It therefore requires no implementation and has immediate legal effect in the member states. Directives, on the other hand, do require further implementation and are addressed to the member states. The means by which a directive is to be transposed into national law is therefore left to the member states. Individuals may rely upon a directive before a national court, although the right is derived from the national implementing measure and not from the directive. A decision of the European Commission also has immediate legal effect and requires no implementing measure. Decisions are more limited in their application than regulations and are only binding upon those to whom they are addressed.

1-8   Community law is capable of creating rights and obligations enforceable before national courts: for example, a number of articles of the Treaty and a large proportion of Community legislation. Where a Community measure creates such rights and obligations it is said to have direct effect. Community law also takes precedence over national law, known as the doctrine of primacy (or supremacy). In the event of conflict with national law, Community law will be supreme.

In addition to the EC and the EU, there is the European Economic Area (EEA) which was created in 1994 and provides for free-movement provisions similar to those in the EEC Treaty (for example, goods, persons, services, capital) and a similar competition policy. Initially there were six members. Austria, Finland and Sweden left to join the EC in 1995, leaving Norway, Liechtenstein and Iceland. The law of the EEA forms part of the Community law and so, in turn, part of the law of the United Kingdom.

The European Court of Human Rights and related institutions, however, should not be confused with the EC. The European Convention on Human Rights (ECHR) was drawn up in 1950 under the auspices of the Council of Europe. The Commission and the Court of Human Rights sit in Strasbourg and have jurisdiction to adjudicate on alleged violations of the Convention. They have no competence under European law and are not institutions of the European Community. The ECHR was recently incorporated into UK law by the Human Rights Act 1998.

THE DIVISIONS OF LAW

It is impossible here to explain why law is divided into various categories **1-9** and why it is divided into the categories that it is. Indeed lawyers often argue about these divisions. For the purposes of this book, however, the main divisions that affect most legal decisions encountered by the sportsperson and discussed in this book can be simply set out. This is, however, a practical exposition and is not intended to be complete.

Criminal law

This is the body of law which tells the subject what he must not do or else **1-10** face the wrath of the state. While there may be a victim, in the Scots system the victim has no real part in the process of prosecution of the wrongdoer save as a witness. In Scotland the victim cannot "drop the charges". There are some criminal offences laid down by statute, such as drinking in a football stadium,[8] but very many, like assault, are laid down by the custom enshrined in judicial decision. Perhaps the most famous sporting examples of recent years are the convictions of the Rangers players Terry Butcher and Chris Woods for breach of the peace (*Butcher v Jessop*[9]) and of the Rangers player Duncan Ferguson for assault. A more routine example is the prosecution of youngsters for playing football in the streets.[10] A person who is the victim of a crime can usually sue for damages in a civil court and may be entitled to compensation under the Criminal Injuries Compensation Scheme. As will be seen below, particularly in the chapter on football, the relationship between crime and sport is live.

Public law

Public law includes criminal law but also other relationships between the **1-11** subject and the state. In English law, as it relates to sport, this distinction is very important because judicial review of decisions—including decisions of

---

[8] See para 2–36 below.

[9] 1989 SLT 593.

[10] *Cameron v Normand* 1992 SCCR 866.

sporting bodies—is restricted to cases with a public law element.[11] However, while Scots law recognises a body of public law, it will be seen in Chapter 3 that the distinction is not crucial in relation to the practical matter of deciding which decisions can or cannot be reviewed.

Private law

1-12 This is the law between one citizen and another (whether individuals or corporations). The main divisions which are relevant to this study are as follows.

Contract[12]

1-13 In Scots law, unlike English law, promises as well as agreements will be enforced. This is so whether they are bilateral, with two sides to the deal—such as sale, which has a seller and a purchaser—or unilateral, a simple undertaking by one party, given to another either with or without consideration. Some contracts require writing for their constitution—for example, those for buying a house. Most others do not. This is the general principle and covers many "deals". The "deal" must, however, be intended to have legal effect and so some sporting deals—such as to play football with your pals on Friday night—are not enforceable. Some put this point differently and say that an agreement will be a legal contract if there is money or property involved—and so, if Rangers agree to play football with Celtic that will be enforceable.[13]

Lawyers deal with people. But they have invented legal persons—the most famous is the limited company. However, many clubs and associations are still unincorporated. They are no more than a group of people getting together for a special purpose. For the local stamp club which owns no property and enters into no agreements this is ideal. However, many unincorporated bodies eventually gain property and webs of agreements often related to a successful social club—junior football clubs are an example. The law as it applies to such clubs and the office bearers is difficult. It is the law of contract which is usually called into play to deal with such problems rather than company law.

Mostly lawyers and clients deal with actual contracts. Unsurprisingly, similar contracts are treated in the same way under a proper system of justice and so, over time, contracts are treated according to their subject-matter. Add to that the fact that Parliament may legislate (and does) for some contracts but not for others and it can be seen that in practice there is really a law of contracts. Some contracts of specific relevance to sport are introduced in the next chapter.

Delict[14]

1-14 The law imposes duties on people regardless of their will. So it is a breach

---

[11] *R v Disciplinary Committee of the Jockey Club, ex parte HH the Aga Khan* [1993] 1 WLR 909.

[12] SE Woolman, *Contract* (2nd edn, 1994).

[13] An untelevised friendly might test the theory.

[14] WJ Stewart, *Delict* (3rd edn, 1998).

of obligation to run a person down by driving without keeping a good lookout. There follows a selection of duties laid down by law which are relevant to one or more of the topics in this book.

Nuisance One must use one's property in such a way as not to cause harm **1-15** to others' use of their land. Land use should not be more than is reasonably tolerable. The court will restrain offending use by interdict. Where damage arises it may be compensated for irrespective of negligence but on proof of the intolerable test—which is an objective one. This obligation is important to sport in that many sports are noisy or attract noisy crowds. Others, like golf, can involve annoying projectiles.[15]

Assault The intentional infliction of harm on another is actionable even if **1-16** done in a spirit of playful fun. Excessive lack of care—which might be categorised as gross recklessness—is a sufficient mental element to constitute the wrong. The application of this delict to contact sports is obvious. Factual situations will raise the possibility of negligence where there has only been inadvertence.

Negligence[16] The law has reached a state where it can generally be said that **1-17** a person must take reasonable care for the physical safety of others where he can reasonably have foreseen when directing his mind to his activities and inactivities that a failure to take such care would cause harm of the kind which has resulted. There are whole books explaining this apparently simple idea of citizenship or civilisation. The key factors at a practical level are as follows. The duty is not one of insurance—only of the kind of care as would be taken by a reasonable person in the position of the defender at the time the injury took place. The mistake must have caused the loss—not just as part of the sequence of events but in a way that an ordinary person would say meant that the wrongdoer was responsible for the event. For example, it may have been because of ice that a car slid into a pedestrian but the legal cause may be that the driver, knowing of the ice, drove far too fast. Unforeseeable events are unlikely to attract liability unless part of a matrix of circumstances which are foreseeable. So if injury by burning is foreseeable, a burning injury by an unforeseeable explosion can infer liability.

There are advanced complexities dealing with unusual cases—cases where the mistake has been made by a public authority and cases where the loss is financial. In these and some other cases the wrongdoer may have made a mistake which has caused the pursuer a loss but there will be no compensation payable because the law may hold that in some cases the pursuer did not owe a duty to take care in the first place.

Employers' liability[17] *and the vicarious liability of employers*[18] Obviously sports **1-18**

---

[15] See the discussion in Chapter 10.

[16] *Stair Memorial Encyclopaedia,* Vol 15, paras 252–391.

[17] *Stair Memorial Encyclopaedia,* Vol 15, paras 331–350.

[18] *Stair Memorial Encyclopaedia,* Vol 15, paras 242 *et seq.*

clubs and similar organisations employ staff. The most famous footballers are employees of their clubs. The main common law duty is to take reasonable care for employees and over time this has been recognised to cover the provision of a safe system of work, safe fellow employees, safe plant and machinery. More recently it has been argued to include such things as protection from passive smoking and repetitive strain injury from typing. Acts of Parliament and legislation inspired by the European Union have provided many more detailed protections, many of which are discussed in more detail in Chapter 2, including the provision of work equipment and protection from injury in manual handling. Often these statutory duties are tougher than the common law standard of reasonable care—sometimes no excuse is permitted at all.

1-19 *Product liability*[19] Irrespective of any contract, the manufacturer of a dangerous product owes a duty to the ultimate consumer, a duty to take reasonable care to keep the consumer safe from physical injury—taking one landmark example, to keep snails out of opaque bottles. Furthermore, Parliament, following European legislation, imposes a duty on the producer of a product to supply goods which are not defective. Liability is for loss, injury or damage, but not for damage to the thing itself nor for cases of non-physical injury of a value less than £275. The legislation does not apply to damage to a product where it was not for private use.

Unjust enrichment[20]

1-20 The law provides a number of remedies which taken together can be said to prevent a person from gaining at the expense of another without a legal justification. If you sell a car you bought for £10,000 to another for £11,000 knowing it only to be worth £9,000 that is a good deal and you are not unjustifiably enriched; if a person sends you £1,000 instead of sending it to his friend then you are so enriched and it must be returned.[21] This area of law does not often arise in sports law but can be important where clubs run by amateurs accidentally or mistakenly pay money they should not, including taxes.[22]

Property law[23]

1-21 Scots law is still feudal although there are moves afoot to abolish this system. Even then, the system is at heart civilian and so ownership is the key concept. At present there may be real burdens—conditions attached to the use of the land—which prevent activity that might be of interest to clubs, such as the sale of alcohol. It does not arise often in advising sports clubs and bodies and when it does there are few specialities.

---

[19] *Stair Memorial Encyclopaedia,* Vol 15, para 196.

[20] *Stair Memorial Encyclopaedia,* Vol 15, paras 10–143; WJ Stewart, *Restitution* (1992; Supp 1995).

[21] Subject to a defence which is gaining more and more recognition—change of position.

[22] See para 1–29, n 46.

[23] *Stair Memorial Encyclopaedia,* Vol 18.

Family law

This topic is almost entirely unimportant in sports law, despite the many **1-22** references to the paternity of referees. Experience suggests that the main significance of sport in this area is as support for the ground of divorce at the instance of "golfing widows". It might also be of relevance in relation to eligibility to play for national teams as some nations spread their net ever wider in the search for talent.

The law of remedies

Scots law prides itself in favouring rights over remedies—where there is a **1-23** right there is a remedy—but the truth is that like any legal system there is a real resistance where the wrong remedy is used. The court will not allow a simple change of remedy when such difficulty arises: an action may have to be abandoned at great expense and the attempt made to raise another.

Some other important legal doctrines and rules

Prescription and limitation

The passage of time can extinguish a claim or allow the defender to have it **1-24** thrown out of court. The rules are so important and detailed that it would be dangerous to set them out in a book which may be read (and possibly misunderstood) by a layman. Legal advice is always needed.

Judicial Review[24]

This is a kind of a hybrid. In England the courts can review the decisions of **1-25** administrative bodies but only if their activities come within the sphere of public law. In Scotland an entirely different test of entitlement to review is used, allowing administrative decisions in both the public and private sphere to be challenged. Thus the Scottish sports administrator should be very wary of English texts or English-based advice.

Environmental law

Clearly, apart from the Hampden Roar,[25] football and rugby do not cause **1-26** major environmental disasters. Of the particular sports considered in this book, golf and skiing are good examples of cases where one man's meat is another's poison. The core legal regime, in this context, protecting the environment is that established by the Town and Country Planning Acts.[26] As a consequence, inquiries at various levels are likely to be held and have been held where it is hoped to build even more golf courses on the green

---

[24] Finch and Ashton, *Administrative Law* (Greens Concise Series, 1997). See Chapter 3 for an exposition of judicial review and sport in Scotland.

[25] Which is now something of a purr by former standards.

[26] See generally, N Collar, *Planning* (W Green, 2nd edn, 1999). A good treatment for the layman can be found in Poustie, Ross, Geddes and Stewart, *Hospitality and Tourism Law* (ITBA, 1999), Chapter 8.

belt or where lift tows are contemplated in the mountains.[27] Most other legal systems face similar problems. An interesting example from England is *R v Watford Borough Council, ex parte Incorporated West Hertfordshire Golf Club*,[28] in which the local authority for "environmental" or public reasons wanted the golf club to allow more public access and so refused to renew the club's lease. This represents the real tensions that exist in relation to sports facilities and golf clubs in particular. It also turns out to be an excellent example of judicial review, introduced above[29] and discussed in some detail below.[30] The club were able to have the decision quashed as being in breach of their legitimate expectations.

Employment and discrimination law

1-27 The ordinary law of contract applies to many of the important working relationships in sport—perhaps the one most frequently seen by the public is that of football manager. These contracts can be and are litigated in the ordinary courts.[31] There is also a substantial statutory code administered by the Employment Tribunals.[32]

Scotland, as with the rest of the United Kingdom, has laws against sex discrimination,[33] race discrimination[34] and disability discrimination.[35] These are very important in relation to sport. Participation in sport outwith some schools is voluntary—generally speaking we do not have to play games with people unless we want to. It is the cultural, political and economic importance that sport has accumulated that arguably gives the state a legitimate ethical right to intervene. There are no quotas and no positive discrimination. The physical aspects of most sports (invented by men) often mean that women (like feeble men) are excluded from competition (even with handicapping as in golf). So far as race is concerned, the state keeps clear where clubs restrict membership to a racial group otherwise than by colour.

Perhaps the most famous case in Scotland in recent years is *Graham v Hawick Common Riding Committee*.[36] The Hawick Common Riding is an annual event which takes place over a period of about one month during

---

[27] The Cairngorm Ski Lift Company has recently been given permission to build a mountain railway after lengthy opposition from a number of conservation and related organisations.

[28] [1990] 1 EGLR 263.

[29] Para 1–11.

[30] Chapter 3.

[31] See, *eg*, *Macari v Celtic Football and Athletic Co Ltd* 2000 SLT 80. See para 8–31 below.

[32] See Chapter 2.

[33] Sex Discrimination Act 1975; Pannick, D, *Sex Discrimination in Sport* (1983).

[34] Race Relations Act 1976.

[35] Disability Discrimination Act 1995.

[36] 1998 SLT (Sh Ct) 42.

May and June. It commemorates a victory over an English war party shortly after the battle of Flodden in 1514. It also has the more common function of being a riding of marches to interrupt the operation of prescription. In modern times it involves dinners and functions. All the functions, even the riding about with the Cornet, were restricted to men only. It was held that the case was legally relevant in terms of the Sex Discrimination Act.

Tax

This is a speciality in which lawyers are often as actively involved as **1-28** accountants; it is not considered in detail in this book. The law is, in general, the same throughout the United Kingdom. This note simply seeks to point towards some practical issues which have arisen and to direct to further reading.[37] Club administrators should always seek professional advice on the tax implications of their activity. Although the Inland Revenue and the Customs and Excise are "the opposition" should it come to a dispute, they often provide helpful information and guidance leaflets on key topics and that service should be used. As Baldwin[38] puts it:

> In many cases volunteers have to deal with complex tax matters which are unfamiliar to them. They can often be tripped up by the myriad forms and numerous deadlines and often officers can be personally liable to substantial tax liabilities, interest and penalties. With the advent of self-assessment for both companies and individuals, the burden on the sporting tax payer is ever increasing.

So far as income tax and corporation tax are concerned, essentially sports people and sports clubs are charged like any other individual or enterprise. Unincorporated clubs are taxed like companies, save for internal transactions.[39]

Most professional sports people will pay Schedule E income tax through the PAYE scheme. Testimonial matches are a good example of how sports people can come into contact with the complexities of the tax system by accident. It was held in *Seymour v Reed*[40] that a benefit match for a cricketer was a gift from a generous appreciative public and not liable to tax. Where, however, the testimonial is provided for by contract on the basis of an automatic provision such as the passing of a certain number of years, this is likely to be taxable.[41] Moore suggests that benefit matches be organised by trustees instead of the club and that admission to the event should be by way of a small admission charge and a donation.[42]

---

[37] The best first port of call for the Scots lawyer is the updated *Stair Memorial Encyclopaedia*, Vol 19, paras 1296–1322. See also E Grayson, *Sport and the Law* (2nd edn, Butterworths, 1994), Chapter 14.

[38] R Baldwin, "Taxation and Sport" (1996) 4 (3) SLJ 95.

[39] Grayson, *Sport and the Law*, p 377. See *Carnoustie Golf Club v Inland Revenue* 1929 SLT 366.

[40] [1927] AC 554.

[41] *Davis v Harrison* [1927] 11 TC 707; *Moorhouse v Dooland* [1955] 1 All ER 93.

[42] Moore, *Sports Law and Litigation* (CLT, 1997), p 31.

1-29   Care has to be taken with terminal payments in sport as in other businesses. There are special provisions allowing "golden handshakes" to be
made tax free but these must be followed carefully or the payment may be
taxable.[43]

Money spent on football transfer fees would look like an expense to be
set against income to the layman. However, Boon has explained that as a
result of a standard issued by the Accounting Standards Board it is compulsory to capitalise such fees. The club can then depreciate this "intangible fixed asset", probably over the term of the contract.[44]

Football and other sports where players are bought and sold can raise
unusual problems for auditors and as it is the owners who have to live with
these it might well be important that the proper view is taken of preparing
the accounts—undue conservatism might adversely affect the view of the
organisation with banks etc.[45]

Value added tax is relevant to sportsmen and sporting organisations.
Non-profit-making sports clubs and charitable organisations are exempted
from charging VAT on services closely linked to sport or physical education—that is, not just membership fees.[46] Other clubs and professional
operations pay VAT on most things—even transfer fees.[47] Programmes are
zero rated as reading matter and this explains the curious practice sometimes encountered of entrance being by programme only. The pie and
Bovril are only zero rated if they are sold for consumption on premises but
for these purposes a grandstand can constitute the premises.[48] For an interesting Scots case on VAT, see the note below.[49]

---

[43] *Shilton v Wilmshurst* [1991] 3 All ER 148.

[44] G Boon, "Capitalisation of Purchased Football Player Registrations. The Effect of FRS 10:
Goodwill and intangible assets (FRS 10) on football club accounting" (1998) 6 (1) SLJ 39. He
points out that capitalisation is optional for "home grown" talent that comes up through the
youth squad.

[45] G Boon, "Is Football a Going Concern?" (1994) 2 (3) SLJ 24. See also Gerry Boon and Dale
Thorpe, "Going concern considerations in relation to football clubs" (1995) 3 (1) SLJ 44.

[46] See E Virgo, "Sport Clubs and VAT: the correction of long-standing errors" (1994) 2 (2) SLJ 17,
citing *inter alia*, Art 13A.1.(m) of the European Council 6th Directive on VAT, 17 May 1977, VAT
notice 701/45/94. The UK Government had to make retrospective correction. See, generally,
R Farrell, "VAT and Amateur Sport" (1993) 1 (1) SLJ 22, Alistair Duff, "Windfall or Not?" (1995)
3 (1) SLJ 33, M Clifford and G Small, "Repayment of VAT – the English position" (1995) 3 (3)
SLJ 26.

[47] Moore reports that the transfer of Alan Shearer from Blackburn to Newcastle scored the
Government £2.25 million.

[48] *Stair Memorial Encyclopaedia*, Vol 19, para 1316.

[49] See Chapter 8. *Celtic Football & Athletic Co Ltd v Customs and Excise Commissioners* [1983] STC
470.

2   LAW FOR THE CLUB SECRETARY

Heather-Anne Barton*

This chapter is written from the perspective of the management of major **2-1** commercial football clubs. Conditions vary across the range of football clubs and across sports. However, many of the issues canvassed in this chapter will be of interest to junior or amateur football clubs or to other commercial sports undertakers like rugby.

There is a general misconception that football clubs work for only 90 minutes on a Saturday and that staff members have summer holidays as long as those of school teachers. Nowadays, football clubs are mature businesses in areas including hospitality, retail and security, with the core integral element being the football squad. These businesses interface with the general public in the form of supporters, diners, visitors and consumers on a daily basis, and as a result many areas of law have major impacts on the successful running of a football club. Equally as important is the club's responsibility towards its staff members to ensure that a safe and secure place of work is provided and that all employees' rights are observed and protected.

The type of organisation

A sports club can be simply an individual's trade, a voluntary association, **2-2** a partnership or a limited company.[1] It might also be a charity. As an example, the club of which the writer has experience, while beginning as a voluntary association,[2] is now a network of limited liability companies. The legal entity of the Celtic Football and Athletic Company Limited was incorporated, that is registered, at Companies House in Edinburgh as a limited liability company and being issued with a certificate of incorporation, on 12 April 1897 when it acquired the assets etc of the original Celtic Football and Athletic Club. On 15 December 1994 this company was re-registered as a public limited company to be known as Celtic plc. Celtic plc is the main holding company with Celtic Football Club as a trading division of the holding company.

---

* The writer is grateful to Rod McKenzie and his team for the section on Licensing.

[1] See C Moore, *Sports Law and Litigation* (CLT, 1997), Chapter 2.

[2] Celtic Football Club was established by Brother Walfrid, a Marist brother, in the late 18th Century with the main purpose being, by playing football, to raise money for the poor and under-privileged people who lived in the east end of Glasgow.

A limited company is a distinct legal entity which is separate from its owners (the shareholders). The company has the ability to enter into contracts, to sue and be sued in the courts, and to own and dispose of property. It is a company limited by shares whose memorandum and articles of association describe it as such. Compliance with the Companies Acts (as amended) is compulsory—such compliance includes the obligation to publish its name and other required details on its business stationery.[3] Failure to comply with the terms of the Acts could result in every officer (*ie* appointed individual of the company) being fined. The Companies Acts affect and govern all aspects of control, functions and existence of a public limited company with the definitive element of that governance relating to the disclosure of information. The corollary of granting a company limited liability on incorporation is that the general public should be able to assess the company and any risks which could be attached to investing or dealing with it. The company satisfies the disclosure obligation by providing certain information on a regular basis to Companies House—for example, confirming details of its directors, company address and so forth. Certain other information is required on an occasional basis—for example, when there are changes to its details, such as a change in its registered office address,[4] resignations or appointments of directors.[5] The general public has access to the information which is held by Companies House on payment of the appropriate fee. Once again, Companies House has powers to penalise non-compliance, including criminal prosecutions and fines, imposing fines without going to court, disqualifying directors and striking the company off the register of companies, thus preventing it from trading as a limited company.

2-3   If the company, like Celtic plc, has shares which are listed on the London Stock Exchange then it also has to comply with the Stock Exchange's own rules which are known as the "Listing Rules" (also known as the "Yellow Book"). The Yellow Book states continuing obligations for fully listed companies, one of its main purposes being to ensure that individuals who deal in the Stock Exchange have access to the same information at the same time. Accordingly, the company is obliged to notify the Stock Exchange immediately of any appropriate information to allow the public and the company's own shareholders an opportunity to assess it.

One important obligation for the fully listed company is that it must issue an annual report and accounts as well as issuing a report covering the first six months of each financial year—thus generally two reports are issued per year. The main annual report and accounts must be published no later than six months after the end of the financial year, whilst the half-yearly report must be issued within four months of the end of the relevant period. This is a more onerous obligation than that specified by the terms of the Companies Act 1985[6] which require only a profit and loss account for

---

[3] s 349 of the Companies Act 1985 states that a company's name must legibly appear on all business letters, notices and other official publications; s 351 requires that the company's place of registration (*eg* Scotland), Companies House's registered number and its registered office address appear on business letters and order forms.

[4] Companies Act 1985, s 287.

[5] Companies Act 1985, s 288.

[6] s 226(1).

each financial year, with a balance sheet as at the end of that period to be prepared. The company is monitored to ensure compliance with the disclosure requirements. In the event that the Stock Exchange considers that there has been a failure to comply, it can censure the company by publishing the fact that it has been censured, and it can suspend or cancel the company's listing on the Exchange, which would be extremely detrimental not only to the company's trading position but to its reputation in the business community. The Stock Exchange could also take action against the individual directors of the company.

Further controls regarding the conduct of companies, particularly those **2-4** listed on the Stock Exchange, come from what is known as the Combined Code. This code is a result of separate committees—Cadbury, Greenbury and Hampel (now including Turnbull)—with their resultant reports and recommendations. These committees were established to review the performance of companies vis-à-vis the information provided to their shareholders, the conduct of their executives and the powers and influence of non-executive directors (*ie* individuals from outside the company who are not employees but who, on request, sit on the company's board of directors in order that the company can benefit from their experience and expertise). Equally as important was the restoration of the general public's faith in the integrity and professionalism of company directors in light of "fat cat" press coverage. The general term for the conduct of companies in this context is "corporate governance".

The Stock Exchange has inserted a new Listing Rule to the effect that, for a listed company with the end of its financial year being on or after 31 December 1998, it is mandatory to comply with the terms of the Combined Code. The company has to disclose in its annual report and accounts how it has applied the principles of the Code and whether or not it has complied throughout its financial year with the provisions of the Code. If it has not complied with some, or has complied for only a part of the period, then this must be explained and justified.[7] The Code itself covers a number of different aspects for the company to follow, ranging from the recommended proportion of non-executive to executive directors on the company's board of directors,[8] the appropriate procedure for the appointment of new directors, to directors' remuneration and periods of notice for directors' service contracts.[9] Not only does the Code cover the internal conduct of such a company but also its approach and attitude to its shareholders, with particular reference to the procedures undertaken at the company's annual general meeting: "Boards should use the Annual General Meeting to communicate with the private investors and encourage their participation".[10] This is important as the Annual General Meeting is usually the only opportunity whereby small shareholders can be fully advised of the company's activities and also the sole opportunity for those shareholders to ask questions directly of the company's directors.

---

[7] In terms of Rule 12.43A.
[8] Provision A.3.1: "Non executive directors should comprise not less than one third of the board".
[9] Provisions B.1.1 and B.1.4.
[10] Provision C.2.1.

The regulatory bodies of the sport

2-5 Thus far, running a company which is a sports business is no different from running any other. However, a sports club will normally have to comply with and take cognisance of its own sector's rules and regulations. In the case of a Premier League Football Club, for example, this means the regulations of FIFA, UEFA, Scottish Football Association (SFA) and Scottish Premier League (SPL). Each body has its own regulations, varying in jurisdiction and exclusivity: *eg* FIFA—worldwide, UEFA—Europe, SFA—Scotland, and SPL—governing the clubs within its league (12 at present). The regulations govern the activities of football clubs. For example, within Scotland this can range from the design of the club's strip (to include logos endorsed thereon),[11] the sale or purchase of players (see below), the capacity of its floodlights and the dimensions of its pitch to the conduct of its players and officials on and off the field of play.

The purpose of all these rules and regulations is to provide a framework, a uniformity and a minimum standard of conduct with which clubs, players and other officials must comply. They also govern the relationship between the club and its players (see below) and also between clubs within their respective leagues by providing procedures for the settlement of disputes with hearings,[12] provision for representation and appeals.

As a member of the SPL, a Premier League Football Club is obliged to comply with that body's regulations, but it is also a member of the SFA and thus is bound to follow that body's rules, which in turn are based on FIFA's and UEFA's regulations as appropriate. The very fact that each club is bound by the same form of regulations is useful in a global context whereby a club in Scotland is equally obliged to comply with them, along with clubs in Spain, France, Brazil or Japan. This element is particularly useful in the situation of player transactions because both the selling and buying clubs are bound to comply in this matter with the FIFA regulations, thus minimising any confusion which could otherwise arise between organisations in different parts of the world with different languages and legislation.

2-6 As with all sets of rules and regulations, as would be expected, there are penalties and sanctions for non-compliance. Discipline is a vital element in the maintenance of standards of behaviour within any sport. Thus, it is quite appropriate that all individuals involved in the sport should be equally subject to these standards. In relation to Scotland, it is, ultimately, the SFA and its rules and regulations which govern and determine the acceptability of behaviour of the participants.[13]

Each player, when signing a contract with his club, contracts and thus agrees to comply with the relevant applicable rules and regulations.[14] Each club being a member of such a regulatory body, a player, football club or an official of a club can be fined, suspended or expelled (permanently or temporarily) for such non-compliance, subject to consideration of the matter at the appeal level of that regulatory body. The decision of the body is final

---

[11] SFA Article 100.
[12] SFA Article 136.
[13] SFA Disciplinary Procedures and Article 86.
[14] SFA Article 108.

and binding with the individual having no recourse to a court of law as the provisions of section 3(1) of the Administration of Justice Act 1972 are specifically excluded in terms of Article 136.2.9 of the SFA Articles.[15]

Supporters and the general public

Working within this gamut of obligations, statutory or otherwise, a major 2-7 commercial sports club can become a multifaceted consumer organisation providing services from retail and catering to publishing. However, even here there is no escape from rules, whether based on statute, common law or industry practice. What follows is based upon the experience of a major Premier League Football Club but many of the points apply to a local cricket or golf club.

Standard terms and conditions

In the case of Celtic, for example, it would be impossible to enter into a con- 2-8 tract with each individual who wanted to purchase a season book (particularly with a season ticket database of over 50,000) and to negotiate specific terms with each person. Thus, standard terms and conditions are prepared which apply to each season ticket. By the act of paying for and receiving the ticket there is the acceptance of the terms, which require full compliance; otherwise the club is entitled to withdraw its use. This method of standard terms and conditions is commonplace when catering for large numbers of people who generally wish to receive the same service. It also gives the club a degree of consistency when providing the service by regulating its relationship with its customer base. However, such terms are only effective if they are tempered by complying with the terms of the Unfair Contract Terms Act 1977 and subsequent legislation. The purpose of the Act is to restrict and on occasion to withdraw completely the right to rely on certain terms which specifically exclude ("exclusion clauses") or limit responsibility ("liability") for certain events.

Celtic Park had over one million visitors in 1997/98 (either attending football matches or using its other facilities). In this context it is considered important to limit Celtic's liability for damages or costs incurred or sustained by such visitors, if possible. This is done by means of notifying visitors of the extent of the club's responsibility by using disclaimer notices whether around car parks or in other areas where the public has access. The purpose of such notices is to make members of the public aware that they also have a responsibility to take care of their possessions and themselves when visiting Celtic Park and thus cannot automatically assume that if there is any form of damage to or loss of possessions and such like they can succeed in a claim against the club for compensation subject to the adequacy of the notice being given.[16]

The Unfair Contract Terms Act 1977 deals solely with liability of business, that is liability for acts carried out by an individual in the course of a business or arising from that person's use of business premises. One of the

---

[15] See, however, Chapter 3 on judicial review.
[16] *Thornton v Shoe Lane Parking* [1971] 2 QB 163.

purposes of the Act is to ensure that liability cannot be excluded or limited for death or personal injury caused by negligence.[17] There are, of course, other terms which are not permitted relating to consumer protection (see below). A clause trying to avoid liability for death or personal injury caused by negligence would be deemed to be ineffective and would not be allowed to operate. Certain other clauses, such as where a ticket allows the club to locate a spectator in a room with no view of the match, would not automatically be ineffective but would have to pass a statutory test of "fairness and reasonableness" before it could be considered to be legally effective.[18]

Data Protection

2-9 Another form of legal protection for the consumer relates to the holding of information. For example, Celtic plc is registered with the Data Protection Registrar and as such is authorised to hold certain information about its employees and its customers in a prescribed form—but consequently it is obliged to comply with the principles and terms of the Data Protection legislation. The applicable Act is the Data Protection Act 1998. The Act's application for Celtic relates to the holding of information about its customers on databases. The eight principles for data protection are:

(1) personal data should be obtained fairly and lawfully;
(2) personal data must only be held for registered purposes;
(3) personal data must not be used or disclosed except as described in the registration;
(4) personal data held for any purpose should be adequate, relevant and not excessive in relation to that purpose;
(5) personal data should be accurate and where necessary kept up to date;
(6) personal data should not be kept for longer than is necessary for the purpose concerned;
(7) the data subjects (customers) should be given access to the personal data (in terms of the procedure set down in the Act); and
(8) appropriate security measures should be taken against unauthorised access, alteration, disclosure, loss or destruction of personal data.

Merchandising

2-10 Visit any sports shop and the reader will appreciate that retailing is an important element in the commercial strength of a football club—whether it is football strips, videos, photos of the players or keyrings. Celtic has a growing number of exclusive retail outlets in Scotland and Ireland. The integrity and reputation of any designs or logos associated with the club are of great importance and require protection. The club's badge with the four-leaf clover symbol, for example, has been associated with Celtic for a

---

[17] s 21.
[18] s 4 of the Unfair Contract Terms Act 1977 and *George Mitchell Ltd v Finney Lock Seeds Ltd* [1983] 2 All ER 737.

considerable period of time. It is vital that the association is protected in order to prevent third parties taking advantage and commercial benefit from it.[19] Time and effort and not insubstantial expense are expended in affording this protection, which in effect preserves Celtic's right of intellectual property in that symbol. It is unfortunately too common for other parties to use such symbols and marks on its items which are not licensed by the club and which are unauthorised. Such use is detrimental to the reputation of the brand, particularly as these third party items are usually of inferior quality. Thus, vigilant monitoring of unauthorised vendors and markets, together with well-maintained relationships with the trading standards departments of local authorities (who can bring criminal prosecutions against these persons) are required. One useful method for such monitoring is to register with Customs and Excise, who will check certain consignments coming into the United Kingdom from abroad and, if satisfied that the goods are counterfeit, will arrange for the goods to be seized and, possibly, destroyed thereafter. The club itself can take action against unauthorised individuals by suing them in a court action for passing off. This remedy is available where the manufacture, distribution or sale of unauthorised and unlicensed goods is likely to cause confusion in the minds of the general public, who are led to believe that the goods are, in fact, authorised and genuine club merchandise, thus affecting the club's business goodwill.[20] Such an action could include claims for interdict (interim or permanent), damages and accounting for profits. Lord Diplock in *Erven Warnick v Townsend*[21] stated:

> "[It is] possible to identify 5 characteristics which must be present in order to create a valid cause of action for passing off:
>
> (1) a misrepresentation;
> (2) made by a trader in the course of trade;
> (3) to prospective consumers of goods or services supplied by him;
> (4) which is calculated to injure the business or goodwill of another trader (in that it is a reasonably foreseeable consequence); and
> (5) which causes actual damage to a business or goodwill of the trader by whom the action is brought or ... will probably do so."

However, rather than simply relying on the common law protection of **2-11** passing off, further protection can be secured by registering certain marks or designs as trademarks in the United Kingdom with the Trade Marks Registry. On application to secure a registration, the company's interest in the use of the design/mark is noted, which should then discourage other

---

[19] See, for a sports related treatment, R Verow, C Lawrence, P McCormack, *Sports Business and the Law* (Jordans, 1999), Chapter 4 ("Intellectual Property Rights and the Law").

[20] See generally, Stewart, *Delict* (3rd edn), paras 3.7–3.13; Stewart, *A Casebook on Delict* (2nd edn), paras 7.1.1–7.4.4.

[21] [1979] AC 731 at 755.

parties from using the mark or anything similar to it. The principal statute is the Trade Marks Act 1994, with s1(1) stating: "trademarks means any sign capable of being represented graphically which is capable of distinguishing goods or services of one undertaking from those of other undertakings. A trademark may, in part, consist of words (including personal names), designs, letters, numerals or the shape of the goods or their packaging".

A company's application should state the classes of goods and services in which the mark is to be registered. There are 34 classes of goods ranging from jewellery (class 14) to clothing, footwear and headgear (class 25). There are also eight classes of services ranging from telecommunications in class 38 to the provision of food and drink in class 42. Once registered the registration lasts for 10 years and is renewable for 10 years at a time without limit. However, it can be removed with the registration being revoked for non-use if the registered mark is not used for more than five years. The trademark itself has several purposes: it allows the trader to create a link in the mind of the consumer with the trader's goods; it gives an entitlement to the use of the design, thus restricting the use of the mark except solely in connection with or associated with the specific classes of the goods/services. In terms of section 10 of the Act, the trademark can be infringed as follows:

(1) by use of an identical mark on identical goods or services;
(2) by use of an identical mark for similar goods or services or similar mark for identical/similar goods or services (this is when the trader needs to show the likelihood of confusion on the part of the general public and includes the likelihood of association);
(3) by use of an identical or similar mark for goods not similar but the mark has a reputation in the United Kingdom and therefore the use "dilutes" the value (there is no requirement of confusion on the part of the general public).

2-12   The health warning against threatening any unjustified action of infringement under the Act is that the "accused" trader has the right to bring an action to prevent groundless threats—thus enabling a person against whom an action of infringement is being threatened, to sue over the threat.[22]

In a trademark, a company has an asset of property which can be licensed (that is, consent given to another person to use the trademark for a specific purpose), sold or used as security for a debt. In Celtic's case a common use for its trademarks is the licensing of the marks to other companies for use on specified items on certain terms and conditions, and in consideration of payment of royalties. Once again it is useful to have standard terms in place in order to regulate the standards of quality and performance of each individual licensee without the necessity of long protracted contract negotiations subject, of course, to the exigencies of each such situation (eg length of licence, level of percentage of royalties and amount of advance royalties, if any).

---

[22] s 21. See F Akers, "When Threats can Backfire" (1998) 43(9) JLSS 22.

The purpose of the terms of any licence agreement is to ensure that the mark, its integrity and the business goodwill and reputation attached to it are preserved, protected. Failure to do so could be a sufficiently material breach of the agreement to entitle the licensing company to terminate the agreement and effectively withdraw its permission to use the mark.

Once the licence agreement is in place, with the licensee now producing the licensed products, the next legal issue which comes to the fore is consumer protection in relation to product liability. There is a plethora of consumer protection legislation in this context, including the Consumer Protection Act 1987, the Sale of Goods Act 1979 and the Supply of Goods and Services Act 1982.

Consumer Protection

The basic premise for most if not all of these statutes is to place responsi- **2-13** bility on the manufacturer or supplier for the safety and quality of goods and services. Thus, from a contractual point of view additional terms are included in a contract by implication in that they apply even although they are not expressly stated in the contract. These implied terms are:

(1) the goods should comply with their description,
(2) the goods are of a satisfactory quality (*eg* state and condition),
(3) if the buyer expressly or impliedly advises the seller of the purpose for which the goods are being bought, the seller warrants that the goods are fit for that purpose,
(4) if there is a sale by sample the goods sold should correspond in quality with the sample provided.

If the buyer "deals as a consumer" in accordance with the Unfair Contract Terms Act 1977 these implied terms cannot be excluded. In the event of failure to comply with these terms the buyer would be entitled to reject the goods and seek damages because such failure normally results in inconvenience and financial loss only. However, if the failure to comply relates to a fault in the goods which causes injury, then there could be a claim for product liability resulting in a claim for compensation. In this context the seller would be responsible even if he had taken every possible care and was not at fault. Furthermore, any effort by the seller to restrict or exclude these statutory rights of the consumer is completely unenforceable. Indeed, it is a criminal offence to display notices etc which try to effect this exclusion or restriction. The application of certain implied terms is also introduced into contracts for the supply of services in terms of the Supply of Goods and Services Act (ss 13–15):

s13: provides that where the supplier acts in the course of a business he will carry out the service with reasonable care and skill,
s14: provides that where the supplier acts in the course of a business and the contract does not specify the time within which the service is to be provided, then such service is to be carried out within a reasonable time,
s15: provides that in the (unlikely) event that the cost for the service is not included in the contract nor set down by the usual practice of the business, then the customer will pay a reasonable charge.

As before, the Unfair Contract Terms Act 1977 applies if efforts are made to exclude the application of these implied terms and, once again, if the buyer "deals as a consumer" no such exclusion can be enforceable.

Catering

2-14 Attending a football match can properly be described as a sensory experience, with attendance at Celtic Park, for example, reaching nearly 60,000 spectators at most home matches. One important element of this sensory experience is the ubiquitous "pie and Bovril". Thus, the safety of the food sold either to the spectators at the many catering units or to diners at the restaurants is of vital importance. The principal piece of legislation for this aspect of consumer protection is the Food Safety Act 1990. The main purpose of the Act is to ensure that all food produced for sale is safe to eat, reaches quality expectations and is not misleadingly presented. It empowers, as appropriate, local authorities to enter into premises to investigate possible offences and to initiate criminal prosecutions and impose penalties. The Act governs all the stages of the operation involved in the selling, having for sale, cleaning, storing, etc of food. Thus, it is an offence to sell any food which fails to meet safety standards. Specifically, the main offences are:

- selling or possessing for sale food which does not comply with the food safety requirements, which means that food must not have been rendered injurious to health, be unfit or be so contaminated either by external matter or otherwise that it would be unreasonable to expect it to be eaten,[23]
- to do anything which makes food harmful to health by adding or removing something,[24]
- selling to the purchaser's prejudice food which is not of the nature or substance or quality demanded,[25] and
- falsely or misleadingly describing or presenting food.[26]

2-15 It is the local authorities who are empowered to enforce the Act.[27] The Trading Standards department attend to the labelling and composition of food whilst the Environmental Health officers attend to matters of hygiene and certain cases of contamination. These officers are able to enter any premises within their area to investigate possible offences. This includes the seizing of records and the taking of samples of food for analysis.[28] If food is suspected of being unsafe it can be seized and if a court of law decides that this is in fact the case it will be destroyed or disposed of at the owner's expense,[29] the converse being that if the food is suspected but then

---

[23] Food Safety Act 1990, s 8 (2).
[24] Food Safety Act 1990, s 7.
[25] Food Safety Act 1990, s 14.
[26] Food Safety Act 1990, s 15.
[27] Food Safety Act 1990, s 6.
[28] Food Safety Act 1990, s 9.
[29] Food Safety Act 1990, s 9 (6).

found to be safe, and in the meantime it has deteriorated, the owner is entitled to claim compensation for any depreciation in value resulting from action taken by the local authority.[30]

The Act also deals with the premises within which food is processed and sold. It empowers the local authority officers to close such premises (after a successful prosecution of the owner) or to require improvements to be made within the premises.[31]

Licensing

For some years now it has been illegal to drink alcohol whilst watching **2-16** football matches and to be in possession of alcohol at football stadiums (see below). However, the sale of alcohol is permitted within the restaurants and function suites all in accordance with the Licensing (Scotland) Act. Obviously the sale of alcoholic beverages can represent an important part of the finance of any sporting club—many workers' sports and recreation clubs the length and breadth of the country rely on such sales to support the core activities. Indeed, it is often the case that the first time some small clubs have to think about their constitutional arrangements is shortly after they decide that it would be a good idea to have a bar for the members!

Licensing in Scotland is regulated by the Licensing (Scotland) Act 1976, as amended, which regulates on-sale and off-sale of alcohol. The main licences available are: hotel licence; public house licence; restricted hotel licence; restaurant licence; refreshment licence; entertainment licence; off-sale licence. The type of licence dictates what the holder is permitted to do, such as bar service/table service; off-sale; regular/occasional extensions; extensions with meals.

Bar service/table service Hotel, public house and entertainment licence hold- **2-17** ers may offer a bar service which allows customers to purchase alcohol at a bar counter without the requirement that they also purchase food. Alcohol may only be served in premises holding a refreshment licence where food and non-alcoholic beverages are also available for consumption. Customers need not be consuming non-alcoholic beverages or food—they must simply be available. Restricted hotel and restaurant licences permit the sale of alcohol, in a dining area, to customers as ancillary to a meal.

Off-sale The option to allow off-sale is a facility available to the holders of **2-18** hotel, public house and off-sale licences and allows the retail sale of alcohol for consumption off the premises. A restricted hotel licence-holder has a very limited ability to make off-sales to a resident—namely they must be consuming a meal, otherwise an offence is committed under the Act.

Regular/occasional extensions All on-sale licence-holders may apply for a reg- **2-19** ular or occasional extension to their licence, which extends the permitted hours in which they may engage in their business as permitted by their

---

[30] Food Safety Act 1990, s 9 (7).

[31] Food Safety Act 1990, ss 10 and 11.

licence. On-sale permitted hours are 11 am to 11 pm, Monday to Saturday, and 12.30 pm to 2.30 pm and 6.30 pm to 11 pm on a Sunday. A period of 15 minutes is also allowed for "drinking-up time" in which customers are permitted to consume alcohol on the premises although no alcohol may be sold or supplied. In restaurant licences, and where the sale or supply of alcohol was ancillary to a meal, a half-hour drinking-up time is available. The premises must be cleared by the end of these drinking-up periods. The licence-holder may apply for extensions to his licence for any hours although licensing boards will commonly grant regular extensions within previously determined policy hours. Trading hours for off-sales are Monday to Saturday, 8 am to 10 pm, and on Sundays, 12.30 pm to 10 pm.

2-20 *Extensions with meals* Extensions can be obtained under the Act for purposes of meal taking only. These are in terms of sections 57, 58 and 60 of the Act and are commonly referred to as chief constable consents.

2-21 *Children's certificates* It is important to note the provisions regarding entry to licensed premises by children. Children under the age of 14 are excluded from bar areas (*ie* areas where there is a bar counter) in licensed premises. The holder of a public house or hotel licence should make an application to the relevant licensing board for a children's certificate in respect of all or part of his premises. There is no provision for children's certificates in premises which hold a restaurant and refreshment licence (as these should not have a bar counter) nor in premises holding an entertainment licence. This certificate may be granted by the licensing board if satisfied that the premises are suitable for children to be present and there is provision for the supply of non-alcoholic beverages and meals. Accordingly, where a certificate is in force, persons under 14 years may be on the premises between 11 am and 8 pm (unless the certificate places other restrictions on the times of access) if in the company of a person of or over the age of 18 and for the purpose of consuming a meal supplied on the premises.

2-22 *Gaming machines* There are different types of gaming machines allowed in licensed premises and different provisions which apply. In general two amusement with prizes (AWP) machines can be installed in licensed premises in accordance with section 34 of and Schedule 9 to the Gaming Act 1968, on application to the Licensing Board for a permit. "Jackpot" machines differ in that they offer far greater cash prizes and, as such, their use is prohibited except on premises licensed under the Gaming Act 1968 or the premises of clubs or minors' welfare institutes registered under Part II or III of the 1968 Act (by section 31 (1)). Accordingly, jackpot machines are of more relevance to registered clubs than licensed premises.

2-23 *Licensing boards* Licensing boards are typically made up of local councillors and a licensing clerk who is legally qualified. Generally, local variations in licensing practice can be found in each licensing board area. Accordingly, whilst it is impossible to cover all such variations, it is important to be aware of the possibility that bye-laws and regulations may be created by each individual board. Each board is also likely to have "policies" on matters such as regular extension hours, etc.

The constitution of a licensing board is of importance. Liquor licensing is a local government function and there is a separate licensing board for each council area. Each board must contain no less than one-quarter of the number of members of the council; however the council may subdivide into licensing divisions. If this happens, that division must have a duly constituted board, in which case the divisional board must contain not less than one-quarter of the total number of councillors for the ward within the area of division. Of this, one-third must be councillors of the ward. In any event, the number of members for a licensing board must be five or more.

A councillor or a member of the council will not be allowed to sit as a member of a licensing board if they hold a liquor licence or if they are a brewer, distiller or dealer in or retailer of alcoholic liquor. A board must elect its chairman who should sit for a period of one year (but in practice usually sits for his full term) and ordinary members who also must be elected at the first meeting following the ordinary council elections. The ordinary members' term of office commences with the date of election to the board and terminates upon the election of the succeeding board—however, termination will not occur when the outgoing board has unfinished business. An outgoing councillor is eligible for re-election.

When a licensing board convenes, a quorum will be established if one-half of the board are present with a minimum of three. It should be noted that when voting, where a majority is not established, the chairman has the casting vote. The voting must take place in public; there must be separate votes for each aspect of the decision and in voting on a motion, the chairman must ensure that all motions have been tabled to ensure all opinions have been canvassed.

Transferring a licence A licence can be transferred by temporary and then **2-24** permanent transfer or permanent transfer alone. The temporary transfer is dealt with by delegated powers, being given to the clerk to the board, the chairman and a board member, normally from the ward in which the premises are situated. If a licence is transferred by way of temporary transfer, a permanent transfer must be applied for at the next available board sitting. If this is not done, or if a permanent transfer is refused, the licence becomes suspended until a fresh temporary or permanent transfer application is not only made, but also granted. A one-step permanent transfer can be applied for at any licensing board sitting. If it is refused, the licence will either be suspended or, if the previous licence-holder is still in possession of the premises, fit and available to act, revert back to them. Different boards approach the transfer procedure in different manners—for example, Argyll and Bute council require two references and a letter of consent from the current licence-holder before they will deem a transfer application to be "competent", whereas other boards will begin processing the application as soon as they receive it but will simply insist on a letter of consent before the transfer is granted.

Confirmation and substitution A licence may be held by an individual or by a **2-25** company, firm or partnership (*ie* a body other than an individual or natural person). A licence may only be held by one individual in Scotland, unlike England where licences may be held jointly. If a licence is held by a firm, company or partnership, an individual must be named. This is in terms of section 11 of the Licensing (Scotland) Act 1976, as amended, and the individual is therefore called the section 11 nominee. This nominee can be transferred by substitution and confirmation. Substitution is similar to a temporary transfer and can be done by delegated powers. A confirmation must then follow at the next licensing board to ensure the substitution is made permanent, similar to a permanent transfer. The substitution must, however, be applied for and granted within eight weeks of the section 11 nominee ceasing to be in control of the premises. If this is not done, the licence ceases to have effect and will not be effective again until a further substitution is granted.

Publishing

2-26 Communication with the club's supporters is vital whether by the usual means of a club magazine, match programmes or by the more "techno" method of a website on the Internet.[32] These are important and useful methods to advise on instructions for attending away matches, providing updates on team and general club news and, of course, the highly valued "exclusive" interviews with the team. The collation, preparation and production of such means of communications are, as you would expect, affected by the law. By various means the articles which appear belong to the club in that when the writer creates the article, he/she has copyright in the piece. Fundamentally, copyright is a right in the creative work[33] which can be sold, licensed and so forth. The club should ensure that the writer transfers this right to the club, thus allowing it to deal with the work as it wishes (within varying degrees. See "moral rights" below). If the writer is an employee then by means of his contract of employment he has already agreed that such rights will automatically pass to the employer if the work has been created in the course of the employment in the absence of an agreement to the contrary[34] (as per the case of *Stevenson Jordan & Harrison Ltd v Macdonald and Evans*[35]). If the writer is an external contributor then by means of his agreement of commission these rights will pass to the club, usually in exchange for a fee.

The principal piece of legislation governing this area is the Copyright, Designs and Patent Act 1988. Under the Act copyright exists in literary, dramatic, musical and artistic works and in published editions. Such a right exists if the work is original to the author[36] and protection is given to the first owner of the copyright.[37] For literary works the copyright protection lasts for the lifetime of the author plus 70 years after the author's death.

---

[32] See, *eg*, www.celticfc.co.uk; www.rangers.co.uk.

[33] This includes a film. See, *eg*, *Milligan v The Broadway Cinema Productions Limited* 1923 SLT 35 re the screenplay of "football daft". See, generally, *Stair Memorial Encyclopaedia*, Vol 18, 931–1150.

[34] Copyright, Designs and Patents Act 1988, s 11.

[35] (1952) 69 RPC 10 (CA).

[36] *eg Iterlego v Tyco Industries* [1989] AC 217.

[37] *eg Cummins v Bond* [1927] CG 167.

The author (or club's) copyright in the work can be breached ("infringed") if it is reproduced without consent and this would then give the author/club the right to sue. For there to be such an infringement the work needs to be copied or substantially copied.[38] This can extend to authorising another person to infringe the work and the importing, distributing and selling of copies of infringed copyright works, knowing that they are infringed. This latter aspect has important implications in the issue of selling counterfeit goods (as above). The usual claims in any subsequent court action are for interdict, damages and accounting for profits. However, there are defences to such an action as specified within the Act which allow certain acts to be done with copyright works which are not considered to be an infringement.[39]

Even if the author has transferred the actual copyright in the work to the club he still retains other rights introduced by the Act which are known as moral rights. These type of rights last for as long as copyright and ensure that the author shall be identified as the work's author (the right of paternity); and that the work is not subjected to unjustified changes (the right of integrity) (which lasts for 20 years after the author's death). There is also the right of ensuring that works are not falsely attributed. There is no registration process for copyright in works (unlike trademarks)—thus, vigilant monitoring is required to ensure that there is no unauthorised infringement. In the case of musicians there are societies (such as the Performing Rights Society—PRS) who on behalf of musicians enforce the rights to ensure that if the works are publicly performed then royalty payments are paid and received. One particularly apposite example is the case of *PRS v Rangers FC Supporter Club Greenock*,[40] when it was held that a performance in a private members' club was a public performance even although the membership was restricted. Generally, where music is played in areas to which the general public has access, an annual licence fee is payable to PRS which is then distributed to its members.

2-27

An important responsibility of a club which produces such publications is to ensure that third party individuals' reputations are not damaged by the terms of any of the articles/photographs which are published. The publisher has the ability to do this mainly by two means: even if the questionable article is from an external contributor, the publisher should have final editorial control with discretion to delete or amend the possibly offending provision or even the whole article in its entirety. Even at that stage the publisher can seek legal advice as to whether the particular element is defamatory. The care and effort which are taken is justifiable as the publication of a defamatory article could lead to an expensive court action where the publisher and the author could be sued.

The subject of defamation is in itself too large to be fully treated in this chapter. Nonetheless, such is the public interest in sport that all too often sports people may well find themselves embroiled in this arcane area of the law.[41] An ill-considered phrase which is published could be an expensive

2-28

---

[38] s 18 of the 1988 Act.
[39] s 20 of the 1988 Act.
[40] 1974 SC 49.
[41] See, *eg, McCann v Scottish Media Newspapers* 1999 SCLR 636; *Peat v News Group* 8 March 1996.

experience for a club and perhaps even for the individual who uttered the offending words. In its widest sense the principle of defamation is the making of a statement which is hurtful or damaging to an individual character or reputation. To be actionable the statement must be untrue—it may be made orally or in writing—but does not necessarily have to be communicated to a third party. The main piece of legislation is the Defamation Act 1996 which states under section 1 that a person has a defence to a court action over an alleged defamatory statement if he shows that:

(1) he was not the publisher of the statement complained of,
(2) he took reasonable care in relation to its publication, and
(3) he did not know and had no reason to believe that what he did caused or contributed to the publication of a defamatory statement.

In addition, under section 1(4) employees of a publisher are in the same position as their employer to the extent that they are responsible for the content of the statement or the decision to publish it.

2-29   The Act prescribes a procedure for the making of offers to amend in that they must include a "suitable correction" and "sufficient apology and pay such costs as agreed".

As a matter of law a judge can decide whether or not a statement can be defamatory but once it has been decided that it can it is a matter of fact for the judge (or a jury if in the Court of Session) to say whether a statement has in fact defamed the pursuer. The whole statement must be reviewed and read as an ordinary reader would read it and so fine print saying that the subject is an angel cannot be expected to negate a "Spawn of the Devil signed by Glasgow Club" headline! Damages in Scotland are not as high as in England, although they can be astronomical if a person's earning capability is affected—the very thing that can happen in football.

Leaving aside the common law of defamation, those who are involved in a sport are usually constrained by the rules of their governing bodies from disparaging each other, their governing bodies and officials with penalties which might be worse than the payment of damages, and so even lawyers versed in the law of defamation must take special care in advising sports people about what they can or cannot say.[42]

The Pools competition

2-30   The "Pools" has been an important part of the football culture in Britain for several decades, with large organisations such as Littlewoods and Vernons becoming virtual institutions in the course of time. The public face of gaming has changed recently, particularly since the introduction of the National Lottery in 1994. The social change has been from supporters checking their coupons on a Saturday night/Sunday morning to "family entertainment" on Saturday and Wednesday evenings. Notwithstanding the introduction of these very popular forms of gaming, an important source of financial support for football clubs in the United Kingdom which,

---

[42] See, *eg*, SPL rule A3 reproduced in the opinion in the Ranger's Huddle investigation: www.scotprem.co.uk. and SFA Articles 99, 127 and 130.

in general, has maintained its loyal support, has been the clubs' own brand pools competitions.[43] Nonetheless, even at this traditional level of support, the clubs have had no option but to rejuvenate their pools operations to effectively compete with the other methods of gaming which appear to be more accessible and understandable than the traditional coupon system. Thus, nowadays, scratch cards linked to clubs and windfall lotteries on match days, together with periodic incentives, have been devised to maintain, and hopefully increase, previous levels of interest and support. The pools operations are in place to provide additional funding to football clubs for the development of sporting activities. Such strategies are as useful to the small local club as any big football club.

No matter how imaginative the existing or new methods may be, they cannot be used unless they comply with the legislation ranging from the Lotteries and Amusements Act 1976 to the National Lottery Act 1993. It may be surprising to note that in spite of the predominance of some form of lotteries in people's lives today, there is no statutory definition of "a lottery". A working definition has been devised in the form of criteria which require to be met—a distribution of prizes by chance where persons taking part, or a substantial number of them, make a payment in return for obtaining their chance of a prize.

Section 1 of the Lotteries and Amusements Act 1976 set the scene by setting down the forms of lotteries which are permissible (subject to certain conditions). The type of lottery generally associated with football clubs is a "society lottery" which in accordance with section 5(1) means a lottery promoted by a society which is established and conducted wholly or mainly for one of the following purposes:

(a) charitable purposes,
(b) participation in support of athletic sports or games or cultural activities, and
(c) purposes which are not described above but are purposes neither of private gain nor for any commercial undertaking.

The whole proceeds of a society's lottery, after deduction of expenses and prize money, must be applied for the purposes of the society. Registration is required with the Gaming Board of Great Britain; registration remains valid indefinitely subject to further fees being paid regularly.

Once registered, the society is not restricted in either the number or frequency of lotteries to be held.[44] However, the total value of tickets sold in any single lottery for a society must not exceed £1,000,000 and the total value of tickets sold in any one calendar year should not exceed £5,000,000.[45] In addition the value of a prize must not exceed £25,000 or 10 per cent of the total value of tickets sold, whichever is the greater; not more than 55 per cent of the actual proceeds of a lottery may be used to provide prizes.[46] The amount of expenses which can be included and further legislation ensures that the maximum percentage of the proceeds

2-31

---

[43] *eg* Celtic Pools, Rangers Pools.
[44] Lotteries and Amusements Act 1976 ("1976 Act"), s10.
[45] 1976 Act, s11.
[46] 1976 Act, s11.

which can be appropriated for expenses and prizes together is 80 per cent—thus ensuring that no less than 20 per cent of the proceeds goes to the specified cause.[47]

Accurate record keeping is imperative to ensure that all expenses are correctly and properly incurred; other details which require to be recorded include the number of tickets ordered and received from a printer, tickets issued from each point of sale, tickets sold, the amount of all income received, of all prizes, and details of winners and winning tickets. All such records are required to be kept for at least two years but generally for as long as possible because the Gaming Board can inspect a lottery operation at any time and can examine in detail all such records. The tickets themselves and their printed details are governed by the Act.[48] At the moment the stake money is laid down by statute at £1—although there is pressure from the operators of lotteries to have this level of stake money increased, particularly in light of the issue of the £2 coin and its increased circulation. In addition, there is a desire from such operators to secure equality with the benefits of the National Lottery—*eg* roll over, unlimited prize money—in order to give such operators an even playing field to attract and maintain their customers.

2-32   Each ticket must be the same price with no part payments nor refunds allowed. Furthermore, each ticket must specify:

(1) its price,
(2) the name of the society promoting the lottery,
(3) the date of the lottery,
(4) the fact that the society is registered with the Gaming Board, and
(5) the name and address of the society's promoter.

Obligations to visitors

2-33   The supporter is one of the most important people to the commercial sports club. His or her safety is morally, commercially and legally very important.[49] For example, Celtic Park now has a certified capacity of over 60,000. It is one of the largest club stadiums in Britain and as such there are legal and practical responsibilities. Before the rebuilding and redevelopment process of Celtic Park started in the summer of 1994, it had a certified capacity of over 50,000: 37,000 standing and 15,000 seated. In light of the terms of the report of the Right Honourable Lord Justice Taylor in 1990 (which recommended that certain football stadia be all seated by 1 August 1994) the North, West and East sections of Celtic Park were demolished. Lord Justice Taylor was appointed by the then Conservative Government to inquire into the events at Sheffield Wednesday's Hillsborough Stadium on 15 April 1989 when 95

---

[47] 1976 Act, s13.
[48] 1976 Act, s11.
[49] See, *eg*, M Phipps and P Patel, "Spectator Safety – Who Cares?" (1997) 5 (2) SLJ 50; S Gardiner, "Managing Safety in Sport and Recreation" (1997) 5 (2) SLJ 49; Gardiner *et al*, *Sports Law* (Cavendish, 1998), Chapter 12; E Grayson, *Sport and the Law* (2nd edn, Butterworths), Chapter 5; C Moore, *Sports Law and Litigation*, Chapter 7; *Stair Memorial Encyclopaedia*, Vol 19, paras 1246–1254; 1276–1278.

people died.[50] He was asked to make recommendations about the requirements for crowd control and safety at sports events. The final report, which was published in January 1990, made 76 recommendations which it was hoped would be "instrumental in promoting better and safer conditions at sports grounds in the future". The report recommended that sports grounds designated under the Safety at Sports Grounds Act 1975 should become "all seater" under a phased programme. There were 31 clubs so designated in Scotland: those grounds designated under the Act as providing accommodation for 10,000 spectators were to become all seated accommodation. For the football clubs within the then Premier League and the national stadium, the report recommended an annual reduction of 20 per cent in standing capacity from their 1989/90 level over each of the following five years in order to eliminate any standing accommodation by August 1994. For all other grounds which were designated, it recommended an annual reduction of 10 per cent to eliminate the standing capacity by August 1999. Lord Justice Taylor also considered that the ruling of FIFA (Federation of International Football Associations) that there should be no standing capacity from the start of the 1993/94 season going forward at "high risk" matches (as defined by UEFA) should apply in the United Kingdom.

Even before the establishment of the various working parties to recommend guidelines on crowd safety there was the "safety net" of the Occupiers' Liability (Scotland) Act 1960. The purpose of the Act was to reform the liability of occupiers/owners of property to the effect that the owners are responsible for damage or injury sustained by parties who enter into or upon that property to the extent that they can prevent this by the exercise of reasonable care.[51] To be made liable the occupier has to be in possession and control. Only where a club has surrendered occupation and control might it be argued that although they are generally occupiers they are not occupiers in law in a particular case—an example might be where contractors have taken over a part of the premises to build a new stand. However, this type of liability may not be upheld if the injured party has notice of the danger or condition of the property and notwithstanding this fact he still enters the property and effectively has agreed to accept the risk and take the chance of sustaining any injury. This is important when, for example, there is ongoing repair/maintenance work on the premises—in the particular area signs are posted to warn members of the public that there are such ongoing works, advising that the area is closed to public access, and the area is usually taped off. If, even after all these precautions, an unauthorised individual still persists in gaining access it could be argued that the obvious risk has been accepted. The mere happening of an accident is not enough to make the occupier liable.[52]

2-34

---

[50] See, *eg*, HJ Hartley, "Hillsborough – A Disaster Unfolds: Implications for Managing Mass Sport and Recreation Events" (1997) 5 (2) SLJ 65.

[51] See, generally, Stewart, *Delict*, paras 7.2–7.11; *Stair Memorial Encyclopaedia*, Vol 15, paras 316–330.

[52] See, *eg*, *McDyer v Celtic Football and Athletic Co* 1999 SLT 2. However, see also two cases (it is understood one is being appealed), in which more exacting legislation protecting workmen has been applied to protect the public: *Banna v Delicato* 1999 SLT (Sh Ct) 84; *O'Brien v Duke of Argyll's Trs* 1999 SLT (Sh Ct) 88.

The veritable bible in the management of sports grounds for the safety of spectators is known as "the Green Guide".[53] Unfortunately, the Green Guide is the result of the lessons which have been learnt from previous crowd disasters. After initial guidance became available in 1972, this was supplemented when Mr Justice Popplewell was asked to set up a working party after the fire at Valley Parade, Bradford in 1985. A further edition was published in 1990 making further changes to the guidelines which were reviewed after the Hillsborough disaster. This responsibility for the safety management of any sports ground is paramount, as the list of serious accidents at grounds is already too long, stretching from Ibrox in 1920, with Heysel in 1985, to Guatemala in 1996.

2-35   The Green Guide has no statutory force but supplements and enhances the already heavy legal burdens on management. Its recommendations, however, do have force by their inclusion in the individual grounds' safety certificates issued by local authorities under the 1975 Act. The main purpose of the Green Guide is to give guidance to the management of sports grounds in order to help in assessing the number of spectators who can safely be accommodated at the grounds. In accordance with section 2(1) of the Safety at Sports Grounds Act 1975 the prime purpose is "to secure the reasonable safety at sports grounds when it is used for the specific purpose". The Green Guide also gives guidance on how the management should follow its recommendations in the design and management of new grounds or newly constructed sections of existing grounds. The Green Guide has not been devised to provide minimum standards but to establish and promote responsibility for spectator safety. It is not enough to prepare manuals to gather dust on a shelf—rather these policies must be used and understood on a daily basis by all relevant staff. However, full compliance with each element of the Green Guide is not necessary—deviations which are reasonable and necessary are permissible subject to there being no reduction in the provision of overall safety. However, a series of such deviations, which could result in lower standards, is not acceptable.

The Green Guide also provides that the management is responsible for the provision of adequately trained staff who are capable of performing their relevant duties. The individuals who are trained and given the tasks of ensuring that spectators are safe, minimising the chances of disorder and attending to emergencies, are the match day stewards. As is only proper for this extremely important aspect in the safety procedure, the Green Guide[54] is very detailed with regard to the specification of the stewards' duties, their appropriate training and criteria for appointment. The stewards deal with spectators and it is vital that they have a detailed knowledge of their ground in order to be able to guide/direct spectators to their seats etc. In the case of emergencies it is highly likely that it will be a steward who has to deal with the incident initially and call upon the emergency services as appropriate—thus knowledge of emergency procedures is equally vital. It may seem to visitors to the sports ground that stewards have one of the

---

[53] Presently in its 4th edition—issued by the Scottish Office and the Department for Culture, Media and Sport.

[54] s 3.

best jobs in that they get paid to attend football matches. However, this is certainly not the case—only after receiving training do stewards get the dubious pleasure of ejecting a 24-stone spectator who has failed to comply with the club's ground regulations as his presence has been "deemed to constitute a nuisance to other spectators".

Surprisingly, the Green Guide even has an impact on the more commer- **2-36** cial aspects of spectator events:

(1) *Tickets*[55]: the design and terms of tickets issued. Again from a safety and security perspective, the Green Guide makes various recommendations, ranging from the recommendation that an easily understandable plan of the stadium be printed on the reverse of the ticket, to the statement that the portion of the ticket retained by the spectator after he/she passes through the turnstile should clearly identify the location of his/her seat.

(2) *Catering*[56]: areas around catering units should be kept free of hazards, reduce the risk of fire, and an adequate number of bins for waste and litter should be provided. Drinks etc sold in the spectator area should be in soft containers as glass, bottles or cans could be used as missiles.

(3) *Alcohol*: possession and consumption is governed by the Criminal Law (Consolidation) (Scotland) Act 1995 which superseded the innovatory Criminal Justice (Scotland) Act 1980.[57] The basic premise of the legislation is that anyone in possession of a controlled container/alcohol or who is drunk and attempts to enter a sports ground commits an offence—within two hours of the start of the football match and up to one hour after the event. Obviously, being drunk whilst within the stadium is an offence, as can be the possessing of alcohol in any part of the stadium from which the pitch can be seen during the above time period. There are also strict guidelines which require to be met regarding the consumption of alcohol in hospitality boxes 15 minutes before and up to 15 minutes after the end of the match.

The football club's relationship with its staff

General

It is not uncommon for visitors to Celtic Park to comment on the unexpect- **2-37** edly high number of staff members who work there on non-match days, that is Monday to Friday. The club employs approximately 320 people as a core staff—which can increase to 1,000 on a match day with additional staff employed for stewarding, catering and retail units. As in any other mature business employee rights and the protection of such rights are important considerations, compliance with the legislation applying equally to the club as with other employers such as shops, offices and restaurants. A full treatment of employment law is well beyond the scope of a general chapter.[58]

---

[55] s 2.25.

[56] s 2.26.

[57] See, generally, *Stair Memorial Encyclopaedia*, Vol 19, paras 1269–1272.

[58] See, generally, Craig and Miller, *Employment Law in Scotland* (T&T Clark, 1996); Gardiner *et al.*, *Sports Law* (Cavendish, 1998), Chapters 7, 8 and 9. *Stair Memorial Encyclopaedia*, Vol 19, paras 1231–1237. For a specially sports related treatment, see R Verow, C Lawrence, P McCormack, *Sport, Business and the Law* (Jordans, 1999), Chapter 5 ("Employment Agreements").

However, lay readers involved in club management should be at least aware of the following key points and should in any event seek to have their legal advisers "audit" their employment law position.

In terms of the Employment Rights Act 1996[59] the employer is obliged to provide a written statement of the employment terms and is obliged to give the employee a minimum period of notice to effectively terminate the employment contract. While governing the working relationship, the Act provides protection to the employee in that if the employer fails to comply with its statutory obligations as specified in the Act—for example, to allow the employee time off work to carry out public duties, for antenatal care or to look for work or arrange for training—the employee is entitled to refer the matter for determination by an employment tribunal. If the tribunal finds the employee's complaint to be well-founded, in certain circumstances an award of compensation can be made against the employer. The old limits have been discarded and tribunals can award up to £50,000. The most well-known and significant right conferred by the legislation is the right, unknown to the general law, for the employee not to be unfairly (as opposed to wrongfully) dismissed.[60] A fair dismissal will require to show at least, among other legally acceptable grounds, that the contract of employment was terminated by the employer for reasons related to the employee's capability or qualifications[61] or the employee's conduct. A redundancy proper is not an unfair dismissal but unfair selection for redundancy can be an unfair dismissal. The protection granted under the Act does not apply to the dismissal of an employee unless he has been continually employed for not less than one year (originally there was a two-year qualifying period but that has been reduced to one year since June 1999). Once again the Act provides the employee with recourse to an employment tribunal to determine if the dismissal was unfair and, if so, to make the appropriate order (of re-instatement or re-engagement) and/or an award of compensation.

2-38   The most recent and well-publicised development for the protection of employees came in the form of the Working Time Directive which came into force on 1 October 1998.[62] Unless employees have given their prior consent in a specified form they should not be required to work more than an average of 48 hours per week, averaged out over 17 weeks. The Directive also specifies that employees are entitled to various forms of rest breaks during the day and on a daily and weekly basis. The Directive also provides employees, for the first time, the statutory entitlement to paid holidays—subject to the qualifying period of service. Failure to comply with these Regulations could result in enforcement action being taken via the Health and Safety Executive, who will monitor the hours of work of employees, or by a referral to an employment tribunal by the employee himself.

---

[59] The Act consolidates existing legislation, some of which goes back to the 1960s.

[60] s 94.

[61] That he was a tennis player and not a footballer, not that he did not score on Saturday!

[62] Obviously many readers will consider this has little application to Premier League football because most of the employees only work for 90 minutes (and some would argue not always the full 90!).

The football perspective on employment

The basic tenets of employment are supplemented by the rules of the regu- **2-39** latory bodies of the sport. This is a matter that even the general legal practitioner might not appreciate. In Scotland this means the rules of the SFA and SPL for Premier League football and other bodies at different levels of the game. Most of the terms of a player's contract of employment are compulsory in that for the contract to be effective and registerable with these bodies, it has to include certain terms. There are strict procedures, as laid down in the rules of the regulatory bodies, relating to the administration involved in the transfer of players between clubs. Each player's contract is submitted to these bodies to ensure that the terms are in order; if so, the player's contract is registered, which then entitles him to play for the club. If these procedures for registration are not followed the club cannot use the player. If it does so it can be censured.[63]

The contracts entered into between the player and the club have to provide in specific and prescribed terms provisions regarding procedures for dealing with misconduct; a statement to the effect that the terms of payment as stated within the contract are the "Player's complete entitlement"[64]; and a statement that the player and club shall observe the rules and regulations of the SPL and SFA. A duplicate of the contract, signed by both parties, is given to the player for his retention in accordance with standard contract law procedures. An important layer of protection for both the player and the club is that in the event of problems in their relationship recourse is available to either party to seek the assistance of the regulatory bodies to determine the matter. This is particularly important as, once again, the right to refer matters to a court of law is not available to either party under the SFA Articles.[65]

Thus, generally, the effect of the inclusion of such clauses and the application of the rules ensure that for each professional player in the country, no matter the position of his club (geographically or in a league context), standard terms of employment apply. This reinforces the image of football as an industry, with its employees on standard contracts with the same rights and protection—a major exception being the individual remuneration packages! The very fact that there should be little, if any, deviation from the standard terms allows the clubs and regulatory authorities greater control and ability to minimise problems, which can arise when every person has materially different terms and conditions of employment. Conversely, it provides comfort and security to players in that they can be assured of uniformity in their terms of employment and the application of those terms.

In these highly competitive times, football clubs need to have a constant **2-40** availability of talented players within the squad. It is more common for clubs to look abroad as there is an unfortunate lack of home-grown talent

---

[63] Possibly by having points deducted from its points total in the League: SPL Rule D1.3.

[64] SPL Rule D10.2.3.

[65] Subject, of course, to issues of natural justice. (See SFA Article 136.2.9).

coming through the ranks sufficiently quickly to satisfy the demands of club fans for immediate success. At times this results in clubs even looking beyond Europe for this talent. No special permissions are required for players who are nationals of countries within the EEA, Gibraltar and certain other territories (subject to certain criteria) to come and work within the United Kingdom.[66] With the expanding globalisation of the sport—matches being transmitted throughout the world through various means, including pay TV—it is inevitable that the free movement of players, not only from club to club within the same territories but from continent to continent, will increase, particularly under the *Bosman* ruling.[67] Thus, a working knowledge of the criteria for securing the requisite permission for a player from outwith the EEA to play within the United Kingdom is becoming more useful. Such permissions, known as work permits, are issued by the Department of Education and Employment once certain criteria have been satisfied. The legislation governing this aspect of football life is the Immigration Act 1971. The application for a work permit requires to be submitted in the prescribed form and sent to the Overseas Labour Service of the Department of Education and Employment. The Overseas Labour Service considers each application to ensure that it satisfies the set criteria (which are reviewed on a regular basis). In the event that the permit is granted, it allows the player of an international standard of the highest calibre who is able to make a significant contribution to the development of the British game at its highest level to join the club in the United Kingdom. The present criteria (as from July 1999) are as follows:

- the player must have played for his country in at least 75 per cent of its competitive "A" team matches for which he was available for selection during the two years preceding the date of application; and
- the FIFA ranking of the player's country must be at or above 70th place in the official ranking list when averaged over the two years preceding the date of application.

The permit, if granted, lasts for certain periods:

- for the first permit, it will now be granted for the duration of the player's contract up to a maximum period of three years, and
- for following applications, after satisfying the criteria again, it will be issued again for a further period of up to three years.

It is the prospective employing club which applies for the permit not the player—thus, if a player is transferred within his contract period to another club the new club requires to apply for a new permit. Permits will not be issued if clubs wish to have players on loan or for trial—separate arrangements have to be made with the Home Office in this connection. In the event that the application is not granted the applicant club can seek review

---

[66] The EEA is considered to include: Ireland, Austria, Belgium, Denmark, Norway, Portugal, Spain, Sweden, Switzerland, Iceland, Germany, France, Italy, Greece, Luxembourg, the Netherlands, Finland, Liechtenstein and the United Kingdom.

[67] See Chapter 5.

of the decision. If this happens, it is referred to a review panel of independent experts whose recommendation is then passed to the Minister of the Department of Education and Employment for final decision. It is inherently risky for the target player to enter the United Kingdom and commence employment while his application is being considered. Such action could lead to the Home Office instructing the Overseas Labour Service to refuse to grant the permit, criminal sanctions against the club for illegally employing the player, and/or the player, himself, being deported if the permit is refused.

Vicarious responsibility

At the heart of the employer/employee relationship lies the responsibility **2-41** which the employer has for the actions of his employee as carried out within the scope of his employment.[68] Thus, if damage is sustained by a third party as a result of an action or a failure to act by the employee, the employer could be liable to that third party in damages. Employers must carry insurance for these risks. However, sports lawyers are aware of the interesting questions which arise in relation to injuries on the field. The first defence is that the victim has only sustained the kind of injury to which he has consented by virtue of playing the game.[69] Where there is, for example, an outrageous tackle, the question is whether, albeit unauthorised and no doubt deprecated by the club, it is still within the scope of the employment. If it is so bad as to be outwith the scope of the employment, then it is possible that some club insurance policies might not cover the case.[70] The footballer himself is always liable for his own acts.

Health and Safety

Considering that, statistically, workers spend a greater portion of their lives **2-42** at their place of work than anywhere else, it is imperative that the place of work is safe and that the worker's wellbeing will not be negatively affected by working there. Employees, themselves, have a duty to take reasonable care of their safety and health at work and also that of their workmates which means co-operating with the employer to ensure that all requisite duties are complied with.

The employer has a basic common law duty to provide a safe place of work for its employees. If the employer fails to comply with its duty and as a result an employee sustains injury, the employer could be found liable in damages to the employee. The duty has been enhanced by the introduction of legislation which has increased the employer's exposure not only to civil liability but possibly to criminal prosecution for such non-compliance.

The Health and Safety at Work etc Act 1974 governs the duties of the employer in this connection. Such duties include: the employer's obligation to protect its workers from risks arising from the actions of its other

---

[68] See, generally, Stewart, *Delict*, Chapter 10; *Stair Memorial Encyclopaedia*, Vol 60, paras 242–251.

[69] See, generally, A Duff, "Reasonable Care v. Reckless Disregard" (1999) 7 (1) SLJ 44.

[70] See T O'Brien, "Sports Liability Insurance" (1997) 5 (2) SLJ 58; JC Green, "Insurance and Sport" 1997 5 (2) SLJ 61.

workers; to control the use and storage of dangerous substances and to control the emission of noxious or offensive substances. The basic premise of the Act has been supplemented in the intervening years by various regulations, including the Workplace (Health and Safety at Work) Regulations 1992 which state that the workplace must be maintained in an efficient state, with repairs and maintenance to be carried out without undue delay. Such regulations also require employers to ensure that there is adequate ventilation, reasonable temperature, adequate lighting (to prevent eye strain), adequate cleaning (as appropriate) and that each worker has sufficient space at their workstation.[71] The list of duties and requirements is not exhaustive and employers are expected to be cognisant of them in order to protect their staff members adequately.

Failure to comply could result in injury to the employee or even death. Under the terms of the Reporting of Injuries, Diseases and Dangerous Occurrences Regulations 1995 certain types of accident and injury require to be reported to the environmental health department of the local authority. Failure to report is a criminal offence. The main body which presides over the environmental health departments countrywide is the Health and Safety Executive (HSE)—as a statutory body it ensures compliance with and enforcement of the regulations. The HSE is empowered to issue notices to employers, requiring improvements to premises to bring them up to the required standard. It can also investigate and bring criminal prosecutions against employers for non-compliance—which could lead to fines and/or imprisonment.

2-43   It is hoped that this chapter has given the reader a brief insight into the legal implications of running a modern football club. While some of the points raised are very specific to a public limited company working in the football sector, it is hoped that they will be of some interest if not of use to individuals who are involved in the running of sports clubs. At the very least, it might have encouraged some individuals charged with looking after a sporting club to consider consulting a sports lawyer!

Whilst not all of the elements discussed above are encountered every single day of the week, most are encountered often enough to confirm the idea that although a football club can be considered a business it has different aspects (not just legal ones) which make it a very special place to work.

So much for the 90-minute week of the sports club secretary!

---

[71] See, generally, Stewart, *Delict*, paras 7.38–7.50.

3 JUDICIAL REVIEW OF DISCIPLINARY DECISIONS OF SPORTING BODIES

Stephen Miller

The governing association of every sport publishes its own rule book and, **3-1** in its disciplinary guise, enforces its terms whilst at the same time promoting and administering its sport (by attracting sponsorship and by facilitating games, fixtures, leagues, tournaments, etc) and this gives rise to certain inherent conflicts. (Not every sport is run by an association but the comments which follow in this chapter apply equally to all governing bodies regardless of constitution.) The modern governing association, therefore, will seek to achieve a situation where disciplinary decisions impinging upon its members' and players' sporting (and usually also patrimonial) interests are ceded to a quasi-autonomous commission or tribunal. Thus, the ideal structure for sports body governance begins closely to model Lord Hope's tripartite paradigm for judicial review[1] which creates the irony that the more an association strives to be fair, the more likely its decision will be susceptible to judicial review. That is an observation, not a problem: no governing body reasonably could seek to dispense with its disciplinary commissions or tribunals simply to deny claimants the opportunity to petition for judicial review; and even if that was done successfully, which is in itself questionable, it is likely that dissatisfied members and players would simply seek to enforce their rights with some private law contractual remedy. There may, at times, be conflict between the association's separate disciplinary and promotional activities; and so the properly functioning governing association will seek to dispatch its disciplinary duties fairly, consistently and only so far as is necessary to maintain the credibility and competitiveness of the sport which it promotes, and to protect the participants. There exists also an unavoidable conflict between the individual rights of the competitor and the collective rights of all the members of the association which means that the properly functioning governing association must discharge its decision-making function objectively and impartially in proceedings which must be formal without becoming legalistic; flexible without being arbitrary; transparent at every stage without being burdensome.

The final conflict for the sporting association is created by the tension between the powers it exercises in its own regulatory function, and the protections afforded by the court poised to exercise its supervisory control over

---

[1] *West v Secretary of State for Scotland* 1992 SLT 636.

the administrative decisions taken. It is hardly surprising, therefore, to see that some have observed within associations the existence of "micro legal systems"[2] containing autonomous legislative, executive and adjudicative functions. In turn, this phenomenon has been described as demonstrating: "a shift toward self-regulatory control mechanisms which are transparent, accountable and enjoy a measure of independence with the Courts performing a 'fail-safe' function of intervening in cases of self-regulatory failure".[3] The court is friend and foe of the sporting association, in equal measure. The authorities demonstrate that the court is consistently unwilling to trespass on territory which is uniquely within the domain of sport because it respects the role of the association as best placed to administer the sport concerned. Equally, however, there is ample evidence that the courts will not shirk from branding decisions unlawful and unenforceable as offensive to the principles of natural justice simply because they may have arisen in a wholly sporting context. No association can operate disciplinary rules without knowing when its decisions will be held as unimpeachable upon the former principle, or reduced by the court according to the latter. Defining the distinction is not easy, and is made more difficult by evidence of a gradual but marked shift in the judicial approach to the decisions made by sports associations in the disciplinary context. This important development is taking place at a time when associations can ill afford to treat their obligation to sportsmen and women lightly. The former British Athletics Federation had to seek an administration order largely as a result of the legal costs it incurred in the lawsuit which followed the suspect positive drug test of Diane Modahl. It is necessary, before going any further, to appreciate the fundamental principles of administrative law as applied in Scotland.

PRINCIPLES OF ADMINISTRATIVE LAW

Generally

3-2 It is trite that the court will not supplant its own decision for that of a decision competently taken by an administrative body and, especially in the sporting context, the court will be slow to afford remedies to those seeking to exploit cumbersome or inadequately drafted rules. In *Wilander v Tobin* the Court of Appeal emphasised that fact: "While Courts must be vigilant to protect the genuine rights of sportsmen in the position of the Plaintiffs, they must be equally vigilant in preventing the Courts' procedures being used unjustifiably to render perfectly sensible and fair procedures inoperable."[4] Unless the court can pass through certain "gateways" (see below) it may be faced with having to endorse an administrative decision which it would not itself have reached on the same facts. The

---

[2] Foster, "Developments in Sporting Law" in Allison (ed), *The Changing Politics of Sport*, Chapter 6.

[3] Morris and Little, "Challenging Sports Bodies' Determinations" (1998) 17 CJQ 128 at 129.

[4] *Wilander v Tobin* [1997] 1 Lloyd's Rep 195 at 195.

landmark case in this area[5] has spawned an eponymous test. The *Wednesbury* principles are the judicial rule of thumb applied to distinguish between those decisions reasonably taken (and so unimpeachable) and those decisions reached by unreasonable means which can be examined by the court; and so form the "gateways" through which the court must pass in order to disturb the decision under consideration.

Judicial review

Generally

The concept of judicial review has been articulated succinctly as: "the **3-3** imposition of compulsory standards on decision makers so as to secure the repudiation of arbitrary powers".[6] The court's examination of the decision brought before it is designed to establish whether or not the decision maker has taken into account matters which it ought not to have taken into account, or, conversely, has refused to take into account matters which it ought to have taken into account. Even if the decision in question survives that analysis it may still be interfered with by the court if the decision maker has reached a conclusion so unreasonable that no reasonable person could ever have come to it. In *Barrs v British Wool Marketing Board*[7] Lord President Clyde made clear what is meant by the court's supervisory jurisdiction: "The test is not 'Has an unjust result been reached?' but 'Was there an opportunity afforded for injustice to be done?' If there was such an opportunity, the decision cannot stand." This last category is difficult to define any more comprehensively with most of the relevant *dicta* emphasising that "you know it when you see it". From the employment precedents the equivalent test is said to be fulfilled when the judge can say "oh my goodness – that is clearly wrong". Recently Lord Diplock described this type of *Wednesbury* unreasonableness thus: "It applies to a decision which is so outrageous in its defiance of logic or of accepted moral standards that no sensible person who had applied his mind to the question to be decided could have arrived at it."[8]

Scottish judicial review procedure

If there is a prospect of challenging a decision against these principles, then **3-4** in Scotland it is likely to be brought out in a judicial review petition before the Court of Session, which has exclusive jurisdiction in such proceedings. In 1985 the Court of Session introduced special rules relating to judicial review. No change was made to the substantive law but there was introduced a flexible and novel procedure for the resolution of judicial review proceedings.

---

[5] *Associated Provincial Picture Houses Limited v Wednesbury Corporation* [1947] 2 All ER 680.

[6] *R v Ministry of Agriculture, Fisheries & Food, ex p First City Trading Ltd* [1997] 1 CMLR 250, per Laws J at para 69

[7] 1957 SC 72 at 82.

[8] *CCSU v Minister for the Civil Service* [1985] AC 374 at 410.

Since 1985 parties have required to plead law and refer to authorities in the pleadings and the court is empowered to grant any remedy it considers appropriate whether it is craved or not. These principles have assisted and encouraged the rapid growth of judicial review jurisprudence in this country. Rapid growth or not, however, there is still scope for looking at cases from other jurisdictions. According to O'Neill[9]: "It is clear that the developing body of administrative law is extraordinarily open to outside influences, particularly from other jurisdictions which have had longer periods in which to develop and refine their notions of administrative law." Certainly, in the sporting context there is much that can be learned from overseas decisions, as will be seen in the course of this chapter. The Scottish practitioner must be careful of the English line of authority which (presently) sees the English higher courts consistently forbidding sportsmen to challenge disciplinary decisions by the judicial review process. (For reasons unimportant here, aggrieved competitors in England and Wales must bring private civil actions in contract relying on the implied obligation of the disciplining association to act fairly. No such public/private distinction is made in Scotland.)

3-5   The case of *West v Secretary of State for Scotland*[10] contained a comprehensive review and taxonomy of the law of judicial review in Scotland and has established that once a party can prove the existence of a tripartite relationship (with the decision complained of having been taken by the external party) then he can competently ask the court to review judicially the decision taken by the external party. In his leading opinion Lord Hope stated[11] that the paradigm case for the exercise of the supervisory jurisdiction involved the Court of Session regulating "the process by which decisions are taken by any person or body to whom a jurisdiction, power or authority has been delegated or entrusted by statute, agreement or any other instrument" for the purpose of ensuring that "the person or body does not exceed or abuse that jurisdiction, power or authority, or fail to do what the jurisdiction or authority requires". Lord Hope was articulating a position which, for sporting bodies, had been clear since, at least, the decision in *St Johnstone Football Club v Scottish Football Association*.[12] In that case the Club had been subjected to disciplinary proceedings without knowing what charge they faced, nor its nature, and they were not even given the opportunity to make representations. The Club sought to reduce the minutes of the SFA which implemented the penalty. The court held that the disciplinary proceedings of a body such as a sporting authority (such as the SFA) were quasi-judicial and thus capable of being scrutinised.

The European dimension

3-6   While Lord Hope's leading judgment in *West* was an exhaustive and admirable synthesis of hundreds of years of administrative law in Scotland

---

[9] A O'Neill, *Judicial Review in Scotland* (1999), p31.

[10] 1992 SLT 636.

[11] at 404.

[12] 1965 SLT 171.

it is relevant to note that constitutional lawyers in Scotland (and perhaps Lord Hope himself) are already looking beyond *West*. Parties are having to look to the implications of the European Convention on Human Rights, and to consider the doctrine of proportionality. At least since the *dictum* of Lord Eassie in *Salah Abdadou v Secretary of State for the Home Department*[13] and certainly once section 2(1)(a) of the Human Rights Act 1998 comes into force, a court considering a judicial review petition will require to have regard to the petitioner's Convention rights, or, as the legislation has it, to take into account any relevant judgment, decision, declaration or advisory opinion of the European Court of Human Rights, or any other convention institution; and that has important implications. Mr Justice Laws has said[14]: "The difference between *Wednesbury* and European review is that in the former case the legal limits lie further back."

In particular, some of the most established principles of administrative law appear susceptible to challenge. In the light of some of the *dicta* in *Smith & Grady v United Kingdom*[15] it is likely that the court will be reluctant to regard the statements of, say, Lord President Clyde in *Barrs* (above) with the same reverence. *Smith & Grady*, which concerned the MOD ban on homosexuals in the Armed Forces, had proceeded along normal lines through the English courts. It was not regarded as remarkable when the Master of the Rolls (Sir Thomas Bingham) said in the Court of Appeal that the court was not entitled to interfere with the exercise of an administrative discretion on substantive grounds: "save where the court was satisfied that the decision was unreasonable, in the sense that it was beyond the range of responses open to a reasonable decision-maker".[16] Sir Thomas Bingham's judicial threshold was regarded by the European Court of Human Rights as having been "placed so high"[17] as to amount to a contravention of the right to an effective remedy under Article 13 of the European Convention.

There is a further conflict between domestic, *Wednesbury* principles of **3-7** review, and the principles which distil from Community law and European Convention law. In the European model exists the doctrine of proportionality, which provides the reviewing judge more scope for interference. The proportionality test, according to O'Neill,[18] "requires judges to consider whether or not there were any significant alternative courses of action which might achieve the same end less oppressively". The extent to which Scottish judges will require to consider the doctrine of proportionality is moot. It has been suggested that the doctrine may only apply in cases where national law directly applies or specifically derives from Community law.[19] Lord Hope, since the decision in *West*, has commented extrajudicially that it is notable that "there has been no opportunity for the Inner House

---

[13] 1998 SC 504.

[14] *R v Ministry of Agriculture, Fisheries & Food, ex p First City Trading Ltd* [1997] 1 CMLR 250 at para 69.

[15] [1999] IRLR 734.

[16] *Smith & Grady v United Kingdom* [1999] IRLR 734.

[17] at 752.

[18] *Judicial Review in Scotland*, p 73.

[19] *ibid* at p 78.

to re-examine the opinion in *West* in the light of subsequent developments".[20] These questions are likely to be litigated in genuine "pure" public
law judicial reviews (such as those involving government departments etc)
rather than in sporting cases and for that reason the Convention and proportionality debates may not imminently touch sporting bodies. Notwithstanding that, most national sports associations are likely to be treated as
public authorities liable to comply with the Convention and so the likely
impact of "Convention rights" suggests that sports bodies would do well to
ensure, now, that, when in disciplinary mode, there is complete separation
between the roles of prosecutor and judge, and that one of these roles
(preferably the latter) be handled by a body with a measure of independence. And, if proportionality is to be given application in Scotland,
petitioners are bound to have the opportunity to scrutinise sporting bodies'
decisions more closely and to seek to persuade judges to form opinions
traditionally left to sports administrators.

3-8   As will be seen below, in Duncan Ferguson's petition to the Court of
Session it had been pled that when his criminal sentence was taken together with his 12-match ban he was suffering from a form of double jeopardy.
When the case came forward for argument that line was not pursued, it
being acknowledged that disciplinary bodies are not obliged to take actual
or potential criminal sanctions into account. If, however, Lord Macfadyen
had had to consider proportionality it is certain the point would have been
insisted upon in the course of an argument that the ban, when considered
alongside the three-month sentence, was more severe than was necessary
to mark the gravity of the offence. There is one important check on the doctrine of proportionality which gives some latitude to decision makers: the
margin of appreciation. Were the doctrine to take hold in Scotland governing bodies would be certain to argue that their closer proximity to, and
greater knowledge of, their own sport (their margin of appreciation)
should make the court slow to interfere even in cases of apparently disproportionate decisions.

In what remains of this chapter it will be assumed that the necessary
tripartite relationship exists and therefore all references to court challenges
will be in the judicial review context. The principles of natural justice
permeate all disciplinary proceedings. Attempts are made here to classify
natural justice in its various forms. For that reason, it is worth remembering that the very exercise of compartmentalising the ingredients of natural
justice is itself offensive as operating in conflict with the need to consider
each individual case on its own merits. In addition, Lord Hope draws attention in *West* to the fact that "[t]he categories of what may amount to an
excess or abuse of jurisdiction are not closed, and they are capable of being
adapted in accordance with the development of administrative law."[21]

---

[20] Lord Hope of Craighead, "Helping each other to make law", 1997 SLPQ 93 at 102, as cited
by O'Neill, *Judicial Review in Scotland* at p15.

[21] *West v Secretary of State for Scotland* 1992 SLT 636.

ESSENTIAL ELEMENTS OF DISCIPLINARY PROCEEDINGS

We have arrived at a stage where it is possible to list for associations those **3-9** fundamental principles which must be observed when disciplining individuals. These principles might be described as the basic rights of the competitor or club being disciplined. A failure, without justification, on any count will lead to a quashing of the decision taken. In short, a competitor is entitled to a fair hearing, which itself has several essential elements:

No bias

The person or panel hearing the case must neither exhibit nor possess bias. **3-10** The former Chief Executive and Secretary of the Scottish Football Association, Jim Farry, was guilty of breaching this fundamental principle[22] when the SFA had cause to examine the conduct of a linesman following an incident of violent conduct during the Scottish Premier Division match between Rangers FC and Heart of Midlothian FC on 21 October 1995. The referee supervisor, Douglas Hope, in the main stand, took the view that the linesman should have seen the incident and should have taken action. The linesman was summoned to a meeting with, among others, Mr Farry, and was told that a recommendation would be made before the Referee Supervisors Executive Committee to have him struck off the list of senior referees. An excerpt from the judicial review petition and answers focuses the flaws:

> "13. The procedure leading to the decision was conducted in a manner contrary to natural justice in that:
>
> the petitioner should have been told at the outset that his general standing and eligibility to act as a senior referee and linesman were in issue. Reference is made to *Turner v Board of Trade (1894) 22 R 18; Moore v Clyde Pilotage Authority 1943 SC 457; and Mahon v Air New Zealand [1984] AC 808.*
>
> Having investigated the matter, discussed it with the petitioner and formed a view leading to a recommendation against the petitioner, Mr Wharton [Chairman of the Referee Supervisors Executive Committee] and Mr Farry should not have taken part in the deliberations of the RSEC. Mr Farry was not a member of the RSEC and, on that basis also, should not have taken part in its deliberations.[23] Notice should have been given to the petitioner that his conduct was to be considered at the meeting of the referee committee on 12th December. He should have been given an opportunity to make representations to the referee committee. Reference is made to *Inland Revenue Commissioners v Hood Barrs 1961 SC (HL) 22.*

---

[22] *McGuire v Scottish Football Association* 586/1996 (unreported) (Case No 586/1996, Court of Session, Outer House, 6/12/96—Lord Coulsfield).

[23] Reference is made to *Somerville v Edinburgh Assembly Rooms Directors* (1899) 1 F 1091, *Barrs v British Wool Marketing Board* 1957 SC 72, *Palmer v Inverness Hospital Board* 1963 SC 311 and *Bradford v Macleod* 1986 SLT 244.

Answer 13. Admitted that the procedure leading to the decision was conducted in a manner contrary to natural justice but only in respect of the ground in paragraph (b). *Quoad ultra* denied. In relation to the ground in paragraph (a), the petitioner ought reasonably to have known as an experienced referee that his eligibility was an issue. He had received a copy of the supervisor's report. In relation to the ground in paragraph (c) the petitioner was given notice that his conduct was to be considered at a meeting with the referee committee on 12th December. He had no legitimate expectation of making representations at that meeting. He had been given a full opportunity to do so at the meeting of the RSEC on 1st December. In relation to the ground in paragraph (b) the RSEC comprised experienced former referees. Their decision was unanimous. Mr Farry did not take part in the making of that decision."

Lord Coulsfield quashed the decision. No evidence was required. The SFA was ordered to consider an application by the linesman for inclusion in the list of senior referees for season 1996/97.

Proper disclosure pre-hearing

3-11 The competitor being disciplined must know the case against him in sufficient detail to answer the charge.[24]

Rules must be followed

3-12 The person or panel must deal with the charge in a manner consistent with its own rules, precedent and pronouncements: that, of course, becomes a very difficult exercise if those rules are complex. The Jockey Club of South Africa had one of its fines quashed largely as a result of its doping rules being held to amount in effect to "an elaborate system of inter-meshing measures".[25]

Rules relied upon must support punishment

3-13 Those rules themselves must support the decision taken and, once a rule has been expressly relied upon, it is of no consequence that other powers may have sustained the decision complained of. In *Ferguson v Scottish Football Association*,[26] the former Rangers' striker Duncan Ferguson famously demonstrated a lacuna within the SFA Disciplinary Procedure (and it merited only passing mention in the ultimate judgment that the SFA had had—unused—powers in its Articles to have lawfully punished the player).

The SFA invoked its rule to visit additional punishment beyond its tariff-based disciplinary scheme following the notorious head-butting incident

---

[24] *St Johnstone FC v Scottish Football Association* 1965 SLT 171.

[25] *Jockey Club of South Africa v Forbes* (1993) (1) SA 649.

[26] 1996 GWD 11–601.

during the Rangers FC versus Raith Rovers FC Scottish Premier Division match on 16 April 1994. Paragraph 3(i) of the SFA Disciplinary Procedure provided:

> "Exceptional cases of players' misconduct.

> Notwithstanding anything stipulated elsewhere herein, the Disciplinary Committee retains discretion to deal with exceptional cases of players' misconduct and to impose *any additional penalties* in such cases as it considers may be merited. The Committee shall determine if a case is to be treated on an exceptional basis and that player shall be called to appear before the Committee" (emphasis added).

The player argued that there could be no additional penalty where no original penalty had been imposed. The SFA resisted the petition relying on detailed provisions within its Articles of Association (which had not previously in this case been relied upon) for the right to discipline; and proposing "other" as an appropriate synonym for "additional"; and by seeking to influence Lord Macfadyen with the likely consequences of the serious lacuna which would be left were he to favour the player's interpretation. In ruling for the player and ordering the SFA to recall the suspension, Lord Macfadyen identified the report of a match official, and a penalty, each as "essential preconditions to the exercise of the power [relied upon by the SFA]".[27] As to the possibility of a serious lacuna thereby being exposed, the judge stated: "while that consideration might tilt the balance of preference between two constructions of almost equal merit, I do not consider that it is sufficient to lead to the rejection of the construction for which the petitioner contends".[28] The judge found it notable that the words in question were "part of a disciplinary code the operation of which can result in the imposition of penalties which can materially affect the player's patrimonial interest".

Before leaving the Ferguson case it is worth noting the second line pursued by the player, which was rejected by the judge. By the time the Disciplinary Appeals Tribunal ratified the decision of the Disciplinary Committee the player had been jailed. The ban was immediately reinstated, and ran during the short period of the player's imprisonment. The player's counsel argued that the tribunal had been guilty of illogicality by failing to backdate the commencement of the ban to include the whole time that the player had been in prison. This line was resisted by the SFA relying on the *Wednesbury* principles (above). Lord Macfadyen had little hesitation in agreeing with the SFA's suggestion that: "it could not be inferred merely from the fact that [the Tribunal] had rejected the submission that the penalty should be reduced that it had acted in a way which no reasonable Tribunal would have acted".[29] Two lines pled but not argued in this case are considered below.

3-14

---

[27] at 17–18.

[28] at 21.

[29] at 24.

Access to all the evidence

3-15　The competitor must have access to all the evidence before the person or panel and must not be denied the right to lead relevant evidence.[30]

Compliance with the *Wednesbury* principles

3-16　The panel determining the case must not breach the *Wednesbury* principles (see above). *Singapore Amateur Athletics Association v Haron bin Mundir*[31] provides a good illustration of a trial judge confining his role to an examination of the decision-making process, and not usurping the jurisdiction of the Association on the merits. The facts of the case, themselves, give a striking example of how not to conduct disciplinary proceedings. Mundir, a former Singaporean sprint champion, was persuaded to train (as part of his attempt to qualify for the 1989 South East Asia Games) in Japan, rather than in the United States of America, his favoured location, on the understanding that Don Quarrie would be there to assist him. After five weeks in Japan with no sign of Quarrie the athlete returned home without the permission of his Association. The Association considered that the athlete's actions had created "an international fiasco" and gave the athlete to understand that if he tendered an apology matters would rest there. Mundir said sorry and then found himself before the Association's disciplinary panel once again, this time to be handed a two-year suspension! The court had little hesitation in quashing the suspension. The proceedings had not only breached the principles of natural justice, they were "farcical".

Importance of loss of livelihood

3-17　Beyond these basic entitlements are many features which are desirable and the absence of which may lead, in special circumstances, to a reduction of the decision to which objection is taken. Before considering these additional features it is worth commenting, at the outset, that professional competitors will rely heavily on the loss of livelihood that often accompanies disciplinary sanctions. Traditionally, the court has not been impressed by the existence of this factor. The *dictum* of Sir Robert Megarry in *McInnes v Onslow Fane*[32] makes that clear:

> "Courts must be slow to allow any implied obligation to be fair to be used as a means of bringing before the Courts for a review honest decisions of bodies exercising jurisdiction over sporting and other activities which those bodies are far better fitted to judge than the Court. *This is so even where those bodies are concerned with the means of livelihood of those who take part in those activities.* The concepts of natural justice and the duty to be fair must not be allowed to discredit themselves by making unreasonable requirements and imposing undue burden" (emphasis added).

---

[30] *Jones and Another v Welsh Rugby Union* [1998] TLR 8.

[31] [1994] 1 SLR 47, referred to in Beloff and Kerr, "Judicial Control of Sporting Bodies" (1995) SLJ (3) 5 at 7.

[32] [1978] 3 All ER 211.

As has already been seen, two decades after that pronouncement Lord Macfadyen has shown a greater willingness to be influenced by the loss of livelihood issue (see above). Similarly in the interlocutory proceedings which brought Ebbw Vale Rugby Football Club forward Mark Jones before the High Court of Justice Queen's Bench Division,[33] Mrs Justice Ebsworth signalled that the court has not been blind to the changes in sport which have occurred over the last 20 years: "sport today is big business. Many people earn their living from it in one way or another. It would, I fear, be naïve to pretend that the modern world of sport can be conducted as it used to be not very many years ago."[34] It is thought that the loss of livelihood is likely to be viewed by the court as the type of special circumstance which might succeed in elevating some of the desirable features discussed in the next chapter to the mandatory category considered above. Ironically, this feature may permit an association to depart from one of the mandatory principles: the obligation to act consistently. Associations may be permitted to disregard as precedents the sanctions that may have been imposed during the amateur era.

DESIRABLE ELEMENTS OF DISCIPLINARY PROCEEDINGS

There are some features of disciplinary proceedings which, presently, cannot be categorised as essential. These features are nonetheless desirable and should be adopted by any association seeking to avoid unnecessary court activity. **3-18**

Legal representation

The authorities make it clear that no party in disciplinary proceedings has an inalienable right to legal representation. Professional representation is not regarded as an essential requirement of natural justice. Associations are injuncted to avoid "legalism". This term is invariably used in a pejorative sense which can be misleading. Morris and Little[35] comment: **3-19**

> "If by 'legalism' critics mean a rigorous, procedurally correct hearing, then, quite frankly, it is to be welcomed. If on the other hand 'legalism' denotes lawyers searching for and exploiting loopholes in sports bodies' substantive disciplinary offences, a re-casting of these offences in order to maximise clarity and precision is the correct solution rather than a policy of excluding lawyers."

Enderby Town Football Club presented an appeal to the Football Association against an adverse finding of the Leicestershire County Association, and requested legal representation before the Appeal Panel.

---

[33] *Jones and Another v Welsh Rugby Union* [1998] TLR 8.

[34] at 25 of full judgment.

[35] "Challenging Sports Bodies' Determinations" (1998) 17 CJQ 128 at 135.

The Football Association refused this request, relying on a provision in its rules excluding such representation (rule 38). In a strong dissenting judgment,[36] the late Lord Denning (in early 1971) sought to prevent such blanket bans on legal representation. The Court of Appeal by majority ruled that the terms of rule 38, and their effect, were not unlawful. What troubled Lord Denning was the complete failure of the Rules to provide for representation even in special circumstances. Since the creation of the Scottish Premier League (SPL), in time for the start of season 98/99, there exists an anomaly in Scottish football as regards the representation of players, club officials and clubs in disciplinary proceedings. A party being brought before the SPL Board or an SPL Commission on a disciplinary charge can have legal representation,[37] whilst in equivalent hearings under the auspices of the SFA no such right exists.[38] The Scottish Football League also does not permit legal representation.[39] In fact, the situation exists where a party, convicted of a breach at SPL level after being legally represented at a hearing, gains the right to appeal the conviction to the SFA Appeals Committee but loses his entitlement to legal representation. The current SFA Chief Executive, David Taylor, is himself legally qualified and this may lead to a change in stance. At every opportunity since Lord Denning's famous *dictum*, the court has declined to give effect to his dissenting judgment by ruling that legal representation is an essential requirement. But there seems to be an increasing acknowledgement by the court that there is some scope for challenging some of these aged precepts of natural justice.

3-20   Even when a lawyer was deemed necessary to represent Mark Jones, a professional rugby player with a speech impediment standing to lose his income, the court was unwilling to foist a barrister, with full rights to represent, cross-question and make submissions, on the disciplining association.[40] Mark Jones, the Ebbw Vale forward, was sent off during his club's match against Swansea Rugby Club on 9 November 1996. He had been exchanging punches with a Swansea player (a former team mate!). Jones took the view that, whilst the referee's decision was one that he was entitled to make, he may not have done anything more than book him had he been aware of all the relevant circumstances. There is a suggestion in the evidence that Jones was not the instigator of the incident. The relevant resolution (13) of the WRU's Rules at that time set down the procedure to be adopted when dealing with a player who had been sent off. The resolution states:

> "... before the case of a player reported by a referee for misconduct is dealt with by the appropriate Committee, he shall be furnished as soon as possible with a copy of the referee's report and invited to forward his observations thereon.

---

[36] *Enderby Town v Football Association* [1971] Ch 591.

[37] SPL Rule G9.

[38] Art 184.3.3.

[39] See *DUFC Ltd v SFA & SFL* 1998 SLT 1244 considered at 3-25 below.

[40] *Jones and Ebbw Vale Rugby v Welsh Rugby Football Union* [1998] TLR 8.

The player must appear before the Committee ... At the meeting, at which he may be accompanied by a Club Official, he may give an explanation or make representations as to the referee's report and the Committee shall invite other persons as it thinks fit to attend and similarly make representations ... no punishment by way of prohibition, suspension or otherwise shall be imposed upon a Club, without the Club's representatives first being given the opportunity of appearing before the Committee to make such submissions as they fit think. The Committee may request or accept any video, film or other visual evidence appropriate to the case.

The decision of the Committee on all matters relating to discipline shall be final, subject to the Committee's right to review its decision at its absolute discretion at any time."

By chance, the Ebbw Vale Treasurer was a practising silk, Patrick **3-21** Harrington, QC, and, whilst he was allowed to attend a disciplinary hearing with the player, he was there as a "shoulder to lean on" and not as an advocate. He was able to speak to the committee on the player's behalf and to make representations on the referee's report and on the video of the game which the committee were due to review. Crucially, however, he was not allowed to ask questions of the referee nor to be present in the room when the committee watched the video. An argument to that effect (that is, that he had no legal representation as that expression is properly understood) was advanced before Mrs Justice Ebsworth and there is some indication[41] that this factor tipped the balance in favour of the injunction which she granted on an interim basis, pending trial. While the judgment makes clear that the judge had no difficulty in principle with the disciplinary decision having been reached following an inquisitorial, rather than an accusatorial, process, she was surprised to note that the player was not entitled to adduce his own evidence or challenge evidence by questioning. The problem for the Welsh Rugby Union was that their disciplinary code, which had not been amended in response to the challenges of the professional era, did not allow even the inquisitorial process to operate fairly. For reasons apparently bound up in custom and practice the video of the incident which brought Jones before the committee was not played during the hearing. Instead, the committee recessed and watched the video in private. By this process, the player was denied the opportunity of making points by reference to the tape as it played. That was plainly wrong. Mrs Justice Ebsworth stated: "It seems to me to be clearly arguable the Committee was wrong to refuse to vary its procedure for no reason other than 'we don't do things that way'."[42] But for this extraordinary and unaccountable procedural lapse the committee's decision might have survived the interlocutory challenge. In the event, Mrs Justice Ebsworth was persuaded to grant the injunction in view of the complications which were bound to arise were the committee's decision allowed to stand, subsequently to be found unlawful. In those circumstances, Jones would require

---

[41] at 24 of full judgment.

[42] at 24 of full judgment.

to claim damages, the quantification of which would have been no easy task.[43]

3-22   It is worth noting that Jones' Club, Ebbw Vale RFC, also applied for injunction. The club claimed that the loss of its star player would, in turn, cause loss to the club and whilst, as a *prima facie* statement of fact, this statement is unarguable, the club were unable to demonstrate any attempt whatsoever to join themselves to the disciplinary proceedings. Further, the club had made no attempt to secure a revisal to the Rules to provide for such a procedure (despite having had an opportunity to do so). Mrs Justice Ebsworth would not have granted the club an injunction for these reasons. While Jones' three-month ban remained suspended pending trial (proof) the Welsh Rugby Union sought to recommence the disciplinary process on the basis that the judge had indicated that the suspension would not remain in abeyance if the Welsh Rugby Union were to reconvene under less restricted rules. Within days of Mrs Justice Ebsworth's ruling, therefore, the Union amended its Rules to permit a player's representative to have the right to question the referee and also to call and cross-question witnesses. It was also stated that any player's request for legal representation would be considered on its merits (a provision which would have satisfied Lord Denning in *Enderby Town FC*[44]). Whilst the Welsh Rugby Union were thus in a position to restart the proceedings against Jones, the player and his representatives took the view that further procedure would be unlawful, standing Mrs Justice Ebsworth's order. That stance was subsequently proved groundless, but not before the disciplinary committee had examined the facts of the case and imposed a punishment of 28 days' suspension during proceedings at which Jones and his representatives were deliberately absent. It is an irony of this case that the second, lawful suspension was imposed after a hearing at which the player was not even present, let alone represented. In the litigation which followed the second suspension Lord Justice Potter commented in the Court of Appeal that Mrs Justice Ebsworth had expressed the view that it was in the interests of Welsh rugby that a second hearing take place. It did not go unnoticed before the court that whilst the Welsh Rugby Union reasonably desired to have matters of discipline dealt with speedily, Jones and Ebbw Vale Rugby Club had commercial and playing reasons for seeking a delay. It was while reviewing the ruling of Mrs Justice Ebsworth that Lord Justice Potter signalled that the courts appear to be ready for some of the traditional boundaries to be rolled back. He noted that Mrs Justice Ebsworth:

> "considered that the matter was well arguable, not least on the basis that, in the days of professional sport now upon us, the requirements of natural justice in relation to disciplinary proceedings may well require further developments.

> At no time in any of the various Hearings in this case was there an attempt by the player's representatives to have the referee's decision changed. For that reason, commentators who suspect that the Jones

---

[43] See para 3-35 below.

[44] [1971] Ch 591.

case has provided scope for just such a challenge will be disappointed. The Judge herself stated that a judicial review of a referee's decision would: 'be one wholly inappropriate for a Court of law'."

The *Jones* case settled before there were any further hearings and so a number of points brought out by the litigation remain unresolved.

Providing reasons for decisions

A failure to give reasons for a decision will not, at least as matters current- **3-23** ly stand, automatically render a disciplinary decision invalid. The weight of the authorities demonstrates that reasons need not be given. It is difficult to reconcile this line of authority with the demand that even summary justice be done transparently. Reasons, however brief, are highly desirable. It is worth noting that the one line pled, but not argued, in the Ferguson Petition depended upon an absence of written reasons for the disciplinary panel's decision. Nevertheless, it is open to competitors facing significant financial loss to argue that a total absence of reasons offends the principles of natural justice.

In August 1996 Dundee United FC signed the Dutch player, Armand Benneker. The club had insisted that the player be medically examined prior to the start of the contract by both the club doctor and the club physiotherapist, as is common. Examinations revealed a medical history which affected the player's left knee. On three occasions before joining the club, Benneker had had medical treatment on his right knee in the form of injections. According to the club's doctor and physiotherapist, the player was asked whether or not he had had any medical treatment to his right knee and he replied in the negative. (Benneker maintains he disclosed one injection during the medical examination.) Within two months of signing for the club, Benneker sustained an injury to his right knee. Whilst he was able to return to training and matches briefly, by December 1996 he was unable to continue playing on account of the condition of his right knee. That event caused the club to examine the circumstances in which the medical examinations had taken place and when the club formed the opinion that there had been a material non-disclosure by Benneker, his contract was terminated—ostensibly because the player stood accused of inducing the club to enter the contract with him by making a material pre-contractual misrepresentation (no injections on his right knee) and, also, because he was in breach of his employment contract by continuing to misrepresent the condition of his right knee.

All professional association football players in Scotland have the benefit **3-24** of a standard form contract which provides for a two-tier review procedure: first, by the Scottish Premier League (SPL) or the Scottish Football League (SFL) and, second, by the Scottish Football Association (SFA). Benneker appealed to the SFL and his case was heard by the SFL's Appeals Committee. In terms of SFL Rule 65: "If any dispute or difference not otherwise expressly provided for in these Rules shall arise between a Club and player, The Scottish Football League Appeals Committee shall upon application made by either party consider and adjudicate upon the matter". No legal representation is permitted before the SFL Appeals Committee nor before the SFA Appeals Committee. At the SFL Appeals Committee

Hearing on 15 August 1997 the committee decided in favour of Benneker having heard submissions on the club's behalf and on the player's behalf. On 19 August 1997 the Appeals Committee issued a decision which was so peremptory as truly to be a conclusion, rather than a decision. There were certainly no *ratio decidendi*:

> "The Scottish Football League Appeals Committee decided that the player did not misrepresent the position as regards his right knee to the Club doctor and Club physiotherapist at the pre-employment medical on 7th August 1996 and did not thereby induce the Club to contract with him and accordingly the Club was not entitled to terminate the Contract of Service between the parties."

Beyond that bare statement no indication was given to the club, orally or in writing, of the reason for the committee's finding.

3-25   The club appealed to the SFA Appeals Committee. The SFA Appeals Committee had no more information as to the SFL Appeals Committee's judgment than that set out above, but the SFA Appeals Committee heard submissions from Campbell Ogilvie of Rangers FC and Eric Riley of Celtic FC, both then members of the SFL Appeals Committee. The proceedings before the SFA Appeals Committee were specifically restricted to a review of the procedure before the SFL Appeals Committee. Whilst the SFA Appeals Committee could permit a rehearing of the case the club had not requested such a ruling. The club sought to challenge the SFA decision by judicial review and the SFA and SFL both responded. The matter came out before Lord Bonomy for a ruling.[45] The club attempted to persuade Lord Bonomy to reduce the decision of the SFA Appeals Committee and to return the case to the SFL Appeals Committee to state reasons for their finding in favour of the player. The ground in which that order was sought was that the SFA Appeals Committee had acted unfairly and in breach of natural justice by refusing to uphold that paragraph of the club's grounds of appeal which had invited the SFA Appeals Committee to return the case to the SFL Appeals Committee for reasons. Although it has been argued elsewhere that the presence of a party who has sat in judgment at first instance ought not then to appear as a witness in any internal appeal proceedings,[46] no similar argument was put forward in this case. At any rate, Lord Bonomy makes no criticism of the presence of two members of the SFL Appeals Committee before the SFA Appeals Committee. In fact he notes that, had they been asked, these SFL Committee members might well have shed some light on the issues being complained of by the club. That no such issues were put to these members and that by far the majority of the club's appeal appears to have concentrated on matters unrelated to the absence of written reasons, lies behind Lord Bonomy's decision to refuse the petition. The club have appealed.

---

[45] *Dundee United Football Club Ltd v Scottish Football Association & Scottish Football League* 1998 SLT 1244.

[46] *Roche v de Waller,* Irish High Court, 23 July 1992, unreported. In *Roche* it was argued that a race steward who had sat on the initial enquiry ought not to have then given evidence at the appeal. It was said that this procedure was equivalent to a judge giving evidence in an appeal against his decision. The Irish High Court concluded that, in that instance, the steward could be described as merely assisting the Appeal Board, not usurping his function.

Although he did not grant relief to the club on this occasion, Lord **3-26**
Bonomy's *dictum* ought not to be regarded as support for the proposition
that reasons need not be given. In fact in some *obiter* comments the opposite view is strongly stated:

> "In my opinion the existence of a right of appeal is a factor strongly
> indicative of an obligation on the decision maker to give reasons for his
> decision. Whether or not there is a duty to give reasons will depend on
> the particular circumstances of the decision being made."[47]

Both the SFA and SFL had argued that a requirement to give reasons for
decisions would render their internal proceedings unduly burdensome.
Parties appearing before the appeals committees might take a much more
legalistic approach to the cases being heard. Lord Bonomy was expressly
not persuaded by that argument. He was unable to square that argument
with the facts of the present case:

> "I found it curious and contradictory that the [SFL and SFA] should on
> the one hand maintain that the League representatives attended the
> Association Hearing to expand upon the reasons for the decision,
> while at the same time maintaining that requiring written reasons
> would encourage unnecessary appeals and technical points and create
> an unnecessary increase in the formality and expense of the pro-
> ceedings."[48]

Lord Bonomy's judgment concludes with his most telling comment:

> "In the affairs of modern day association football it is easy to envisage
> a case where, in the absence of written reasons for a decision affecting
> the livelihood or major commercial interest of a party, the failure of the
> League to give written reasons for their decision or to explain the
> position at the appeal hearing before the Association could lead the
> Court to conclude that the Association were acting unfairly by adjudi-
> cating on the appeal without insisting on the reasons for the original
> decision being made known to the appellant."[49]

It can safely be stated that any disciplinary body choosing not to communicate the reasons for its decision (either verbally or in writing) to the
parties appearing before it runs a high risk of being challenged successfully,
on this ground, in the court.

Right of appeal

That the decision of the disciplinary committee of any association, at first **3-27**
instance, be capable of internal (or preferably external) review is in line
with modern principles of administrative law. It has been said, however,
that "the Rules of natural justice do not require that there should be a right

---

[47] at 1244.

[48] at 1244–5.

[49] at 1245.

of Appeal".[50] It was in recognition of this line of authority that counsel on behalf of Jones put no reliance on the fact that there was no appeal from the disciplinary committee's decision. It is in the interests of an association to provide for an appeal structure, particularly in view of the fact that procedural defects at an initial hearing may be cured at an appeal stage. This is a principle familiar to employment lawyers. The judgment of Lord Wilberforce given in the Privy Council case of *Calvin v Carr*[51] expressly countenances the approach in sporting cases. In this case it was the Australian Jockey Club which had its decision challenged. The part-owner of a racehorse was disqualified from the club for one year after an inquiry established that the horse and jockey had not tried hard enough to win a handicap race. The trial judge established that the stewards who reached this conclusion had failed in some respects to observe natural justice. The subsequent proceedings before the Jockey Club appeal committee were, however, flawless and the judge, in a decision fully supported by the Privy Council, deemed the previous defects to have been "cured".

3-28 If an association is successfully to rely on an appeal to cure initial hearing defects then it is essential that the association can demonstrate that the appeal consisted of a rehearing and not simply an examination of the decision of the disciplinary committee. This distinction calls into question, for example, the provisions of SFA Article 184.1 which stresses that the appeal structure therein provided does not give rise to a right of rehearing: "An appeal hearing shall neither be conducted as a rehearing of the case nor shall fresh evidence be permitted except with the permission of the Appeals Committee."

UNNECESSARY ELEMENTS IN DISCIPLINARY PROCEEDINGS

3-29 Some omissions in disciplinary proceedings are quite permissible depending on the circumstances.

No right of cross-examination

3-30 It has already been seen that disciplinary proceedings may be set up in a non-accusatorial way, without legal representation. In addition, the panel need not permit parties the right of cross-examination. It is sufficient that the competitor has an opportunity to put his case and that the panel satisfactorily test that case with such witnesses as appear before it, so long as the competitor has a say in who those witnesses are. If a competitor is disciplined over a number of stages it is not regarded as essential that natural justice be observed at each and every stage in the process.[52]

No right to public hearing

3-31 No competitor can demand the right to a public hearing.

---

[50] *Ward v Bradford Corporation & Others* [1972] LGR 27 at 37.

[51] [1980] AC 574.

[52] *Modahl v BAFL* [1999] TLR 552 (HL).

No obligation to heed double jeopardy rule

The second line pled but not argued on behalf of Ferguson related to **3-32** double jeopardy as has been seen above. It seems to have been accepted on Ferguson's behalf that disciplinary panels have no obligation to take into account the fact that competitors may face criminal sanctions for the same misconduct which has given rise to the disciplinary proceedings. Interestingly, the converse will not necessarily be the case. In his instructions to chief constables of 10 July 1996, the then Lord Advocate specifically urged the chief constables to take into account, when deciding to prosecute players, any punishment imposed by the governing body.[53] It can safely be assumed that a similar statement was made privately by the Lord Advocate in his guidelines to procurators fiscal.

OTHER REMEDIES

There are a number of remedies open to aggrieved competitors other than **3-33** judicial review. When the many principles of natural justice prove too nefarious to rely upon, competitors will turn to other legal principles. If a professional competitor is banned from taking part in his sport there will likely be adverse financial consequences. Thus, any court called upon to review the ban must conclude that the competitor's trade is being restrained, temporarily.

Restraint of trade

No court will reduce a decision on the ground of restraint of trade alone. So **3-34** long as the ban complained of goes only so far as is necessary to punish the disciplinary offence then the court will have no difficulty in upholding the restraint in the public interest. A similar defence is open to anybody facing the argument that a suspension from a sport contravenes Article 59 of the Treaty of Rome, as was suggested in *Wilander v Tobin*.[54] Associations are more likely to run up against restraint of trade arguments in the application of their rules[55] rather than in the operation of their disciplinary proceedings. In similar circumstances, national and European law can be pled to avoid the onerous impact of rules of membership.[56]

Damages

Generally

There will be times, regardless of whether or not a judicial review petition **3-35** is raised, when competitors will seek damages from associations. So far, the

---

[53] para 8.

[54] [1997] 1 Lloyd's Rep 195.

[55] *eg Eastham v Newcastle United FC* [1964] Ch 413.

[56] *eg Union Royale Belge des Sociétés de Football Association ASBL & Jean-Marc Bosman*, Case C-415/93, 15 December 1995; *Wilander v Tobin* [1997] 1 Lloyd's Rep 195.

scope of challenge to disciplinary proceedings has focused on the judicial review hearing. As has been seen in the *Jones* case,[57] arguments will sometimes be presented in the interlocutory context, on the basis of *ex parte* statements. That distinction will not alter the fundamental legal principles involved, but, in practice, it is likely that the competitor's arguments will be taken *pro veritate*. The court is aware that it is very difficult, but not impossible, to assess damages if a ban, once served, is found to be unlawful. Jones, the Ebbw Vale star player, was said to be so important to his side that his absence might lead the club into relegation trouble. As with all sports, relegation definitely brings patrimonial loss (and *solatium*?) and so there was clearly the possibility of a significant financial claim if the injunction had not been granted.

Loss of chance to perform

3-36 Whilst the court is prepared to entertain litigation on the basis of the loss of a chance to perform,[58] the complexity, difficulty and ultimately arbitrariness of such claims means that the court will almost invariably grant interim interdicts should a *prima facie* case be made out. The "loss of chance" caselaw is sparse, but does include a sports claim. In May 1964 an American club professional golfer joined the European tour and had an accident in a taxi. He injured his left hand and had to return home before completing his programme of tournaments. Thompson J recognised that the golfer's object in joining the tour was to gain experience of tournament play in Europe, to improve his game, to acquire publicity and prestige and to win some of the money prizes. He agreed that damages fell to be awarded for loss of opportunity of competing in tournaments (and the consequent loss of experience and prestige), and the loss of his chance to win prize money. Damages were assessed at £1,000.[59]

CONCLUSIONS

3-37 One does not have to look very hard to find a sportsman or administrator who will testify that lawyers in sport means bad news. So-called sports lawyers stand accused of single-handedly extinguishing Corinthian values. Less apparent, however, is the benefit which sport gains as a result of increased legal scrutiny. Morris and Little cited anecdotal evidence to support their conclusion that: "Previous and increasing Court scrutiny has prompted sports bodies to re-appraise their decision-making procedures."[60] With each reappraisal of the disciplinary procedure, proceedings become fairer, and competitors' rights are bolstered. Some organisations are keeping ahead of the legal issues. As has been seen,[61] the Scottish Premier

---

[57] para 3-21 above.

[58] *Chaplin v Hicks* [1911] 2 KB 786.

[59] *Mulvaine & Another v Joseph & Another* (1968) Sol Jo 927.

[60] "Challenging Sports Bodies' Determinations" (1998) 17 CJQ 128 at 129.

[61] para 3-19 above.

League permit legal representation. International rugby also boasts mature procedures: at the 1999 Rugby World Cup every match was attended by a legally qualified Disciplinary Commissioner appointed by the tournament organiser (and independent of the teams involved in the fixture) to hear any disciplinary matters arising from the match in question. In their article, Morris and Little report on a small survey which they carried out as part of their research. The resultant data almost unanimously reflected good practice and revealed the presence of significant safeguards. Notably, however, six out of eight of the associations questioned do not require reasons to be given for decisions,[62] lending weight to the theory that this may be the next fruitful basis of future challenges.

One issue which arises from internal hearings which has not yet been the **3-38** subject of litigation in this country is the recording of proceedings, particularly evidence. Ordinarily, a minute of proceedings and a record of evidence is kept by an official of the association. These records are never verbatim and issues are bound to arise because of inbuilt and subconscious prejudice on the part of the official of the association. In all but a few cases it will be unworkable to have an independent recorder of evidence present, if only because of the cost. For these reasons associations would be well advised to devise means to secure agreement to the minute of proceedings and the recording of evidence. More and more disciplinary committees are allowing the use of video evidence and, presuming that the video is played in open session allowing the competitor an opportunity of comment, that must surely be a good thing. When considering video evidence, however, it is worth recalling the problems encountered in *Elliot v Saunders and Another*.[63] Countless rewinds of the video of the tackle, at normal speed and slow motion, did not assist the court. The OB Producer informed Mr Justice Drake that that was because if he knew the tackle was going to occur at that point in the field at that particular time he would have had his cameras placed in totally different positions! Many associations will rightly rely on the court's message, often repeated, that justice can be done better by good laymen than bad lawyers. If lawyers were to dominate disciplinary proceedings disciplinary chaos would ensue. A backlog of cases would be created. The role of the lawyer, therefore, should realistically be viewed as a form of check and balance and if this ultimately makes good laymen better at dispensing summary decisions affecting the livelihood of others then justice is served. There may be a price which associations have to pay for the sanctity of their internal disciplinary proceedings. The corollary for the association which sets up its own micro legal system to prevent court challenge may be liability: the risk to the body which sees itself as giver and enforcer of the rules of the game. In the *Hyde*[64] case the Supreme Court of New South Wales have allowed a case to go to trial which relies upon, among other things, the responsibility of the drafters of the International Rugby Code, the International Rugby Football Board, for culpable failures

---

[62] at 137.

[63] High Court of Justice, unreported.

[64] *Hyde v Agar & Others; Worsley v Australian Rugby Football Union Ltd & Others*, Supreme Court of New South Wales (Court of Appeal), 19 October 1998.

in the Rules which, it is said, lead to injuries in the scrum. If liability can attach in these circumstances it may also attach to the association which, in dealing with the discipline of violent competitors, acts arbitrarily or capriciously or inconsistently with the risk that innocent participants are not protected, as far as is practicable, from the foreseeable risk of physical harm. Persistent physical offenders must be controlled, and participants are entitled to rely on disciplinary committees to do this. But we are far from this conclusion being likely to diminish the role of the sports association; instead, in practice, this will become merely another compulsion to discipline strictly and consistently and so long as this is done in a fair manner with due weight being given to all the issues the association is likely to survive court challenge.

4 THE COURT OF ARBITRATION FOR SPORT: A STUDY OF THE EXTRAJUDICIAL RESOLUTION OF SPORTING DISPUTES

Philip Morris and Paul Spink*

Of all the contributions to this volume our chapter is the one which has **4-1** perhaps the strongest international flavour and is accordingly difficult to justify as distinctively Scottish. Nevertheless, the supranational extrajudicial mode of redress furnished by the CAS[1] is as relevant to sportsmen in Scotland as anywhere else in the United Kingdom or indeed overseas. While it is true that Scottish sportsmen enjoy more extensive public law protections in relation to determinations by sports' governing bodies than

* The writers would like to thank those officials at the Court of Arbitration for Sport (hereafter "CAS") who kindly responded to our requests for information and materials. Completion of this chapter was considerably facilitated by a personal interview with Jean-Philippe Rochat, Secretary-General of the Court of Arbitration for Sport, held in Lausanne, Switzerland on 4 August 1999 (hereafter "personal interview"). Needless to say, all views expressed in this chapter are, unless otherwise indicated, to be attributed to the authors alone.

[1] The existing academic literature on the CAS is mainly American in origin, is vast and constantly growing. See, for example: JAR Nafziger, "International Sport Law as a Process for Resolving Disputes" (1996) 45 ICLQ 130; J Paulsson, "Arbitration of International Sports Disputes" (1993) 9 *Arbitration International* 359; A Samuel and R Gearhart, "Sporting Arbitration and the International Olympic Committee's Court of Arbitration for Sport" (1989) 6 *Journal of International Arbitration* 39; AT Polvino, "Arbitration as Preventative Medicine for Olympic Ailments: The International Olympic Committee's Court of Arbitration for Sport and the Future for the Settlement of International Sporting Disputes" (1994) 8 *Emory International Law Review* 347; SA Kaufmann, "Issues in International Sports Arbitration" (1995) 13 *Boston University International Law Journal* 527; JAR Nafziger, "International Sport Law: A Replay of Characteristics and Trends" (1992) 86 *American Journal of International Law* 489; IS Blackshaw, "Resolving Sports Disputes by ADR" (1992) 142 NLJ 1753; NK Raber, "Dispute Resolution in Olympic Sport: The Court of Arbitration for Sport" (1998) 8 *Seton Hall Journal of Sport Law* 75; T Castle, "The International Court of Arbitration for Sport" (1994) *New Zealand Law Journal* 400; S Netzle, "The Court of Arbitration for Sport – An Alternative for Dispute Resolution in US Sport" (1992) 10 *The Entertainment and Sports Lawyer* 1; JAR Nafziger, "Resolving Disputes Over Financial Management of Athletes: English and American Experiences" (1996) 3 *Villanova Sport and Entertainment Law Journal* 413; S Ansley, "International Athletic Dispute Resolution: Tarnishing the Olympic Dream" (1995) 12 *Arizona Journal of International and Comparative Law* 277; B Simma, "The Court of Arbitration for Sport", in KH Bockstiegel *et al* (eds), *Liber Americorum honouring Ignez Hoheweldein* (1988), pp 573–585; E Grayson, *Sport and the Law* (3rd edn, Butterworths, 2000), pp 358–360; and S Gardiner *et al*, *Sports Law* (Cavendish, 1998), pp 244–248.

their English counterparts,[2] as well as the same private law remedies embedded in delict and especially the restraint of trade doctrine,[3] the same compelling reasons exist for them to have recourse to the CAS as apply for sportsmen generally, irrespective of the legal jurisdiction in which their governing body is domiciled. First, use of the CAS is cheaper and more expeditious than litigation in the court system. Secondly, making use of the CAS is more likely to preserve continuing relationships between the sports governing body and sportsmen than litigation, which all too often brings in its wake antagonism, bitterness and ill-will. Thirdly, the high level of sports law acumen and arbitration experience to be found amongst the pool of CAS arbitrators means that the standards of justice dispensed by the CAS is at least as high if not higher than that found in the court system.

4-2   At the time of writing only one case concerning a Scottish sportsman has actually reached and been resolved by the CAS, namely the long-running saga concerning Glasgow Celtic's claim for a transfer fee in respect of the transfer of Scottish international John Collins to Monaco, which turned upon the scope of the famous *Bosman* ruling.[4] It is possible, however, for the CAS rulings to generate a "spillover" effect in the sense that Scottish sportsmen may invoke favourable CAS precedents in other dispute resolution fora. Thus, at the time of writing, Dougie Walker, the Scottish and British international sprinter, is about to take his doping dispute with the British Athletics Federation and the IAAF to the IAAF's independent arbitration panel where the centrepiece of his case will apparently be a recent CAS ruling, concerning the Swiss triathlete Olivier Bernhard, holding that small quantities of the banned steroid nandrolene can occur naturally in the body.[5] Looking to the future, many Scottish sportsmen are members of United Kingdom-wide governing bodies which have subscribed to the CAS

---

[2] By virtue of the fact that, following *West v Secretary of State for Scotland* 1992 SLT 636, sports bodies domiciled in Scotland are amenable to judicial review even if operating on a United Kingdom-wide basis. Full accounts of the role of judicial review in the sporting arena in Scotland can be found in: WJ Stewart, "Judicial Review of Sporting Bodies: Scotland" (1995) SLJ (3) 45 and S Miller, in Chapter 3 of this volume. Contrast the position of sports bodies in England, deriving their jurisdiction from contract and exercising powers of a non-governmental nature which are not exposed to the discipline of judicial review despite their monopolistic character: *Law v National Greyhound Racing Club Ltd* [1983] 1 WLR 1302; *R v Disciplinary Committee of the Jockey Club, ex p Aga Khan* [1993] 2 All ER 207; *R v Jockey Club, ex p RAM Racecourses* [1993] 2 All ER 225; *R v Football Association Ltd, ex p Football League Ltd* [1993] 2 All ER 833; and *R v Jockey Club, ex p Massingberd-Munday* [1993] 2 All ER 207. For arguments supporting the extension of judicial review to sports bodies, see M Beloff, Pitch, Pool and Rink, *et al* "Court – Judicial Review in the Sporting World" [1989] PL 9.

[3] On which see further Gardiner, *Sports Law,* pp 231–236; Grayson, *Sport and the Law* (3rd edn), pp 391–394; and P Morris and G Little, "Challenging Sports Bodies' Determinations" (1998) 17 CJQ 128 at 140–142.

[4] Case C-415/93, *URBSFA v Jean-Marc Bosman* [1996] CMLR 645. On the John Collins case, see further P Spink, "Post-*Bosman* Legal Issues" (1997) 42 JLSS 108. For a general discussion of *Bosman* and its ramifications, see PE Morris, S Morrow and PM Spink, "EC Law and Professional Football: *Bosman* and its Implications" (1996) 59 MLR 893; and K Middleton, in Chapter 5 of this volume.

[5] *The Herald,* 14 May 1999.

jurisdiction, participate in international competitions held under the auspices of International Federations (IFs) which have accepted the dispute resolution authority of the CAS or participate in Olympic Games on condition that all disputes are resolved by the CAS rather than in the local courts. This trio of institutional fora represents fertile ground in which disputes involving Scottish sportsmen may eventually be definitively settled by the CAS.

Turning to the reasons for the creation of the CAS, the key driving force **4-3** was evidently Juan Antonio Samaranch, the then President of the International Olympic Committee (IOC), and one of the few individuals with the politico-administrative authority in the international sports community able to transform his vision into a reality. The CAS is unquestionably his "brain child".[6] Apart from this essentially personal initiative, there were concerns at the time in the IOC regarding the increasing quantity of sports-related litigation, the quality of judicial decision-making in sports disputes and the need for a dispute resolution mechanism demonstrably independent of national and international sports' governing bodies.[7] The CAS was officially born on 30 June 1984, though it did not deliver its first arbitral ruling until 1986. It is headquartered in Lausanne, Switzerland and Swiss law governs its operations unless the parties specify otherwise in their arbitration agreement or clause. We now turn to a detailed case study of the CAS, examining its institutional structure, jurisdiction, operating standards, nascent jurisprudence, remedial powers and basic functions. We conclude by reflecting on the achievements of the CAS to date and the challenges it seems destined to face in the near future.

INSTITUTIONAL STRUCTURE AND JURISDICTION

The CAS can be broadly characterised as an international arbitration body **4-4** composed of 150 arbitrators selected for their expertise in sports law and arbitration. These individuals are duty bound to act independently and objectively in the discharge of their arbitral functions.[8] A major problem confronting the CAS during its first few years' operations was the absence of perceived independence given that its architect and paymaster was the IOC itself. This issue was referred to by the Swiss Federal Tribunal in *Gundel*,[9] where one of the key issues was whether the CAS was sufficiently independent from the IOC for its awards to be enforceable, in terms of Swiss law, as valid arbitrations. The Tribunal noted that the CAS was

---

[6] M Reeb (ed), *Digest of CAS Awards 1986–1998* (Staempfli Editions, 1998) p xxiii.

[7] Personal interview.

[8] Court of Arbitration for Sport, *Code of Sports-related Arbitration* (December 1995), R33; Court of Arbitration for Sport, *Guide to Arbitration* (not dated), p 12.

[9] *Gundel v International Equestrian Federation* (1993) 8 *International Arbitration Report* F-12, which is fully analysed in Paulsson, "Arbitration of International Sports Disputes" (1993) 9 *Arbitration International* 359 at 364–367 and Kaufmann, "Issues in International Sports Arbitration" (1995) 13 *Boston University International Law Journal* 527 at 539–543.

created and funded by the IOC, which also nominated a proportion of its arbitrators. Despite these "organic and economic" ties between the IOC and the CAS, the Tribunal concluded that the CAS enjoyed the requisite measure of independence for its arbitral awards to be recognised, largely because the CAS was independent of international sports federations and it was possible for a party to challenge an arbitrator on the ground of lack of independence. Influenced by the concerns expressed in *Gundel*,[10] the IOC acted promptly to bolster the perceived independence of the CAS. Responsibility for the financing and administrative stewardship of the CAS was vested in the International Council of Arbitration for Sport (ICAS) which is intended to perform a "buffer" function between the IOC and the CAS. Moreover, the cadre of CAS arbitrators was increased from 60 to 100 and in 1997 to 150 with a broader range of nominating organisations. Essentially the IOC, the IFs and the National Olympic Committees (NOCs) are permitted to nominate 30 arbitrators each. A further 30 arbitrators are selected by ICAS with a view to safeguarding the interests of athletes. The remaining 30 are chosen from persons independent of nominating organisations. These sweeping constitutional reforms and the stronger athlete input have surely laid to rest any lingering doubts regarding the genuine independence of the CAS.

4-5   Turning to jurisdiction, the CAS enjoys the power to resolve any sports or sports-related dispute unless it falls under the settlement provisions of the Olympic Charter or technical issues such as the rules of the competition.[11] Thus the CAS can and has resolved a myriad of disputes such as doping, eligibility for competition, nationality questions, selection disputes, sponsorship contracts, merchandising, transfer fees and disciplinary sanctions, etc. The mechanism via which the CAS is invested with jurisdiction is a separate arbitration agreement between the sportsman and the relevant governing body or, more commonly, an arbitration clause contained in the governing body's statutes compelling submission of disputes to the CAS. On the international plane the spectacular growth in the activities of the CAS can be ascribed to a series of agreements between it and IFs whereby the latter have acceded to the CAS jurisdiction on a wide range of issues. These agreements both endow the CAS with jurisdiction and provide a basis for the enforcement of its awards because the eligibility of sportsmen for international competition depends on the membership of national federations. Such federations include in their licensing contracts with individual sportsmen mandatory arbitration clauses that effectively implement

---

[10] Personal interview.

[11] *Code of Sports-related Arbitration*, R 27 where the expansive nature of the CAS jurisdiction is made clear, namely that it enjoys jurisdiction in relation to any dispute which "may involve matters of principle relating to sport or matters of pecuniary or other interests brought into play in the practice or the development of sport and, generally speaking, any activity related or connected to sport". It is noteworthy that the CAS has yet to experience a single instance where it has had to decline competence on the ground of the dispute not being related to sport: see M Reeb (ed), *Digest of CAS Awards*, p xxix.

the agreement between the IFs and the CAS, thus ensuring that CAS awards are binding on individual sportsmen.[12]

Within the CAS there are essentially four different categories of sub-jurisdiction, the fundamental characteristics of which are as follows.

First, there are ordinary arbitration proceedings,[13] which are essentially a **4-6** first instance hearing of a dispute submitted to the CAS pursuant to a distinct arbitration agreement between the governing body and the sportsman and are heard by the Ordinary Arbitration Division of the CAS. The procedure has distinct written and oral stages, which makes full provision for both parties to set out their cases in full. Cases can be heard in front of a sole arbitrator or a panel of three arbitrators depending on the terms of the arbitration agreement. Where three arbitrators are required the parties select their chosen arbitrator from the ICAS list and these two arbitrators then select a president of the panel. Hearings are conducted in camera, are strictly confidential and in general may not be publicised unless the award permits or the parties consent. The costs of the ordinary procedure are the basic CAS fee of 500 Swiss francs and all other costs of the arbitration including the costs of witnesses, experts and interpreters, etc. The precise proportion of costs to be borne by each party is decided by the panel at the conclusion of the proceedings and takes into account the outcome of the case together with the resources and conduct of the parties.

Secondly, there are appeal arbitration proceedings,[14] which arise when there is an appeal against a disciplinary organ of a sport's governing body, and are heard by the Appeal Arbitration Division of the CAS. In specific terms, this sub-jurisdiction is invoked when the regulations of the sports body allow for it or when the parties have concluded a specific arbitration agreement and the appellant has exhausted all available internal legal remedies prior to the appeal. In general a three-person arbitration panel is required unless the parties have agreed to a sole arbitrator or the president of the division considers that the matter is an emergency requiring resolution by a sole arbitrator. Where the arbitration agreement provides for the appointment of a sole arbitrator, it is the president of the division who exercises the power of appointment. If three arbitrators are required the president of the division appoints the president of the panel and confirms the parties' choice of arbitrators upon being satisfied as to their independence. During the hearing the parties are able to make written and oral submissions amid a regime which is scrupulous in its observance of due process. Given that the sub-jurisdiction focuses on appeals against disciplinary tribunals' determinations, it is scarcely surprising that the president of the

---

[12] Full discussion of this technique, which has both expanded the influence of the CAS and conferred real binding force on its rulings in relation to sportsmen, can be found in Nafziger, "International Sport Law as a Process for Resolving Disputes" (1996) 45 ICLQ 130 at 143–144.

[13] On which see the detailed procedural regime in *Code of Sports-related Arbitration*, R38–R46; and *Guide to Arbitration*, pp 14–17.

[14] On which see the detailed procedural regime in *Code of Sports-related Arbitration*, R47–R59; and *Guide to Arbitration*, pp18–20.

panel enjoys the power to request transfer of the file of the tribunal whose decision forms the subject-matter of the appeal. Two significant points of departure from the ordinary arbitration sub-jurisdiction are, first, that the parties (though not CAS officials) are not subject to strict rules of confidentiality, with the result that they can divulge information to third parties and the award can be publicised unless the parties object. Secondly, in relation to costs,[15] the parties are required to pay the basic CAS fee of 500 Swiss francs; thereafter the proceedings are in principle free of charge. The parties do, however, in practice advance the costs of their witnesses, experts and interpreters, and at the conclusion of the hearing the panel apportions the costs between the parties taking into account the outcome, the conduct of the parties and their respective financial resources.

4-7   Evidently arbitration hearings under both the ordinary and the appeals sub-jurisdiction take on many of the accoutrements of an ordinary court.[16] Quite apart from oral presentation of argument, it seems that the calling and cross-examination of witnesses, legal representation and detailed legal and factual argument are commonplace. Even so, all panels strive to ensure that the atmosphere is as informal as possible and that cases are resolved in an expeditious manner. The CAS is acutely aware of the need to guarantee a fair hearing. Hence if a sportsman cannot afford legal representation and the governing body is represented by a lawyer it draws on its own "legal aid fund" to pay for legal representation for the sportsman. Awards given under both procedures are required to be in writing and reasoned.[17] A study of those which are published reveals that many are akin to court judgments with a summary of the parties' arguments, citation of legal sources, reference to relevant academic writing and discussion of previous pertinent CAS rulings. Finally, enforcement teeth for awards is furnished by the fact that they are final and binding with, in general, no further right of appeal,[18] and that as valid arbitrations they are enforceable in the courts of those large number of states which are contracting parties to the New York Convention on the Recognition and Enforcement of Foreign Arbitral Awards 1958.

Thirdly, the CAS may deliver an advisory opinion at the request of the IOC, an IF, an NOC or any association recognised by the IOC "about any legal issue with respect to the practice or development of sport or any activity related to sport".[19] Once a request for an advisory opinion has been filed the President of the CAS is required to view it. If he thinks that an opinion is necessary he is required to constitute a panel of one or three arbitrators drawn from the ICAS list. Then he is required to "formulate, in his

---

[15] The full provisions as to costs at the CAS can be found in the *Code of Sports-related Arbitration*, R64–R66, which are summarised in the *Guide to Arbitration*, p 22.

[16] The following points are derived from personal interview.

[17] *Code of Sports-related Arbitration*, R46 and R59; and *Guide to Arbitration*, pp 16 and 20.

[18] *Code of Sports-related Arbitration*, R46 and R59; and *Guide to Arbitration*, pp 16 and 20.

[19] *Code of Sports-related Arbitration*, R60.

own discretion, the questions submitted to the Panel and forward those questions to the Panel".[20] Once an opinion has been given it may be published with the consent of the body requesting it but it does not constitute a binding arbitral award.[21] One leading commentator has noted the rich potential of this competence depicting it as "a fertile source of principles and norms in the development of international sports law".[22] Indeed the CAS has made a start on such a project[23] by: in the context of doping disciplinary offences, reducing the minimum sanction provided for under the regulations of an IF in order to suit the circumstances of each particular case[24]; declaring that in the event of a clash the rules of an IF prevail over those of a national governing body in the interests of ensuring uniform standards for a specific sport[25]; and in the context of benchmark standards to be applied in doping regulations, holding that the IOC Medical Code should take priority over internally based rules, at least in relation to multi-sports competitions.[26] Moreover, the CAS has been careful to preserve the purity of this facet of its jurisdiction, emphasising that it is not to be used to resolve a concrete dispute and thereby usurp its arbitral function.[27] It is fair to say, however, that the full potential of the advisory opinion power as a vehicle for the dynamic development of a code of international sports law has yet to be realised.

Finally, ICAS launched an innovative initiative in 1996 at the Olympic **4-8** Games in Atlanta, namely the CAS ad hoc division (AHD) entrusted with binding resolution of disputes on the spot within a 24-hour period.[28] Such divisions also sat during the Winter Olympic Games in Nagano in 1998 and the Commonwealth Games in Kuala Lumpur in the same year. While doubts have been aired regarding the validity of the mandatory arbitration clause, which compels athletes wishing to compete in the Games or event where an AHD is sitting to surrender their right to pursue their grievances in the local courts and accept instead the exclusive jurisdiction of the CAS

---

[20] *Code of Sports-related Arbitration*, R61.

[21] *Code of Sports-related Arbitration*, R62.

[22] JAR Nafziger, *International Sports Law* (Transnational Publishers, 1988), p 37.

[23] The following and all subsequent examples of arbitrations and page references are taken from the *Digest of CAS Awards 1986–1998*.

[24] Advisory Opinion 93/109, 31 August 1994, pp 467–475.

[25] Advisory Opinion 94/128, 5 January 1995, pp 495–511.

[26] Advisory Opinion 95/144, 21 December 1995, pp 523–531.

[27] Advisory Opinion 95/145, 10 November 1995, p 537.

[28] Full discussion of this initiative, in particular its role during the 1996 Olympic Games in Atlanta, can be found in: M Beloff, "The Court of Arbitration for Sport at the Olympics" (1996) 4(2) SLJ 5; RT Rowan, "Legal Issues and the Olympics" (1996) 3 *Villanova Sport and Entertainment Law Journal* 395; MR Bitting, "Mandatory Binding Arbitration for Olympic Athletes: Is the Process Better or Worse for Job Security?" (1998) 25 *Florida State University Law Review* 655; RC Ruben, "And the Winner Is ... " *ABA Journal*, April 1996; and J Pilgrim, "The Competition Behind the Scenes at the Atlanta Centennial Olympic Games" (1997) 14 *Entertainment and Sports Lawyer* 19. The detailed rules for the operation of the CAS AHD at the 1998 Winter Olympics in Nagano are reproduced in the *Digest of CAS Awards 1986–1998,* pp 653–660.

AHD, on the ground that such consent is illusory,[29] there are significant benefits both from the perspective of sports administrators and athletes. For sports administrators disputes are kept out of the local courts and the smooth operation of the competition is facilitated since disputes are rapidly resolved.[30] Athletes benefit from a remedy which is far more effective than a court action months or years later since the AHD is usually able to order immediate relief such as restoration to the competition or the award of a medal which may be far more important to the athlete than court-ordered compensation at some point in the distant future. AHD arbitrators are recruited from the ICAS list, are paid travel, accommodation and subsistence expenses. In terms of calibre they are at least of the same standard as CAS arbitrators sitting in the ordinary and appeals procedures; indeed it is arguable that their calibre is slightly higher given that a deliberate policy of selecting the most well qualified and experienced arbitrators is followed.[31] Moreover, the AHDs have started to make their own distinctive contribution to the emerging jurisprudence of the CAS. Thus AHDs have, for example: approved flexible practice on timely submission of entries for Olympic events and identified the harshness caused by a rigid adherence to the strict letter of the rules[32]; enforced rule 66 of the Olympic Charter which vests powers of accreditation of athletes and officials and withdrawal of it in the IOC Executive Board, so that attempts to withdraw accreditation by NOCs are invalid[33]; ruled that where withdrawal of accreditation is threatened the individual should be notified of the case against him and be given due opportunity to contest it in view of the important rights and privileges which accreditation confers[34]; stressed that while decisions turning on the rules of the game (in this instance an alleged "low blow" in a boxing match) fall within its jurisdiction, purely technical decisions by referees and umpires etc will generally not be interfered with because the AHD "is less well placed to decide than the referee in the ring or the ring judges"[35]; and concluded, on the general issue of consumption of cannabis by competitors, that while this is a matter of "serious social concern" the CAS is not a criminal court and therefore, in the absence of an agreement between the IOC and the relevant IF designating consumption of cannabis as a doping offence, not in a position to take effective action.[36]

---

[29] See, for example, Kaufmann, "Issues in International Sports Arbitration" (1995) 13 *Boston University International Law Journal* 527 at 544–547 and Raber, "Dispute Resolution in Olympic Sport: The Court of Arbitration for Sport" (1998) 8 *Seton Hall Journal of Sport Law* 75 at 95–96.

[30] This consideration was a key influence in the decision to create the CAS AHDs: personal interview.

[31] Personal interview.

[32] Arbitration 001 (AHD), 22 July 1996, pp 377–381.

[33] Arbitration 002 (AHD), 27 July 1996, pp 389–392.

[34] Arbitration 005 (AHD), 1 August 1996, pp 397–402.

[35] Arbitration 006 (AHD), 1 August 1996, pp 413–415.

[36] Arbitration 002 (AHD), 12 February 1998, pp 419–425.

In terms of future developments concerning constitutional and jurisdic-   **4-9**
tional issues, the CAS is anxious not to be seen as an over-centralised "Euro-
centric" dispute resolution mechanism. Accordingly in 1996 it started to
decentralise its operations by creating two permanent offices in Denver,
Colorado and Sydney, Australia though both are attached to the CAS seat
of government which remains located in Lausanne. Within the CAS secre-
tariat there is a strong aspiration to embark on a rolling programme which
hopefully involves the opening of CAS offices in third world countries.[37] So
far as jurisdictional developments are concerned, the CAS has recently
added a mediation facility to its services.[38] The procedure is non-binding
and informal. It requires a mediation agreement in which "each party
undertakes to attempt in good faith to negotiate with the other party, and
with the assistance of a CAS mediator, with a view to settling a sports-
related dispute".[39] The mediation facility is confined to disputes related to
the CAS ordinary procedure. Determinations by a sports body are not
subject to the mediation facility nor are disciplinary or doping issues. These
twin developments are significant steps along the road to the CAS becoming a multi-faceted, truly global, alternative dispute-resolution institution.

OPERATING STANDARDS, EMERGING JURISPRUDENCE, REMEDIAL POWERS AND BASIC FUNCTIONS

In performance of its arbitral functions the CAS draws upon a raft of legal   **4-10**
standards as well as its own subjective notion of fairness or equity. The
primary legal standards it has recourse to are the Code of Sports-related
Arbitration, provisions of the Olympic Charter, national legal rules and
rules of the sports governing body which is a party to the dispute. Judged
in terms of relative importance, it seems that the Code is by far the most
influential; indeed officials at the CAS characterise it as "the Bible"—a comprehensive, authoritative legal framework for the operation of the CAS.[40]
Even so the Code is clearly a document predominantly *procedural* in character which is supplemented in terms of *substantive* legal norms by, in
relative order of priority, provisions of the Olympic Charter, national legal
rules and the statutes of the sports governing body which is a party to the
dispute. Clearly in the vast majority of disputes these standards will prove
an adequate and satisfactory basis for resolving the matter. The CAS, however, glossing over the fact that this is strictly speaking improper for an
arbitral body, consciously makes use of a rather amorphous concept of fairness or equity where the application of legal standards leads to an unfair or
harsh outcome, usually for the individual sportsman. So powerful is this

---

[37] Personal interview.

[38] The full details of which can be found in Court of Arbitration for Sport, *CAS Mediation Rules* (July 1999).

[39] *CAS Mediation Rules*, Art 1.

[40] Personal interview.

concept that the CAS is even prepared in appropriate cases to use it to override legal rules.[41] If this leads to a measure of legal uncertainty it seems that the CAS regards this as an acceptable price to pay for achieving individualised justice, that is to say a solution which strikes an appropriate balance between on the one hand the emerging corpus of international sports law and on the other the legitimate expectations of individual sportsmen.

During the process of exercising its arbitral functions since 1986 the CAS has incrementally developed an embryonic jurisprudence which can be accessed via a commercially published digest which it is intended to update on a regular basis.[42] The digest is *de facto* the equivalent to a series of "law reports" for the CAS and embodies its key fundamental tenets on a plethora of sports law issues. The following specific arbitrations provide us with useful illustrations of the emerging CAS case law.

4-11 In analysing the nature of a sponsorship contract, the CAS has stressed that these contracts are typically not a single contract but rather a bundle of contracts including licensing, agency and commission contracts. It has also ruled that a contract signed for an established period of time cannot be terminated except on just grounds, and that a sportsman under contract with a sponsor is in breach of his duty of care if he fails to inform the sponsor that he engages in another sports activity which involves wearing clothing marketed or manufactured by another sponsor.[43]

Dealing with the vexed issue of dual nationality,[44] the CAS has posited two fundamental principles: (i) each country enjoys the prerogative to determine its own nationality rules, and flowing from this it is entirely possible that an individual may possess two or more nationalities; and (ii) where an athlete has dual nationality the athlete can elect which NOC to compete for, so that when the athlete has not participated in competition for either of the two countries he is free to elect which of the two he wishes to represent.

In grappling with controversial strict liability doping offences of IFs,[45] the CAS has endeavoured to mitigate their often draconian consequences while not hindering the effective fight against doping, which threatens the integrity of so much international sport. Thus the CAS has read a natural justice requirement into such offences so that the sportsman is given an

---

[41] Personal interview.

[42] *Digest of CAS Awards 1986–1998.*

[43] Arbitration 91/45, 31 March 1992, pp 33–46.

[44] Arbitration 94/132, 11 March 1996, pp 53–64.

[45] For useful discussion of this type of disciplinary offence, see further: A Wise, "Strict Liability Drugs Rules of Sports Governing Bodies: Are They Legal?" (1996) 4(3) SLJ 70; and P MacCutcheon, "Sports Discipline, Natural Justice and Strict Liability" (1999) 28 *Anglo-American Law Review* 37. The courts have also tried to soften the impact of these offences by adopting a benevolent interpretation where this is necessary to avoid individual hardship: *R v British Athletics Federation, ex p Hamilton-Jones* (High Court, QBD, 30 April 1992, unreported, available on *Lexis*); and *Gasser v Stimson* (High Court, QBD, 15 June 1988, unreported, available on *Lexis*).

opportunity to provide an explanation or written evidence for his defence and to seek a personal hearing after hearing the result of a confirmatory analysis.[46] Even though the CAS has accepted the reversal of the burden of proof in doping offences, it has fashioned a "general principle of law" whereby the sportsman can clear himself through counter-evidence such as proof that the prohibited substance is the result of ill-will by a third party or that the sampling or analysis procedure was in some way defective. Where the sportsman is able to do this the legal presumption of guilt is effectively rebutted.[47] The CAS has balanced these opportunities to rebut the presumption of guilt, though, by casting "due diligence" obligations on sportsmen to take all reasonable steps to ensure that prohibited substances are not administered and, if they are, promptly to inform competition organisers.[48] In terms of the substance of strict liability doping offences, the CAS has insisted that they must be cast in precise terms, accessible to affected sportsmen and promulgated in a proper constitutional manner.[49] On the other hand, the CAS has insisted that subjective intention on the part of a sportsman to engage in doping is not necessary and the fact that he was doped without his knowledge is irrelevant. Proof of such intent would render the fight against doping "practically impossible".[50] The CAS has, however, intervened at the level of sentencing by reading into doping offences a principle of proportionality whereby the severity of the sanction should reflect the gravity of the infraction, and arrogating to itself a power to vary a sanction imposed if this is necessary to reflect the special circumstances of each case and to ensure a measure of consistency in sentencing policy.[51]

The CAS has also resolved complex nationality disputes, depicting the **4-12** regulations operated by FIBA, the International Basketball Federation, as analogous to a regime of private law not affected by rules of national public law and leaving intact the power of states to define nationality. It then proceeded to uphold a regulation stipulating that a basketball player may only have one *basketball* nationality at any given time and imposed a three-year waiting period before he can switch nationality. For the CAS such provisions, far from being arbitrary, answers "the legitimate concern to prevent changes of basketball nationality from being dependent on the wishes or interests of the players and reserve the option of choosing another sports nationality".[52] On those same regulations the CAS has not been averse to filling in gaps and clarifying uncertainty: it has ruled that while a basketball player may have one or more *legal* nationalities he can only have one

---

[46] Arbitration 91/53, 15 January 1992, pp 79–91.

[47] Arbitration 91/56, 25 June 1992, pp 93–97; Arbitration 92/63, 10 September 1992, pp 115–123.

[48] Arbitration 92/71, 20 October 1992, pp 135–144; Arbitration 92/73, 10 September 1992, pp 153–160.

[49] Arbitration 94/129, 23 May 1995, pp 187–204.

[50] Arbitration 95/141, 22 April 1996, pp 215–224.

[51] Arbitration 95/141, 22 April 1996, p 223.

[52] Arbitration 92/80, 25 March 1993, pp 297–305.

basketball nationality, which exists purely for sports purposes, though no player can have a basketball nationality without having the same legal nationality. In resolving uncertainty in the regulations, the CAS opined that if a basketball player has more than one legal nationality he shall be deemed to have the basketball nationality of the country in which he was born unless he played basketball in any of the countries whose legal nationality he holds on or after his nineteenth birthday—in this case he shall be deemed to have opted for the basketball nationality of this country.[53]

4-13   In dealing with selection disputes the CAS has abnegated any responsibility for deciding which athlete is better equipped to win a medal, stressing that this is a matter for those properly qualified to make such a judgment in the national federation. Rather, the role of the CAS is to ensure that the federation has exercised its selection procedures properly and fairly while showing due deference to the national federation's procedural autonomy. This, however, is subject to the proviso that the CAS "must necessarily ... enter into the procedural affairs of the relevant domestic body if the agreement between the parties requires it to do so".[54] Where a sporting organisation opts to depart from its established rules of selection procedure and in doing so nominates a particular athlete for a particular event, expectations and obligations are created which bind the sporting organisation unless there are compelling justifications for reversing its nomination.[55] Here the CAS appears to be applying a principle akin to the doctrine of legitimate expectations which features in most developed systems of public law.

Similar restraint by the CAS can be found in a case involving a challenge to disciplinary sanctions meted out by FINA, the international swimming federation.[56] The CAS posited the following principles: (i) the CAS can only intervene if the sanctions dispensed pursuant to the rules of the IF are contrary to general principles of law, if their application is arbitrary or if the sanctions provided by the rules may be deemed excessive or unfair; (ii) provided the properly constituted decision-making body of the IF acts within the parameters of the rules laid down, the CAS cannot reopen scrutiny of the issue of whether the sanction imposed is fair and appropriate given the facts found by the decision-making body; and (iii) it is for the IF itself to evaluate whether its rules and sanctions are fair given the nature of the violation.

4-14   We can see from this selection of rulings that the CAS pursues a balanced approach which respects the institutional autonomy and specialist expertise of sports bodies while insisting that the fundamentals of due process are observed when athletes are on the receiving end of disciplinary powers or administrative powers which may adversely impact on their rights, expectations and interests. Furthermore, the CAS possesses a keen appreciation

---

[53] Arbitration 94/123, 12 September 1994, pp 317–322.

[54] Arbitration 96/153, 22 July 1996, pp 335–349.

[55] Arbitration 96/153, 22 July 1996, pp 348–349.

[56] Arbitration 96/157, 23 April 1997, pp 351–360.

of the need for substantive equity in resolving disputes, and in suitable cases has no qualms in drawing on its own subjective notion of fairness, which appears to have no legal foundation, to achieve an equitable outcome even if this involves overriding legal standards. In doing this the CAS comes closer to the ombudsman than a court of law model of dispute resolution. On the other hand the CAS more closely resembles a court than an arbitral body in terms of its attitude towards precedent. Clearly sensitive to the need for a measure of predictability and consistency in international sports law, the CAS, while not formally bound by its own previous rulings, appears to operate an *informal* system of precedent. Under this system the Secretary-General and counsel to the CAS regard it as part of their duties to collate and draw to the attention of particular panels past CAS rulings which appear relevant.[57] Indeed the published *Digest of CAS Awards* is the public face of this activity. While not modelled on the strict system of *stare decisis* typically encountered in common law jurisdictions, it appears that past CAS rulings are highly persuasive and will generally be followed unless there has been some intervening change in international sports law, or the policy upon which the previous ruling is founded is now regarded as flawed in some way. Perhaps the closest analogy is with the European Court of Justice (ECJ): as with the ECJ, previous rulings are regularly cited and discussed, tend to be followed if only in the interests of consistency, but will be departed from without any agonising if there are compelling legal or policy reasons to do so. This informal and implicit system of precedent seems to strike the correct balance between on the one hand furnishing sports officialdom, sportsmen and sports lawyers with the necessary measure of predictability regarding exercise of the CAS's arbitral functions, while on the other hand granting the CAS sufficient licence to make a full contribution to the development of a modern, responsive and sophisticated corpus of international sports law.

Moving on to the wholly separate but crucial issue of remedial powers, the CAS appears to be unfettered in its capacity to grant the aggrieved sportsman an effective remedy. The usual remedy sought and awarded is the lifting of the suspension from competition imposed in earlier proceedings by the disciplinary organ of the sports body. In addition, though, the CAS enjoys the power to order the award of compensation to the successful party. There is no ceiling on the quantum of awards, and the CAS takes into account losses under an extensive range of headings recognised in the national law governing the arbitration such as loss of earnings (often not merely from competition but also lost sponsorship income), damage to reputation, and distress and inconvenience, etc.[58] In quantifying compensation in this way the CAS is virtually indistinguishable from an ordinary court. Obviously the CAS cannot and probably would not wish to order events or competitions to be replayed, even though in many situations this would in fact be the optimal remedy for the aggrieved sportsman. Prompt and effective redress of this sort is arguably only achievable by a continuing expansion in the activities of the CAS AHDs so that they eventually cover most major global and regional competitions.

---

[57] Personal interview.
[58] Personal interview.

4-15   Finally, it is worthwhile discussing the CAS's basic functions. In particular, does the CAS regard itself as confined to a grievance-resolution function or is it prepared to embrace a more expansive "quality control" role whereby individual arbitrations are also used, where appropriate, to identify and rectify systemic deficiencies in sports bodies' rulebooks or the exercise of their administrative powers? The answer appears to be pretty clear-cut: the CAS is predominantly, if not exclusively, a grievance-resolution mechanism.[59] It does not regard itself as having a quality control mission since the content of sports bodies' constitutions and the manner in which their administrative powers are exercised are the exclusive prerogative of their duly constituted organs. Moreover, if the CAS were to assume such a quality control mandate it would inevitably give rise to a conflict of interest given that in performing its arbitral function the CAS must, if only to preserve its perceived independence, at all times act in a neutral manner by maintaining an equal arm's length relationship with both parties. Such residual quality control activity that the CAS *does* engage in is inextricably linked to its arbitral function and takes the form of identifying seriously defective regulations or administrative practices of the sports body and suggesting that the sports body might consider reappraising them in the future, if only to prevent the repetition of similar disputes to the one in hand. This is an extremely muted form of quality control that in any event is fairly commonplace in the ordinary courts. Perhaps more fundamentally, there is of course the long-term and intangible impact of the CAS rulings acting as the catalyst for sports bodies to overhaul their internal regulations and practices, though precise measurement and proper ongoing monitoring of this effect is virtually impossible in the absence of a dedicated unit within the CAS institutional structure which tracks the wider effects of its rulings.

CONCLUSIONS

4-16 After 15 years' operations there can now be little doubt that the CAS has established its credentials as *the* leading extrajudicial dispute-resolution mechanism in the field of international sports law. It dispenses speedy, procedurally meticulous, high quality justice in a field of human activity, professional and amateur sport, which has been undergoing a rapid process of juridification in the wake of the massive commercial interests which now have an entrenched stake in its structures, processes, organisation and outcomes.[60] For an institution that is still relatively youthful the CAS can take pride in establishing its independence from the IOC, its original architect and paymaster, and its significant continuing contribution to the evolution of a coherent body of legal doctrine which can be broadly characterised as international sports law.

---

[59] Personal interview.

[60] Gardiner *et al*, *Sports Law*, pp 66–70; D Griffith-Jones, *The Law and Business of Sport* (Butterworths, 1997), p 68.

Despite its impressive achievements to date, the CAS faces several challenges which it will have to tackle in the near future.[61] First, it must embark on a concerted profile-raising and provision of information campaign designed to assuage lingering suspicion amongst some sportsmen and their legal advisers that the CAS is somehow "in the pockets" of the federations and distinctly "second best" as an avenue of redress compared with the courts. Officials of the CAS are aware that such prejudice can still be found and can only be dispelled by an effective marketing strategy drawing attention to the CAS's constitutional arrangements and even-handed approach to dispute resolution. Secondly, the CAS needs to work hard to encourage those major international sports federations which have yet to fully subscribe to its jurisdiction, such as the IAAF and FIFA, to do so; only when this happens will the CAS be able to assert with confidence that its services are available to the vast bulk of the international sports community. Thirdly, in terms of the CAS's institutional structures, it is fair comment that athletes' interests are still not adequately represented; this needs to be examined as part of an ongoing project to build trust and confidence amongst athletes, so that the CAS is widely perceived as an independent, impartial and effective dispute-resolution mechanism. Fourthly, the CAS needs, in collaboration with national and international sports bodies, to consider the means by which the quality control potential of extrajudicial dispute-resolution institutions in sport can be fully exploited. It may be that the objections articulated above to the CAS performing such a role are insuperable. Even so, there is considerable room for sports bodies themselves to create their own distinct arbitration schemes (the IAAF, the Rugby Football Union and the Central Council for Physical Recreation have already done this and there are even ambitious plans for a wide-ranging British Sports Arbitration Panel[62]) or even ombudsman structures,[63] which could inject a greater measure of independence into dispute-resolution arrangements at a lower level than the CAS, open up the prospects of combined grievance-resolution and quality control functions and limit disputes reaching the CAS to those involving novel or contentious issues of sports law and policy.

In concluding this chapter there is one point that we would like to **4-17** underline above all: that the CAS for all its faults and the future challenges which it faces is surely preferable to the long-running, acrimonious and

---

[61] The following first three points are derived from personal interview.

[62] Requiring sportsmen to have recourse to such panels can be achieved by use of a *Scott v Avery* (1856) 5 HL Cas 811 clause inserted into the sporting organisation's rulebook whereby exhaustion of the arbitration mechanism is necessary before litigation may be commenced. Such clauses, however, cannot purport to oust the jurisdiction of the courts; a clause attempting to do so would be deemed contrary to public policy: *St Johnstone Football Club v Scottish Football Association Ltd* 1965 SLT 171, 175 (Outer House, Court of Session).

[63] For an excellent and exhaustive exposition of the merits of the ombudsman as a dispute-resolution technique compared with arbitration and conciliation, see further, SA Wiegand, "A Just and Last Peace: Supplanting Mediation with the Ombuds Model" (1996) 12 *Ohio State Journal on Dispute Resolution* 95.

expensive court battles we have seen recently with high profile sports personalities such as, to name but a few, Butch Reynolds,[64] Tonya Harding,[65] Alex Higgins[66] and Diane Modahl.[67] In all these *cause célèbre*, if the services of the CAS had been available or utilised at an early stage it is highly likely that the disputes would have been settled in a more expeditious and harmonious manner which fully vindicated the legal rights and obligations of both sides. The stark contrast between these sagas and the recent prompt and decisive resolution of the Michelle de Bruin case by the CAS,[68] notwithstanding the bitter disappointment of the swimmer with the substantive outcome, provides convincing support for the proposition. This alone justifies both the current role and probable increasing prominence of the CAS as an instrument of justice in sporting disputes.

---

[64] *Reynolds v Athletics Congress of the USA Inc*, 1991 WL 179760 (SD Ohio) vacated 935 F2d 270. For full discussion of the affair, see HJ Hatch, "On Your Mark, Get Set, Stop! – Drug Testing Appeals in the International Amateur Athletics Federation" (1994) 16 *Loyola of Los Angeles International and Comparative Law Journal* 37; S Mack, "*Reynolds v International Amateur Athletics Federation*: The Need for an Independent Tribunal in International Amateur Athletics Disputes" (1995) 10 *Connecticut Journal of International Law* 653.

[65] *Harding v United States Figure Skating Association* 851 F Supp 1476, 1479 (D Or, 1994). On which, see MJ Greenberg and JT Gray, "The Legal Aspects of the Tonya Harding Figure Skating Eligibility Controversy" (1994) 2(2) SLJ 16.

[66] On which see the account in C Everton, "Cueless and still fighting", *The Guardian*, 14 March 1997.

[67] For details of the long-running conflict, see "The Modahl Case" (1995) 3(2) SLJ 6; Editorial (1996) 4(1) SLJ 3; and T Knight, "Sad saga of the running battle", *Electronic Telegraph*, 23 July 1999.

[68] Which is fully reported in *The Guardian*, 8 June 1999.

5 EUROPEAN COMMUNITY LAW AND SPORT

Kirsty Middleton*

"We have our rules and our traditions. We are asking: why should the **5-1**
EU interfere? The interests of sports are not necessarily best served by
EU rules."[1]

Sport is now a multi-million pound business. Over the last few years sport,
and professional football especially, has become increasingly commercialised. The astronomical fees paid for football's top players, and the
revenue generated by the sale of television rights, have, however, attracted
the attention of the competition authorities in the European Union ("EU")
and beyond. The EU authorities have tended to regard sport like any other
area of European economic activity, although this view is increasingly
being questioned. The sporting organisations, for instance, believe that
sport occupies a unique position in the EU because of its important social
and cultural functions. This has been recognised in a Declaration on the
social significance of sport attached to the Treaty of Amsterdam 1997, which
notes "[its] role in forging identity and bringing people together".[2] A recent
consultation document on sport, published by the European Commission,
also highlights the role of sport in the EU: "Sport represents and strength-
ens national or regional identity by giving people a sense of belonging. It
unites players and spectators giving the latter the possibility of identifying
with their nation. Sport promotes social stability and is an emblem for
culture and identity."[3] The challenge facing the EU authorities and the
sporting organisations is how to balance regulation of sport with the provisions of the EC Treaty, which provide for free movement. In a speech to
the European Forum on Sport, the former Competition Commissioner, Karl
Van Miert, outlined the EU's approach:

---

* The writer extends special thanks to her research assistant Paul McQuade.

[1] M Benz, Legal Adviser to UEFA, *Financial Times*, 24 March 1998, p 24.

[2] The Treaty of Amsterdam ("ToA") was concluded in 1997 and came into force on 1 May 1999.
The ToA "simplified" and renumbered all of the Articles of the Treaty on European Union
("TEU") and the European Community Treaty (EC). This chapter refers to the old and new
numbering, with the pre-Amsterdam numbering indicated in parentheses.

[3] *The European Model of Sport: Consultation document of DG X* (1999).

"One must underline that the application of Community law to sport does not aim to cause the national character of sport to disappear in order to replace it with a Community dimension. But it is clear that the economic aspects of sport, driven by a commercial logic and not by a logic which is purely sporting, social or cultural and which cross national frontiers cannot escape the application of Community law. In sum, only the economic aspects of sport are subject to the competition rules of the Treaty and the application of these rules takes into account on the one hand the specific characteristics of each sport and on the other hand the principles of proportionality and subsidiarity."[4]

5-2   Contrary to the widely held view, the application of Community law to sport is not a new phenomenon.[5] The European Court of Justice ("European Court") decided in *Walrave and Koch v Association Union Cycliste Internationale* in 1974 that the provisions of the EC Treaty applied to sport "in so far as it constitutes an economic activity within the meaning of Article 2 of the Treaty".[6] The Court also confirmed in *Donà v Mantero*[7] that the activities of professional or semi-professional footballers where they are in gainful employment or provide a remunerated service are to be considered as economic activities for the purposes of Community law. However, it was not until the European Court's decision in *URBSFA and others v Jean-Marc Bosman* in 1995,[8] and the extensive media coverage that followed, that the application of Community law to sport received any particular attention. *Bosman* is best known for its ruling that professional football transfer fees for out of contract players and the nationality rules limiting the number of foreign players who may be fielded by a club, are contrary to Community law.[9] The case has irrevocably changed the way sport in the EU is organised and financed.[10]

---

[4] Karl Van Miert, "Sport et concurrence: 'Dévéloppements recents et action de la Commission'", Presentation to the Forum Europeen du Sport, 27 November 1997, available from DG IV's website, January 1998.

[5] For example, in 1989 the European Parliament drew attention to the compatibility of the football transfer system with Community law, which it described as a "latter day version of the slave trade, a violation of the freedom of contract and the freedom of movement guaranteed by the Treaties": Janssen Van Raay, *Report of the Committee on Legal Affairs and Citizen's Rights on the Freedom of Movement of Professional Footballers in the Community* (European Parliament, Session Documents Series A, 1 March 1989).

[6] Case 36/74 [1974] ECR 1405; [1975] 1 CMLR 320. The Court concluded: "when such activity has the character of gainful employment or remunerated service it comes more particularly within the scope of Articles 48 to 51 or 59 to 66 of the Treaty." See S Weatherill, "Discrimination on Grounds of Nationality in Sport" [1989] 9 YEL 55.

[7] Case 13/76 [1976] ECR 1333; [1976] 2 CMLR 578. See also the more recent cases of *Christelle Deliège v Ligue Francophone de Judo et Disciplines ASBL* (joined cases C-51/96 and C-191/97) and *Jyri Lehtonen and Others v Fédération Royale Belge des Sociétés de Basket-ball ASBL* (C-176/96).

[8] Case C-415/93 [1995] ECR I-4921; [1996] 1 CMLR 645 (hereafter referred to as "Judgment").

[9] For a full discussion of the case, see R Blanpain and R Inston, "The Bosman Case: The End of the Transfer System?" (Sweet & Maxwell, Peeters, 1996); P Spink, "The Bosman Case" (1996), 41 JLSS 71; R Farrell, "Bosman Opinion – What does it Mean?" (1995) 3(3) SLJ 17; R Reid, "FA Premier League Seminar on the Bosman Case, London, 8 January 1996", SLJ 4; D Osborne and P Keefe, "The European Court Scores a Goal" (1996) *The International Journal of Comparative Labour Law and Industrial Relations* 111; and N Bitel, "After *Bosman*–They think it's all over" (1996) 4(1) SLJ.

[10] See A Schaub, "EC Competition Policy and its Implications for the Sports Sector", Speech to the World Sports Forum, 8 March 1998. Available from DG IV's website.

Five years after the Court's landmark judgment in *Bosman* and as opposition to the ruling intensifies, finding a solution which accommodates the commercial interests and the cultural and social dimension of sport within the parameters of Community law remains top of the EU agenda. This chapter examines some of the issues involved in applying Community law to sport. It examines the substantive Community law issues in *Bosman*; considers the impact of the Court's ruling on professional football; looks at recent developments in the transfer system, and examines the issue of broadcasting under the competition rules. The chapter comments briefly on recent developments in the United Kingdom and assesses the likely impact of the new Competition Act 1998 on the regulation of sport at a domestic level. The emphasis is on professional football, although references are made to other sports where appropriate.

THE *BOSMAN* CASE

Although it is unusual for judgments of the European Court to make much **5-3** of an impact on the ordinary man on the street, its ruling in *Bosman* prompted an unprecedented level of public attention that continued long after the legal proceedings had ended.[11] The case established that professional football transfer fees for out of contract players are contrary to Community law. The Court's ruling was based exclusively on Article 39 (ex 48)[12] of the EC Treaty which provides for the right of EU nationals to work and reside anywhere in the EU on equal terms with nationals of the host member state. The case also raised important issues regarding the application of the competition provisions of the EC Treaty, namely Articles 81 and 82 (ex 85 and 86).

Although much has been written about *Bosman*, some readers may be unfamiliar with the facts; a brief resumé might serve as a useful reminder.

Facts and procedure

Jean-Marc Bosman was a Belgian professional footballer employed by the **5-4** Belgian club, RC Liège, on a contract expiring at the end of June 1990. He earned an average salary of 120,000 Belgian francs per month ("BFR"), including bonuses. Towards the end of his contract, Bosman was offered a new one-year deal on a significantly reduced salary. Bosman refused to accept this offer: he was placed on the club's transfer list and a transfer fee set. No transfer bids were received and, at his own instigation, Bosman contacted a French club, second division US Dunkerque, who expressed an interest, first taking up a temporary transfer deal of one year at a price of BFR 1,200,000, plus an option for a full transfer. Both contracts, RC Liège/Dunkerque and Bosman/Dunkerque, were conditional on the Belgian

---

[11] See, for example, F Miller, "Beyond Bosman" (1996) (4)3 SLJ 45.

[12] Provisions of the EC Treaties are directly applicable and hence Article 39 (ex 48) is enforceable by national courts and tribunals.

Football Association, URBSFA, providing international clearance by 2 August—the French club wanted Bosman to play in an important match on 3 August. It emerged later in court that RC Liège doubted US Dunkerque's ability to pay and, consequently, the club did not ask the Belgian FA to send the necessary certificate to the French football association.[13] Bosman's transfer did not take effect and he was at this point effectively suspended from play in accordance with the rules of the Belgian FA.

In August 1990, Bosman commenced what was to become a marathon litigation against RC Liège for damages based, first, on losses he was supposed to have suffered as a result of the defendant's breach of contractual obligations and, secondly, on the unlawfulness of the transfer rules. He asked *inter alia* for a declaration in the Belgian courts that the transfer rules and nationality clauses violated Articles 39 (ex 48), 81 and 82 (ex 85 and 86) of the EC Treaty, which concern free movement of workers, control of anti-competitive agreements and prohibition of the abuse of a dominant position. Subsequently UEFA and the Belgian Football Association became parties to the case as both bodies argued that their respective rules regarding transfer were lawful.

5-5   Five years after legal proceedings had commenced, the Cour d'Appel in Liege sought a "preliminary ruling" from the European Court[14] following a request by UEFA on the interpretation of Articles 39 (ex 48), 81 and 82 (ex 85 and 86) as regards transfer fees for out of contract players and the restrictions on access of EU players to UEFA competitions.[15]

The questions put to the European Court in terms of the Article 234 (ex 177) reference were as follows.

"Are Articles 39 [ex 48], 81 and 82 [ex 85 and 86] of the Treaty of Rome to be interpreted as:

1. prohibiting a football club from requiring and receiving payment of a sum of money upon the engagement of one of its players who has come to the end of his contract by a new employing club;

---

[13] See generally Advocate General Lenz's Opinion of 20 September 1995, points 42–44 (hereafter referred to as "Opinion" and S Weatherill, Amicus Curiae, 1999 13 (Jan) 24–27 at 25 "Do sporting associations make law or are they merely subject to it?").

[14] Article 234 (ex 177) allows national courts to refer any question of Community law to the European Court if clarification of that matter is essential to the determination of the case. The European Court is merely assisting the national court and is not therefore deciding the case on appeal. The question, or questions, may be referred to the European Court at any stage before the national court hands down its final judgment. The ruling of the European Court is therefore a step in the proceedings before the national court and, although it is binding on the national court, the national court has discretion to apply the ruling in its own final disposal of the case. Thus, the ruling of the European Court may be regarded as "preliminary". See A Arnull, "References to the European Court" (1990) ELR *Rev* 380–387.

[15] UEFA has responsibility for organising the European Championships for national teams, the European Champion's Cup and the UEFA Cup for clubs. UEFA's members are the football associations of Europe (18 in total). In addition to the football associations in the member states, UEFA has around 50 members. FIFA is responsible for the organisation of football at the world level and is subdivided into confederations (for example, UEFA), which have responsibility for a particular continent. Both associations are based in Switzerland.

2. prohibiting the national and international sporting associations or federations from including in their respective regulations provisions restricting access of foreign players from the European Community to the competitions which they organise."[16]

By this stage in proceedings, Bosman's challenge to the transfer system had gained him unwanted notoriety. All the evidence seemed to point to a boycott of Bosman by other European clubs,[17] and by the time the case reached the European Court, Bosman was playing for a third division club in Belgium. Nine years after legal proceedings commenced Bosman finally received compensation from URBSFA in 1999.

The European Court's judgment

Generally

In line with its previous judgments on "sports law" the European Court **5-6** held that Community law is applicable to sport in so far as it constitutes an economic activity within the meaning of Article 2 of the Treaty.[18] In addition, the Court concluded: "the activities of professional or semi-professional footballers, where they are in gainful employment or provide a remunerated service are to be considered as economic activities."[19] The Court recalled previous decisions that established free movement of workers as one of the fundamental freedoms under the EC Treaty.[20] The Court noted that the provisions of the Treaty relating to freedom of movement for persons "are intended to facilitate the pursuit by Community citizens, and preclude measures which might place Community citizens at a disadvantage when they wish to pursue an economic activity in the territory of another Member State."[21] The Court went to say: "Provisions which preclude or deter a national of a Member State from leaving his country of origin in order to exercise his right to freedom of movement therefore constitute an obstacle to that freedom even if they apply without regard to the nationality of the workers concerned."[22] Accordingly, the Court concluded that the right of a national to enter another member state in pursuit of an economic activity would be restricted by measures which made it difficult for the national to leave his member state.[23]

---

[16] Judgment, para 49.

[17] Even Advocate General Lenz believed that "there are clear grounds for suspicion that Bosman was boycotted by all European clubs who could have taken him in": Opinion, 20 September 1995, point 47.

[18] Judgment, at point 73.

[19] *ibid.*

[20] Case 36/75, *Rutili* [1975] ECR 1219; [1976] 1 CMLR 140; Case C-370/90, *R v Immigration Appeal Tribunal and Surinder Singh* [1992] 1 ECR 4265.

[21] Judgment, para 94.

[22] Judgment, para 96.

[23] The Court cited earlier decisions, Case C-10/90, *Masgio* [1991] ECR I-1119 and Case 81/87, *Daily Mail* [1988] ECR 5483.

"Since they provide that a professional footballer may not pursue his activity with a new club established in another Member State unless it has paid his former club a transfer fee agreed upon between the two clubs or determined in accordance with the regulations of the sporting associations, the said rules constitute an obstacle to freedom of movement for workers."[24]

5-7   However, the Court gave the football associations the opportunity to justify the continued existence of the transfer rules and set out what it perceived to be the qualifying criteria: (i) the transfer rules must be compatible with the aims of the Treaty, (ii) they must be in the public interest, (iii) they must ensure achievement of that aim, and (iv) must not go beyond what is strictly necessary for their purpose. UEFA and URBSFA presented several arguments in defence of the transfer system. First, they submitted that the transfer rules were justified by the need to maintain financial and competitive balance in the game, and to support the development and training of young players. The Court concluded, however, that despite the social importance of football in the community, the transfer rules did not meet the aim of ensuring a balance between football clubs. The Court endorsed the view expressed by Advocate General Lenz:

"[that] it is of fundamental importance to share income out between the clubs in a reasonable manner. However, I am of the opinion that the transfer rules in their current form cannot be justified by that consideration. It is doubtful even whether the transfer rules are capable of fulfilling the objective stated by the associations. In any event, however, there are other means of attaining that objective which have less effect, or even no effect at all on freedom of movement."[25]

Secondly, UEFA and URBSFA suggested that the transfer system should be preserved in that it compensates clubs for costs incurred in training and developing players. The Court concluded, however, that the search for new talent and encouragement of training could not be met by the transfer system, and further that "the same aims can be achieved at least as efficiently by other means which do not impede freedom of movement for workers".[26] The Court suggested that there existed an alternative and less restrictive means of achieving the aim of training young players by the redistribution of income from TV rights.[27]

---

[24] Judgment, para 100.

[25] Opinion, point 223.

[26] Judgment, para 110.

[27] This was a view shared by Advocate General Lenz, Opinion, point 226, and is one which the European Commission has since endorsed. Karl Van Miert, for example has spoken of: "the need to guarantee the uncertainty of the results of competitions and the interdependence between competing clubs are therefore aspects which are completely peculiar to sport which justify the restrictions on competition, but which do not exclude the existence of competition between clubs. This competition is, in any case, both singular and paradoxical because each club aims to end the season with the best score, but at the same time, each club has a direct interest that the success of other clubs of the same standard should also continue. A club cannot aim simply to maximise its financial benefits and to remove competitors from the market." (Speech to the European Forum on Sports, 1997.) See also the Commission's orientation document, "Broadcasting of Sports Events and Competition Law", *EC Competition Policy Newsletter* (No 2, June 1998), p 18.

Although the Court has been prepared on previous occasions to accept **5-8** that nationality discrimination may be permitted on "non-economic grounds, concerning only the sport as such"[28] it was not suggested in *Bosman* that the transfer rules were applied for purely sporting considerations. Consequently, the Court concluded that the transfer system was motivated for economic reasons.

Nationality clauses

The second part of the reference concerned the legality of the nationality **5-9** rules. The Court held that the rules limiting the number of players from other member states whom a club can play in a match[29] were of a discriminatory nature and prohibited by Article 39(2) (ex 48(2)).[30] The Court rejected UEFA's argument that the rules did not restrict a club's freedom to employ foreign players. It said:

> "The fact that those clauses concern not the employment of such players on which there is no restriction, but the extent to which their clubs may field them in official matches is irrelevant. In so far as participation in such matches is the essential purpose of a professional player's activity, a rule which restricts that participation obviously also restricts the chances of employment of the player concerned."[31]

UEFA sought to justify the "3 + 2" rule on non-economic grounds. First, it argued that the rules guaranteed the availability of a pool of top-class players to maintain and develop national teams. The Court rejected this notion claiming that "whilst national teams must be made up of players having the nationality of the relevant country, those players need not be necessarily registered to play for clubs in that country to play for the national team."[32] Secondly, UEFA claimed that the nationality clause served to maintain the traditional link between each club and its country; UEFA alleged that this was a factor of great importance in enabling the public to identify with their favourite team and ensuring that clubs taking part in international competitions effectively represent their countries.[33] Again the Court rejected this argument, noting that there are no such rules restricting the right of

---

[28] See *Walrave* [1974] ECR 1405; [1975] 1 CMLR 320.

[29] UEFA's regulations stipulated that a club may only field three foreign players plus two "assimilated" players in European club competitions. The regulations define an assimilated player as one who has lived in the country for five years or, alternatively, has played in that club's youth team.

[30] The Court also referred to Article 4 of Council Regulation (EEC) No 1612/68, which supplements the fundamental rights articulated in Article 39 (ex 48) by providing that provisions which restrict by number or percentage the employment of foreign nationals in any undertaking, branch of activity or region, or at national level, shall not apply to nationals of other member states. See F Miller n 11.

[31] Judgment, para 120.

[32] Judgment, para 133.

[33] Opinion, point 123.

clubs to field players from other regions or towns in national competitions, and that a club's link with its hometown or locality cannot be regarded as any more inherent in its sporting activity than any link with the member state in which it is based.[34]

5-10 Finally, the Court rejected UEFA's third submission that the nationality clauses maintain competition by preventing the richest clubs engaging the best foreign players. The Court held that this proposition was insufficient to justify the restrictions on free movement, since those rules would be incapable of achieving the aim of maintaining a competitive balance in view of the lack of equivalent clauses limiting the recruitment of the best national players.[35]

The consequence of the Court's ruling was to prohibit with immediate effect UEFA's quota limits on nationals of other member states. UEFA therefore abandoned the "3 + 2" rule although clubs still in UEFA competitions observed a gentleman's agreement until the end of the season.[36] Further, while the transfer system was not to be retrospectively affected, any transfer negotiations not already agreed by 15 December 1995 were immediately subject to *Bosman*.[37]

Free movement issues

5-11 The decision of the Court to outlaw transfer fees as an obstacle to the free movement provisions of the EC Treaty means that once his contract expires a national of a member state is free to move to a club in another member state,[38] without a transfer fee being payable to the former club. Thus, a Scottish player, on the expiry of his contract, could move from Rangers FC to a French club without payment of any fee.

The Court's decision did not, however, make clear whether a domestic transfer system, operated within the territory of *one* member state, was compatible with Article 39 (ex 48). This was of particular relevance to the United Kingdom, which is a member of the European Community, comprising four countries, each of which has its own governing body for football. The Court's ruling suggested that the provisions on free movement, articulated in Article 39 (ex 48), could not be applied to activities which are confined in all respects to a single member state. Thus, if an out of contract Scottish player sought a move from Aberdeen FC to an Italian club no

---

[34] Judgment, para 131.

[35] Judgment, para 135.

[36] UEFA and FIFA have consistently argued that, as they are based in Switzerland and therefore outside the EU, they are not subject to the application of Community law. This interpretation is wrong in law. See, for example, Case 114/85, *A Ahlstrom Oy v Commission* [1988] ECR 5193; [1988] 4 CMLR 901 ("*Woodpulp*") in which the European Court held that it was immaterial that the companies involved in alleged anti-competitive practices were based outside the EU, provided the agreement had been implemented (or produced effects) within the EU. Since UEFA and FIFA conduct most of their business within the EU, Community law clearly applies to their activities.

[37] Temporal effects of the Judgment, paras 139–146.

[38] This includes EEA states, Iceland, Liechtenstein and Norway.

transfer fee would be payable since this would be an inter-state transfer under *Bosman*. If, however, the same player sought a move to Manchester United, a club situated in the United Kingdom, a fee would be payable because the transfer would be effected in one member state: an intra-state transfer.[39]

At a conference held shortly after the Court pronounced its decision in   **5-12** *Bosman*, it was suggested that Article 39 (ex 48) of the EC Treaty is only concerned with access *to* a market rather than with behaviour *within* the market, once access has been obtained.[40] Article 39 (ex 48) does not, therefore, apply to behaviour within a member state—for example, the United Kingdom. It is difficult to follow this reasoning; if an out of contract player wishes to move to another club within the same member state and this is prevented yet remains open to players coming in from other member states, it is quite clear that this amounts to discrimination as envisaged by Article 39 (ex 48).[41] Article 39 (ex 48), for example, talks in general terms of "the abolition of any discrimination based on nationality between workers of the Member States". It is hard to see in the above circumstances how the matter could be "wholly internal" as suggested by the Court in *Bosman*. The overriding purpose of Article 39 (ex 48) is to prevent discrimination, as the Court in *Bosman* noted, and the provision contains no explicit reference to the right against discrimination only being available to workers moving between member states. In any event, the Court did not address this intra-state issue and the domestic transfer system was unaffected by *Bosman*. A number of players, for example, sought to challenge the domestic position prior to the introduction of Community-compatible domestic rules at the end of the 1997/98 season.[42]

Community competition rules

Although sport affects a number of areas of Community competence (it is   **5-13** estimated that 18 out of the 23 Directorates in the European Commission

---

[39] It should, of course, be remembered that while the United Kingdom has four nationalities according to UEFA, it has only one nationality for EU purposes.

[40] R Reid, "FA Premier League Seminar on the Bosman Case" (London: Middle Temple Hall, 8 January 1996) p 6.

[41] The same point may be made of Regulation 1612/68, [1968] (II) OJ Spec Ed 475, which was cited by the Court at para 118 of the Judgment. The Regulation, for instance, provides in Article 1 that "workers should be treated with the same priority as nationals of that state". Article 4 further states that provisions "which restrict by number or percentage the employment of foreign nationals in any undertaking, branch of activity or region, or at national level, shall not apply to nationals of other Member States". See F Miller, "Beyond Bosman" (1996) 4(3) SLJ 45.

[42] Vinnie Jones and Des Walker, for instance, commenced legal proceedings in 1997 against the application of the domestic transfer rules to them by their respective clubs, Wimbledon and Sheffield Wednesday. Both players argued that they were disadvantaged compared to foreign players who are more likely to be prepared to move to another country on expiry of their contracts. The cases settled out of court. Chris Honor mounted a similar challenge in Scotland in 1997 against Airdrie FC, which, at the time of writing (September 1999), is still ongoing. Airdrie are also facing a similar challenge from Wes Reid, a former midfield player (reported in *The Scotsman*, 17 June 1999).

have some impact, direct or indirect, over sport in Europe),[43] the Community's competition policy probably has the biggest impact, covering ticket sales by agencies, transfers and restrictions on foreign sports persons, product endorsement and exclusive broadcasting rights. Contrary to the advice of the Advocate General, who is obliged to offer his opinion to the Court in Article 234 (ex 177) references, the European Court did not consider the application of the competition rules of the EC Treaty to the transfer system.[44] Given that the vast majority of players transfer between clubs situated within the territory of one member state, or at least at the time of *Bosman* the Court's decision to focus exclusively on free movement issues was surprising. Transfer rules are clearly anti-competitive restrictions and fall within the ambit of Articles 81 and 82 (ex 85 and 86). It has been suggested that a reliance on the competition rules would have resolved the anomalous situation described above, whereby intra-state transfers remained subject to the payment of transfer fees. In these circumstances, Article 39 (ex 48) need not have applied.[45]

The primary purpose of the competition rules of the EC Treaty is to create "a system ensuring that competition in the common market is not distorted".[46] The competition rules complement the free movement provisions of the EC Treaty and are therefore inimical to the integration of national markets. Article 81(1) (ex 85(1)) of the EC Treaty provides that: "all agreements between undertakings, decisions by associations of undertakings and concerted practices, which may affect trade between member states, and which have as their object or effect, the prevention, restriction or distortion of competition shall be prohibited."[47]

5-14   First, there would be no difficulty in finding that professional football clubs qualify as undertakings within the meaning of Article 81(1) (ex 85(1)). According to established Community caselaw, the term "undertaking" embraces "every entity engaged in an economic activity, regardless of the legal status of the entity, and the way it is financed".[48] Given that professional football clubs are now multi-million pound businesses and some clubs, predominantly in the English Premier League (for example, Manchester United and Chelsea), are listed on the stock exchange, the Advocate General had no difficulty in rejecting the assertion that football clubs are non-profit-making organisations.[49]

---

[43] Schaub, "EC Competition Policy and its Implications for the Sports Sector", Speech to the World Sports Forum, 8 March 1998.

[44] The Court's decision not to address the competition issues also contradicted the Commission's position that with respect to the transfer rules only the competition provisions of the EC Treaty should be applied.

[45] P Spink, "Blowing the Whistle on Football Transfer Systems", 1999 JR 73.

[46] EC Treaty, Art 3(g).

[47] Agreements which fall within the scope of Article 81(1) are null and void unless they meet the criteria for an exemption from the competition rules under Article 81(3). See generally, R Whish, *Competition Law* (3rd edn, Butterworths).

[48] Case C-41/90, *Hofner and Elser v Macroton GmbH* [1991] ECR I-1979, para 21; [1993] 4 CMLR 306, cited by Advocate General Lenz in *Bosman*, Opinion, point 255.

[49] Opinion, point 255. In any event, the European Court has held that it is not necessary that the undertaking does not operate for profit for the purposes of Community competition law: Joined cases 209/215 & 218/78 *Van Landewyck v Commission* [1980] ECR 3125; [1981] 3 CMLR 134.

Secondly, the European Commission considers that a number of activities organised by sports clubs constitute economic trade for the purposes of Community competition law—for example, the sale of entrance tickets for matches, sale of TV broadcasting rights and commercial exploitation of logos.[50] UEFA and the Scottish Football League would also qualify as "associations of undertakings" since they too engage in economic activities—this point is endorsed by the recent investigation by the European Commission into the 1998 World Cup ticket fiasco (and, of course, the 1990 investigation).[51]

Thirdly, it is clear from *Bosman* that domestic transfer systems qualify as **5-15** "agreements" or "decisions by associations of undertakings" for the purposes of Article 81(1). It is also clear that the effect of the "agreement", in this case the transfer rules, amounts to a restriction of competition within the meaning of Article 81(1). This view is supported by Advocate General Lenz who noted in *Bosman* that "it is quite obvious that the restriction of competition is not only the effect of the rules in question, but was also intended by the clubs and associations."[52] Further, the full text of Article 81(1) refers to agreements which "make the conclusion of contracts subject to acceptance by other parties of supplementary obligations which, by their nature or according to commercial usage, have no connection with the subject matter of such contracts."[53] Transfer fees paid after the expiry of a contract clearly amount to "supplementary obligations".[54] Alternatively, the payment of a transfer fee might amount to the application of "dissimilar conditions to equivalent transactions with other trading parties, thereby placing them at a competitive disadvantage."[55]

Finally, Article 81(1) stipulates that an agreement must "affect trade between member states" or at least have the potential to affect trade.[56] At first glance, it is hard to see how a domestic transfer system confined to the territory of one state can produce that effect. However, like much of Community competition law, the European Court has interpreted the

---

[50] See, for example, Commission decision of 27 October 1992: *Distribution of package tours during the World Cup* [1992] OJ L326, at point 44.

[51] *ibid*. See also the Advocate General's Opinion, point 257, where he refers to the decision of the Court of First Instance in *Scottish Football Association/Commission* Case T-46/92 [1994] II-ECR 1039. The SFA raised various objections to the Commission's decision taken pursuant to Regulation 17/62 which implemented Articles 81 and 82 (ex 85 and 86), although it did not dispute the fact that the Commission could rely on Article 81 as applicable to undertakings.

[52] Opinion, point 262.

[53] Article 81(1)(e) (ex 85).

[54] See, "Blowing the Whistle on Football Transfer Systems", 1999 JR 73.

[55] Article 81(1)(d) (ex 85).

[56] If there is no inter-state aspect the matter will fall to be dealt with by the relevant member state.

phrase expansively.[57] The fact that all the parties to the agreement are based in one member state will not preclude the application of Article 81 (ex 85). The Court's rationale for this interpretation is that the particular member state is compartmentalised from the rest of the Community and trade patterns are adversely affected.[58]

The European Court has also held that Article 81 (ex 85) will apply to an agreement that actually results in an *increase* in the volume of inter-state trade.[59] In fact, any change in normal trading patterns seems to be sufficient for the purposes of the Community competition rules.[60] Although there has been a marked increase in player mobility since *Bosman* it makes no difference for Community competition law purposes whether cross-border mobility has actually led to an improvement in trade patterns. The important point is that conditions in the domestic football market are distorted as a direct consequence of the transfer rules.[61]

Concluding remarks on the case

5-16 From a legal perspective, the Court's ruling was unsatisfactory and resulted in significant market anomalies. As previously noted, the Court did not deal with the payment of compensation for transfers effected in the territory of *one* member state. Nor did it consider the legality of transfer fees paid *during* the validity of a contract of employment. It is also regrettable that the Court declined to comment on the application of the Community competition rules given the apparent simplicity of the above analysis.

Despite the legal shortcomings, the final outcome of the case was to elevate sport to the top of the Community agenda and raise public awareness of the issues involved in the application of Community law to sport.

THE IMPACT OF *BOSMAN*

Generally

5-17 The *Bosman* ruling has had a significant impact on the organisation of professional sport. The ruling applies to *all* sports in the European Union, which impose restrictions on the mobility of a player and is not confined to

---

[57] The standard test was set out in Case 56/65, *Société Technique Minière v Maschinenbau Ulm* [1966] CMLR 357; [1966] ECR 235, in which the Court held that the test was whether "it was possible to foresee with a sufficient degree of probability on the basis of a set of objective factors of law or of fact that the agreement in question may have an influence, direct or indirect, actual or potential, on the pattern of trade between Member States" (at 249). See also Case 193/83, *Windsurfing International Inc v Commission* [1986] ECR 611; [1986] 3 CMLR 489.

[58] See Case T-66/89, *Publishers Association v Commission (No 2)* [1992] ECR II-1995; [1992] 5 CMLR 120.

[59] See Cases 56 and 58/64, *Consten and Grundig v Commission* [1966] ECR 299 at 341.

[60] Case 19/77, *Miller v Commission* [1978] ECR 131; [1978] 2 CMLR 334.

[61] Spink, "Blowing the Whistle on Football Transfer Systems", 1999 JR 73 at 78.

professional football. The Court's ruling is of particular relevance, for instance, to rugby league, which has become increasingly commercialised in recent years.[62]

Celtic FC was one of the first football clubs to feel the full effect of *Bosman*. In 1996, the former Scotland midfielder, John Collins, sought a transfer from Celtic to AS Monaco. Although the player was out of contract Celtic asked for a transfer fee of between £2 million and £3 million, contrary to the ruling in *Bosman* the previous year. AS Monaco claimed that, as they played in the French first division and were members of the Federation Française de Football ("FFF"), they were subject to Community law and no fee was payable to Celtic under *Bosman*. Celtic's Fergus McCann sought FIFA's intervention and in November 1996 Celtic presented their case to the Player and Status Committee at FIFA in Switzerland. The Committee found that AS Monaco had no alternative to membership of the FFF, as the Principality of Monaco did not have its own national association. As members of the FFF, AS Monaco therefore came under French jurisdiction in football matters. Accordingly, FIFA concluded that the *Bosman* ruling applied to the transfer since both clubs were members of national football associations located in the European Union.[63] Celtic lost their claim for compensation. The decision may seem harsh but it has a sound legal base.[64] Community law does not apply to the principality of Monaco, despite the fact that the principality relies on France for foreign relations and currency. This, however, is irrelevant; the central issue is whether Community law binds AS Monaco, the football club. As a member of the FFF, and in turn UEFA, both of which fall within the jurisdiction of Community law, Celtic's assertion that the *Bosman* ruling does not apply is untenable.[65] It is irrelevant for the purposes of Community law that the entity in question is geographically located outside the European Union if it operates within EU territory.[66] The case was referred to the Court of Arbitration for Sport in Lausanne and it was expected that the Court would uphold AS Monaco's claim. However, Celtic settled the case out of court in January 2000.

---

[62] For example, in 1998 Steve Molloy threatened to take his former club Featherstone to court because the transfer fee, set at £100,000, prevented him from taking up a position elsewhere. The case settled out of court and pressure is now mounting within rugby league to revise the transfer system in line with *Bosman*. Tim Adams, the chairman of Sheffield Eagles, has said "the sooner rugby league gets into the 21st century and adopts the Bosman ruling the better" (*Electronic Telegraph*, 28 January 1998: "Eagles Chairman calls for adoption of Bosman rule"). See also Spink, 1999 JR at 68. For similar developments in British Basketball League, see *The Electronic Guardian Unlimited*, 2 May 1999—the article notes the concern of clubs over the League's rules, which allow clubs to field up to five Americans, introduced in response to the *Bosman* ruling. See also the *Deliège* case cited in n 7.

[63] The European Commission has also confirmed that the *Bosman* ruling applies to the John Collins transfer and that a transfer fee is not payable (reported in *The Herald*, 18 April 1997).

[64] *Cf* the views of P Spink, "Post-Bosman Legal Issues" (1997) 42 JLSS 108.

[65] See *Electronic Telegraph*, "UEFA to answer Celtic's claim", 11 April 1999.

[66] This is the same argument used to reject UEFA and FIFA claims that they do not fall within the ambit of Community law because they are located outside the EU: n 36.

5-18   Initially it was predicted that the *Bosman* ruling would devastate professional football and, with the loss of valuable income, many smaller clubs would go to the wall. It is certainly the case that the ruling has adversely affected some sports, and professional football in particular; rarely a week goes by without some reference to the case in the sporting press.[67] That said, *Bosman* has not precipitated widespread destruction of the transfer system as first assumed. Although English clubs are estimated to have lost over £98 million immediately following the ruling, most of it due to the loss of transfer fees, this figure is not altogether surprising given the propensity of clubs simply to write off transfer fees over the course of a player's contract. Previously clubs retained an asset value for a player on the expiry of his contract to reflect the transfer fee which they would normally expect to receive. Clubs also rushed to take advantage of the open market and many bought overseas players, which led to increased costs. Because the ruling only applies to out of contract players, a fee is still paid by clubs to buy players who are still in contract. This can be seen by the vast quantities of money which continue to be exchanged by clubs to buy the very best players.[68]

It is football's top players who have probably gained the most from the new market conditions post-*Bosman*. No longer mere employees at the mercy of their club, players have experienced a dramatic increase in their bargaining power, particularly in the final few months of their contract.[69] Some of the top players, for example, are able to command huge salaries as an incentive to see through their contract whilst others are exercising their right to see out their contract in order to get a free transfer, contrary to the wishes of their club who may be desperate for a sale.[70]

5-19   However, the boom conditions enjoyed by many of football's top players and clubs have not been shared by many of the smaller and less wealthy clubs. Five years after the Court's ruling, the gap between the rich clubs and the smaller clubs has never been greater. Accountants, Deloitte & Touche, in a review of English football warned:

> "football finance will become even more distinctly polarised between the big clubs at the top of the Premier League, and the small clubs in the Football League. To put it all in perspective there won't be a big difference between what Premier League clubs generate from TV next

---

[67] See, for example, *The Herald* "Football faces cash crisis in new era of player power", 5 August 1999.

[68] The former Arsenal striker, Nicolas Anelka, transferred to Real Madrid for £21 million in July 1999, and as this chapter went to press Luis Figo transferred from Barcelona to Real Madrid for a reputed fee of £37 million, smashing all previous records.

[69] A good example is the attempt by Manchester United in August 1999 to re-sign their captain Roy Keane. The club eventually broke their wage structure in order to keep the player.

[70] An obvious example is Paul Ritchie of Hearts who made it clear at the beginning of the 1999/2000 season that he would not sign a new deal with the Edinburgh club at the end of his contract. Although the Scotland player is entitled to exercise his right to stay for the duration of his contract, cash strapped Hearts are desperate to sell him on for a fee. Ritchie subsequently moved to Bolton on a three-month contract worth £50,000 before agreeing a transfer to Rangers FC. He finally moved to Manchester City at the start of the 2000/2001 season for £500,000.

season, and what the whole of the Football League was able to turnover for the 1995/96 season. In financial terms the trapdoor has nearly closed."[71]

Moreover, the principle of solidarity between large and small football clubs that both the European Court and the Advocate General advocated in *Bosman* has not translated into practice. John Hall, Chairman of Newcastle United, has noted that "the trickle down effect is a bit of a myth … the really big money has circulated in the last five years … in the Premier League or the top of the First Division".[72] Instead, the larger English clubs have preferred to expand their business activities to include their own TV stations, become quoted companies on the stock exchange and generally put more distance between themselves and the smaller clubs. In Scotland, there is certainly plenty of evidence to suggest that the top clubs are growing richer and the smaller clubs are getting poorer. Rangers and Celtic not only dominate Scottish football; in financial terms they are also by far the wealthiest, and the gap is growing. A recent report by PriceWaterhouse-Coopers on the financial state of Scottish football for the 1997/98 season[73] warns of spiralling wage bills over the next few years which smaller clubs cannot match.[74]

Traditionally, the transfer system has provided smaller clubs with vital **5-20** revenue, with many clubs acting as a feeder to the richer teams. Post-*Bosman*, this view has clearly diminished. Many of the smaller clubs, for example, have scrapped their reserve teams due to reduced revenues and the realisation that they are unlikely to get any money for their players. The smaller clubs are also offering far fewer contracts compared to the climate before *Bosman*.[75] Although the under-24 rule, currently in force in the United Kingdom, ensures smaller clubs receive compensation for developing young players, the present structure has a limited shelf-life under Community competition law and the new UK Competition Act 1998 ("1998 Act") (see below).

There have, however, been some positive consequences. *Bosman* has, for instance, led to a significant increase in player mobility. The number of international transfers within the European Economic Area (EEA) has increased significantly since 1995. In 1993 there were only 11 international

---

[71] Deloitte & Touche, Annual Review of Football Finance, 1997, discussed in Gardner *et al*, *Sports Law* (Cavendish, 1998), Chapter 5, at pp 253–259.

[72] "Bosman the Man for Hall Seasons", *Independent on Sunday*, 10 December 1995.

[73] PriceWaterhouseCoopers (Edinburgh), August 1999.

[74] Compare, for example, Rangers' wage bill of £20 million in 1998 with Motherwell's in the same year of £1.4 million, reported in *The Herald*, 5 August 1999. The same article notes that Rangers' retail turnover of £6.5 million was greater, with the exception of Celtic, than every other club's entire turnover for the full 1997/98 season. *Cf* the plight of First Division Clydebank, who are currently homeless: only 29 fans turned up to watch Clydebank in their first game of the 1999/2000 season (see *The Electronic Telegraph*, 2 August 1999).

[75] According to the Professional Footballers Association almost 20% of the 2,500 professional footballers registered to play in England found themselves unemployed and out of contract at the end of the 1998/99 season: "A game of two halves", *The Guardian*, 2 August 1999.

players in the English Premier League; in 1999 there were over 200, an increase of 1800 per cent. This has prompted complaints that cheap foreign imports have stifled the development of home grown talent, a matter of particular concern for smaller countries like Scotland.[76] FIFA's President, Sepp Blatter, recently announced proposals to ensure that in every team more than half of the players on the pitch (at least six) should be eligible for selection by the national team for the country where the championship is being played.[77] However, since these proposals fly in the face of the *Bosman* ruling, it is unlikely that they will be endorsed by the EU authorities. The influx of foreign players has also affected a number of sports such as British Basketball and Rugby League.

Recent developments

5-21 The Court's ruling left some scope for legal manoeuvre, despite its apparent rigidity. Post-*Bosman*, UEFA proposed that national associations should implement, with effect from 1 July 1997, a pattern contract for club players divided into two periods (three years training and three years as a first professional contract). The contract would include a system for the payment of compensation for transfers which take place at the end of the first contract period. The Commission has, however, voiced concerns over the compatibility of this system with Article 39 (ex 48) of the Treaty as the payment of "transfer compensation" at the end of the first phase of the contract still amounts to an obstacle to free movement and a distortion of competition. It is clear that the EU authorities will only accept this system provided the fee reflects actual training costs and is unrelated to the player's market value. The Competition Commissioner at the time, Karl Van Miert, indicated that the Commission would not:

> "shy from the solution of a pattern contract of a reasonable duration, on condition that the transfer compensation at the end of the first period reflects the costs of training the player in question and is not affected by the relationships between the clubs. At this stage, it appears that the pattern contract implemented by UEFA allows for this compensation to be affected by the relationship between the two clubs concerned and does not reflect the real costs of training."[78]

Interestingly, in the same speech Van Miert also suggested a salary cap in respect of the salaries of the players in order to avoid the concentration of

---

[76] In August 1999, the UK employment select committee heard evidence that the influx of foreigners is damaging the development of British talent, in response to concerns over the government's relaxation of work permit requirements in respect of non-EU football players. Work permits are to be granted for the length of the player's contract rather than year by year (*The Electronic Telegraph*, 23 August 1999).

[77] The Italian coach, Dino Zoff, has also recently voiced concerns about the effect of the *Bosman* ruling on the availability and quality of players for the national team: "Italy is especially vulnerable to foreign imports because of the high wages on offer. With trade barriers across Europe being pulled down the *Bosman* ruling is biting harder than ever." Zoff was referring to the English football club Chelsea who regularly field a team comprising nine or ten foreign players (CBS soccer live website, 2 March 1999).

[78] Speech to the European Forum on Sports, 1997. See also the Advocate General's Opinion, n 80.

good players in rich clubs. Thus, the overall expenses of each club would be limited. Unfortunately, in the post-*Bosman* era, where players are seemingly able to hold clubs to ransom, this proposal is unlikely ever to be implemented. It is also difficult to see how this proposal would be compatible with the Community competition rules since clubs would no longer be able to compete on salary.

At the end of the 1997/98 football season, the UK Home Unions devised   **5-22** a similar plan to UEFA's proposal which sought to correct the anomaly between inter- and intra-state transfers. The new structure allows out of contract players over the age of 24 to move without fee between domestic clubs. Clubs still have to pay a compensation fee for players under 24 and, of course, for players who move within contract. The same scheme is also used in Rugby League. Although this new position has some merit in that it guarantees money to clubs which invest in training and development, it remains susceptible to challenge under Community law or, certainly, the UK Competition Act 1998.[79] Indeed, the Advocate General's endorsement of this type of fee structure in *Bosman* was subject to certain qualifications, most of which have not been implemented in the new scheme.[80] Moreover, as Spink notes, "there is nothing in the Treaty of Rome about the age of 24, or any other age, as qualifying a worker for economic or legal majority."[81] He concludes: "the new transfer regime offers no more than a dilution of the fundamental criticisms attached to the old system."[82] The under-24 rule is unlikely to escape legal challenge under the new UK Competition Act which came into force on 1 March 2000.[83]

Finally, one issue currently of great interest in professional football is the   **5-23** legality of the payment of a fee for transfers effected before the expiry of the player's contract of employment with his club—the unilateral termination of the contract on the part of the player. *Bosman*, of course, did not affect the payment of transfer fees for players in contract because the European Court did not address the issue. Although the debacle concerning the transfer of the former Arsenal striker Nicolas Anelka to Real Madrid in July 1999 did much to publicise this issue, the legality of such a fee has not been tested in the courts. Midway through his contract with Arsenal,

---

[79] According to Spink, the structure was apparently based on the French model, which itself is in clear breach of Community law. Under Article 18 of the French Professional Football Charter, a player's first club is entitled to a transfer fee up to the age of 24—this is, however, doubled in the event of a transfer abroad, which would appear to be in direct conflict with the aims of Article 48. See Spink, "Blowing the Whistle on Football Transfer Systems", 1999 JR 73 at 85.

[80] The Advocate General stipulated that the transfer fee would have to be limited to the amount expended by the previous club for the player's training before it would be compatible with Community law. The transfer fee would, in addition, have to be reduced proportionally for every year the player had spent with that club after being trained, since during that period the training club will have had an opportunity to benefit from its investment in the player. Opinion, 20 September 1995, point 239.

[81] "Blowing the Whistle on Football Transfer Systems", 1999 JR 73 at 85. See also S Weatherill, "Sport, Money and EC Law" (1998) EBLR 220.

[82] 1999 JR 73 at 85.

[83] See below.

Anelka announced his intention to join the Italian club, Lazio. Represented by Jean-Louis Dupont, the lawyer who acted for *Bosman*, Anelka threatened legal action that would allow him to break his contract with Arsenal at two months' notice provided compensation was paid to the London club. In the end, Arsenal agreed a fee of £21 million with Real Madrid in July 1999. Although Anelka threatened legal action it is doubtful that his claim would have stood up in court. British courts are rarely minded to extend sympathy to individuals who break a fixed-term contract and, in these circumstances, Arsenal would have been entitled to sue for damages for breach of contract. It is highly unlikely that Anelka's contract with Arsenal contained a clause allowing either party to terminate it on the giving of notice, much less on the payment of a sum in lieu of notice. On the other hand, clubs cannot realistically force players to stay if they do not want to and, if nothing else, the Anelka saga is indicative of a growing trend that is forcing the football authorities and clubs to look closely at this issue, albeit reluctantly.[84] Holland has already introduced legislation that allows a player who has signed a contract from 1 January 1999 onwards to terminate his contract by giving four weeks' notice. Provided the appropriate notice has been served no transfer fee is payable and the player is free to leave. Clubs enjoy similar powers. The new law puts an end to huge transfer deals in Holland, the last being the sale of the de Boer brothers from Ajax to Barcelona for £14 million.

5-24   In an article published by a British newspaper in April 1999, it was alleged that FIFA was planning to give players complete freedom of movement with a new transfer system to be implemented in 2000/2001.[85] The article claimed that FIFA had plans for standard contracts which would contain provisions not only for players whose contracts have expired to have freedom of movement but extending this freedom to allow any player to leave a club at any time. The report also suggested that clubs could also terminate the contract of a player at any time, much like the new Dutch rules. FIFA, however, rigorously rejected such claims as "utter nonsense". Although FIFA is currently revising the regulations regarding transfer of players as a whole with a view to including provisions compatible with EU law for those players whose contracts have ended, FIFA have claimed that the so-called *"Bosman* Mark-II" plan, "would not only endanger clubs but even more so, the players, who would no longer have any employment protection."[86] However, if press reports are accurate, these developments are potentially far more damaging than *Bosman*. [As this book went to press, FIFA finally unveiled plans to bring the transfer system in line with Community law. The Commission has made it clear since *Bosman* that it regards transfer fees for players in contract and in respect of under-24 players as contrary to Community rules on free movement and competition. It intends to set out its view in a forthcoming case in September 2000 before the European Court, the so-called "Perugia case".]

---

[84] For example, the Dutch player Pierre van Hooijdonk refused to turn out for Nottingham Forest at the start of the 1998/99 season in order to secure a move back to Holland, and in August 1999 Leeds Utd moved swiftly to prevent their contract dispute with Jimmy Floyd Hasselbaink developing into a similar situation (*The Electronic Telegraph*, 5 August 1999).

[85] *The Mirror*, 20 April 1999.

[86] FIFA Communications Division, 20 April 1999, website: www.fifa.

UK competition law—the 1998 Act

In light of the anomaly caused by the European Court's reluctance to con-   **5-25**
sider the Community competition rules in *Bosman* the domestic transfer
system in respect of under-24 players remains unaffected, despite condem-
nation of the system.[87] Whereas it is quite possible that the domestic transfer system would fall foul of the restraint of trade doctrine, following the
decision in *Eastham v Newcastle United* in 1964,[88] or, alternatively, the
Community's competition rules, the new Competition Act 1998, affords
players an alternative course of action based on domestic law.[89]

The 1998 Act brings domestic competition law in line with the Community model, Articles 81 and 82 (ex 85 and 86). A Chapter I prohibition
will catch anti-competitive practices, whereas a Chapter II prohibition will
apply to an abuse of a dominant market position. The Chapter I prohibition, for example, mirrors Article 81 and provides in section 2 (1) that
"agreements between undertakings, decisions by associations of undertakings or concerted practices which: (a) may affect trade within the United
Kingdom; and (b) have as their object or effect the prevention, restrictions
or distortion of competition within the United Kingdom, are prohibited
unless they are exempt in accordance with the provisions of this Part."

The 1998 Act also contains a mechanism to ensure both domestic prohi-
bitions are interpreted in line with Community law for the sake of consistency, and the national courts and competition authorities will be required
to follow established Community rules and concepts.[90] This will be
achieved by means of section 60, the so-called "governing principles"
clause. Neither prohibition offers an explanation of key concepts such as
"undertaking" or "agreement" and Community law must be consulted.
Thus, transfer systems, quotas or any other restrictive rules may be
challenged in the United Kingdom without recourse to the Community
provisions (or common law doctrines). A player who wishes to challenge
the rules of a sporting association implemented in the United Kingdom
would be advised to base their claim under the 1998 Act, since the jurisdictional requirement that trade be affected is much easier to satisfy than is the
case under Community law. A challenge to the domestic transfer rules is
anticipated now that the Act is in force.[91]

---

[87] During his time in office, the Competition Commissioner, Karl Van Miert, condemned "the maintenance of the national transfer systems even if their effects are normally limited to one member state" under Community law. This clearly refers to the position in the UK. (Speech to the European Forum on Sports, 1997.)

[88] [1964] Ch 413. See P Morris, S Morrow and P Spink, "EC Law and Professional Football: *Bosman* and its Implications" (1996) 59 MLR 893 at 900.

[89] The new Act repeals the outdated and inflexible Restrictive Trade Practices Acts 1976 and 1977 and the much criticised Restrictive Practices Court has been dissolved. The Act received Royal Assent on 9 November 1998 and came into force on 1 March 2000.

[90] See KG Middleton, "Competition law Reform: Harmonisation with Community law", 1999 JR 225 and KG Middleton, "The Euro-Clause" in *The UK Competition Act–A New Era?* BJ Rodger and A McCulloch (eds) (Hart, 2000).

[91] A number of commentators support this view. See, for example, Spink, "Blowing the Whistle on Football Transfer Systems", 1999 JR 73 at 80–81.

IS SPORT A SPECIAL CASE FOR EUROPEAN LAW?

5-26 In *Bosman*, the European Court rejected the claim that sport should be granted an exemption from the Community rules excluding nationality discrimination. The Court did, however, acknowledge that sport is a different case from "other industries" subject to Community law.[92] The Commission has also indicated that it is not indifferent to the special characteristics of sport.[93]

However, the problem for the Commission, as outlined at the beginning of this chapter, is how to devise a policy that is sensitive to the commercial considerations and the social aspects. Although there are numerous industries in the Community which merit special attention such as insurance, the media and transport, the sports sector is particularly problematic given the need to ensure a degree of uncertainty as to the outcome of a competition. Moreover, unlike ordinary commerce, clubs depend upon each other for survival—it is not in the interests of football's big clubs or the game itself that so many of the smaller clubs are presently under threat. It is, of course, a moot point whether the clubs are prepared to take this view. Although it may be possible to identify some common restrictions—some, for example, which relate exclusively to sport and some to commercial considerations— the additional problem for policy makers is the differences in how each sport is organised; different rules apply in different contexts.[94]

Prior to the conclusion of the Treaty of Amsterdam, the sports sector pressed for sport to be included in the EC Treaty. The aim was to introduce a treaty article to ensure that sport would be taken into consideration in the framing of EU policies. However, it became clear at the Amsterdam intergovernmental conference that sport was subordinated to what were perceived to be more important issues such as institutional reform and the single currency. The outcome fell substantially short and, instead, a Declaration was attached to the Treaty, which formally recognises the social significance of sport. Although this declaration is not legally binding, it nevertheless represents a significant development and commits the Community institutions to take into account the unique characteristics of sport when formulating policy.

5-27 The Commission clearly does not believe there is merit in offering sport a specific exemption from the EC rules. This view might change, however, given the strength of opposition to *Bosman*. European sports ministers are reportedly united in their opposition to the Court's ruling and the French government pledged that it would reform *Bosman* and step up pressure to

---

[92] In any case, the European Court always narrowly construes exceptions to the free movement provisions of the EC Treaty since they amount to derogation from the fundamental objectives of the Community. See R Parrish, "The Amsterdam Treaty: Declaring an Interest in Sport", 1997 (5)2 SLJ 25.

[93] Schaub, "EC Competition Policy and its Implications for the Sports Sector", Speech to the World Sports Forum, 8 March 1998.

[94] See D Brinckman and E Vollebregt, "The Marketing of Sport and its Relation to EC Competition Law"(1998) ECLR 281.

exempt sport from Community law when it assumed the EU presidency in June 2000.[95] However, a review of the *Bosman* ruling would need to be compatible with Community law; European ministers cannot simply set aside a decision of the European Court. For now at least, the Commission seems content to adopt an incremental approach.[96]

BROADCASTING

This chapter would not be complete without a brief look at the current **5-28** "hot" topic in competition law. Post-*Bosman*, football clubs have been looking elsewhere for a source of income.[97] Greater wage costs, for example, in the new football climate have placed demands on the big clubs—who tend to have the best players on the highest wages—for guaranteed income from the sale of TV rights for domestic and European competitions. The larger clubs recently threatened to form a breakaway "European SuperLeague" to increase their income through TV sales. It is also arguable that greater player mobility in the post-*Bosman* climate has seen an increase in demand for coverage of sports taking place in other member states. Consequently, vast amounts of money have been injected into sports such as football, rugby league, cricket and formula one racing in recent years from the selling of television rights.[98] Although the Commission's involvement in the application of the Community competition rules to the broadcasting activities of sports organisations spans three decades,[99] the proliferation of TV stations coupled with the increase in sports coverage has prompted the Commission to take a closer look at the treatment of broadcasting rights under Community law.[1]

The central issue for a competition authority is to determine who owns **5-29** the broadcasting rights to sports events.[2] This has become increasingly important as some football leagues make it a condition of participation that

---

[95] "Europe moves to overturn Bosman", *The Guardian*, 23 November 1999, p 34.

[96] However, see "The Helsinki Report on Sport" (COM (1999) 644 and /2) discussed by S Weatherill (2000) 25 EL Rev June 282.

[97] Deloitte & Touche note in their 1997 Annual Review of Football Finance that "the principal reason that the game has been able to continue is the amount of money now coming into football from BSkyB", and, "[it] is clear that the banks were prepared to lend to clubs in 1996 in anticipation of the funds coming through in later years."

[98] The four-year deal the English Premier League struck with BSkyB in 1996, for example, is worth £670 million to English football. A new deal is anticipated to be in place by June 2000, worth over £1 billion.

[99] The first case involved a complaint to the Commission about the grant of exclusive rights to record and broadcast football league matches: *English Football League/London Weekend Television*, Ninth Report on Competition Policy (April 1980-E420, Edc), Chapter IV, Main Decisions, 1979.

[1] "Broadcasting of Sports Events and Competition Law", EC Competition Policy Newsletter (No 2, June 1998).

[2] See generally H Fleming, "Exclusive Rights to Broadcast Sporting Events in Europe" (1999) 3 ECLR 143 and D Brickman and E Vollebregt "The Marketing of Sport and its Relation to EC Competition Law" [1998] 5 ECLR 281.

the broadcasting rights are assigned to the league and marketed centrally. This prevents clubs from entering into individual arrangements with broadcasters. Instead, the broadcasting rights to matches or competitions are often marketed centrally, or sold in exclusive bundled form by a league or association representing the clubs or participants.[3] This practice, however, has been challenged in some of the national courts as evidenced by recent cases in Holland, the United Kingdom and Germany. The German Supreme Court recently upheld the view that the rights belong to the clubs and that under German competition law the associations are joint agents effectively operating sales cartels.[4] A similar conclusion was reached by the Dutch High Court of Amsterdam, which determined that the television rights belonged to the home team in principle at least.[5] These decisions would appear to reinforce the view of football clubs that they are entitled to a share of the profits.

The exclusivity of broadcasting rights is an accepted commercial practice in the broadcasting sector.[6] Exclusivity guarantees the value of a programme and is particularly important in the case of sports, as the broadcast of a sports event is valuable for only a short time. Provided the duration of such contracts is short and limited in scope and effect the exclusivity of the agreement is unlikely to be restrictive of competition. Where, however, exclusivity is longer than, say, one season, serious competition concerns are raised. The Commission in these circumstances must carry out a balancing exercise because the long duration of a contract may be necessary for those companies in taking out a large investment risk.[7] This was the justification put forward, and which the European Commission accepted, in respect of the exclusive five-year agreements between BSB (now BSkyB), the BBC and the FA for the showing of live matches of English football, between 1988 and 1993. The broadcasting companies were not prepared to invest in previously untried technology without a certain degree of exclusivity over a substantial period.

---

[3] *ibid.*

[4] *Deutscher Fubball-Bund, UFA Film and ISPR v Bundeskkartellamt*: decision of the Bundesgerichtshof 11 December 1997. The court concluded that teams are the natural owners of the broadcasting rights in respect of their particular games. The court did not, however, address the question as to whether associations may also have a claim to ownership in different circumstances.

[5] Decision of the High Court of 8 November 1996. Section 31 of the new German competition statute GWB 1998, for example, exempts "the collective sale of television broadcasting rights to sports competitors organised under the authority and pursuant to the regulations of sports federations which, in compliance with their socio-political responsibility, are committed to the promotion of youth and amateur sports and fulfil this responsibility by means of a reasonable participation in the revenues generated by the collective marketing of television rights."

[6] See D Brinckman and E Vollebregt, "The Marketing of Sport and its Relation to EC Competition Law" [1998] 5 ECLR 281 and S Weatherill "The Helsinki Report on Sport" (2000) 25 EL Rev June 282 at 290.

[7] The European Commission is currently examining a number of exclusive agreements, including the central selling of broadcasting rights, relating to the Formula One Championships. Formal proceedings were opened in June 1999 concerning the FIA's alleged abuse of a dominant position and anti-competitive practices: *The Week In Europe*, the European Commission, 1 July 1999, IP/99/434.

At a domestic level, the competition authorities have taken a tough **5-30** stance to protect competition in sports broadcasting. In January 1999, the Director General of Fair Trading, John Bridgeman, referred the FA Premier League rules and the agreements between the Premier League and BSkyB/ BBC for televising football to the Restrictive Practices Court ("RPC") on competition grounds. The Director General had previously highlighted the Office of Fair Trading's concerns:

> "Developments in broadcasting have intensified the importance of sport in the market for television programmes. Within that market the Premier League has a major, if not unique position. By selling rights collectively and exclusively to the highest bidder it is acting as a cartel. The net effect of cartels is to inflate costs and prices. Any other business acting in this way would be subject to competition law and I see no reasons why the selling of sports coverage should be treated differently."[8]

Earlier in the year, the Monopolies and Mergers Commission (now the Competition Commission) held that the proposed merger between BSkyB and Manchester United was against the public interest. The Monopolies and Mergers Commission stated:

> "We have based our public interest conclusions mainly on the effects of the merger on competition among broadcasters. However, we also think that the merger would adversely affect football in two ways. First, it would reinforce the existing trend towards greater inequality of wealth between clubs, thus weakening the smaller ones. Second, it would give BSkyB additional influence over Premier League decisions relating to the organisation of football, leading to some decisions which did not reflect the long-term interests of football. On both counts the merger may be expected to have the adverse effect of damaging the quality of British football."[9]

Contrary to expectations, the RPC upheld the rules of the Premier League which prevent member clubs from selling their TV rights to broadcasters without first seeking permission from the Premier League.[10] The OFT had argued that it is in the public interest for football to show more games and clubs should be allowed individually to contract with broadcasters to screen matches. Under the BSkyB deal only 60 out of a possible 300 games are screened. The RPC's decision means that the Premier League can continue to act collectively on behalf of the 20 clubs and the existing arrangement continues unaffected until 2001. This is the first case the OFT has lost before the RPC, at a cost of over £20 million.

---

[8] John Bridgeman (6 February 1998), quoted in an Office of Fair Trading ("OFT") briefing note concerning Football Broadcasting Agreements, dated 8 January 1999.

[9] Cm 4305 (1999), para 1.13.

[10] Press reports prior to the decision indicated that the RPC would rule in favour of the OFT. See *Independent on Sunday*, 25 July 1999: "Sky set to lose grip on football".

5-31   The decision has not, however, dampened interest from media companies in investing in British football clubs. In September 1999, Scottish Media Group acquired a 20 per cent stake in Heart of Midlothian, representing an £8 million investment in the club, small in comparison to the bid for Manchester United. As clubs look elsewhere for financial backing post-*Bosman*, this recent acquisition is indicative of a growing trend in professional football. Whether it is in the long-term interests of the game itself is another matter.

CONCLUSIONS

5-32 This chapter has sought to identify some of the issues involved in the application of Community law to professional sport; it is obvious that these issues are complex and subject to rapid development. The European Commission has, however, enjoyed moderate success in applying Community law to the sports sector and its involvement in a number of issues affecting the organisation of professional sport has ensured a fairer deal for EU citizens. The recent investigation into the 1998 World Cup ticket fiasco is one such example.[11] The much publicised saga between UEFA and the larger European football clubs who wanted to establish a European SuperLeague would have also raised some interesting legal issues, although UEFA's concessions to extend participation in their competitions appear to have headed off the competition concerns, at least for now.[12]

---

[11] This has been more a question of discrimination than competition law, although the Commission and Karl Van Miert played a prominent role. Members of the public tried to purchase tickets through the French Minitel network and gave an address in France to receive them. It was suggested that this favoured the local public and created a monopoly for the French Post Office to deliver the tickets. The investigation also found that certain other practices, which included advising the non-French public that tickets could only be obtained from national football federations and tour operators, reinforced the discrimination. When the Commission challenged the organising committee (CFO) a special hotline was set up for national and international calls to sell the remaining 110,000 tickets. The Commission wanted all the tickets to be sold abroad to compensate for the previous bias against the non-French public. The CFO refused as it argued this would discriminate against the French! In July 1999 a symbolic fine was imposed on the CFO for infringing the free movement provisions of the EC Treaty. The Commission justified the light fine on the basis that it was the first time it had reviewed ticket sales for a sporting event and the organisers could not have foreseen their legal problems. The fine is therefore meant to send a message to other organising committees, in particular the Dutch and Belgian organisers of the Euro 2000 football championships who have already offered tickets on a European-scale, posting application forms on the Internet in early 1999. See *The Week In Europe*, the European Commission, 6 May 1999, IP/99/304. For commentary, see P Spink, "World Cup Ticketing", 1998 *Business Law Bulletin* 33–4.

[12] The top football clubs wished to set up a SuperLeague mainly because they were unhappy with UEFA's allocation of revenue from the Champions League. Van Miert noted, "There were indeed talks about inviting certain clubs to participate [in Media Partners' proposed European Superleague], which is in complete contradiction with the qualification system. Sport has its unique qualities, which must be fully recognised. The purpose behind all competitions lies in the uncertainty of result together with the threat of relegation for clubs at the bottom of the table. Creating a new system would, I believe, be contrary to our essential principle." (Reported in *Le Monde*, 27 October 1998.)

Other issues likely to require attention from the EU authorities in the next few years include product endorsement or sponsorship and multiple ownership of clubs.[12] The Commission has yet to decide whether either of these issues is compatible with Community law. With over 50 cases involving sports currently before the Commission, greater legal clarity in EU policy is essential. Certainly, the *Bosman* ruling has had a severe impact on professional football that nobody could have predicted and many smaller football clubs are clearly suffering. That said, the Court's ruling cannot be overturned or set aside and any review must be compatible with the rules of the EC Treaty. The football organisations and the competition authorities must therefore find a way of separating the economic and commercial aspects of sport from its social and cultural functions or devise a policy which accommodates both. The Amsterdam Declaration and the Commission's follow-up communication "The Helsinki Report on Sport" is a step in the right direction although it remains to be seen how much significance will be attached to it. Five years after the Court's landmark decision in *Bosman*, the future of professional football has never looked less certain.

---

[12] ENIC, an English based financial firm which owns 25% of Rangers, recently lost a court battle against UEFA concerning the multiple ownership of clubs. The Court of Arbitration for Sport in Lausanne upheld UEFA's decision to prevent two or more clubs controlled by the same company competing in the same European competition. ENIC is now trying to dispose of its holding in Rangers. (Reported in *The Electronic Telegraph*, 24 August 1999.)

6   SPORTS CONTRACTS

Robin Fletcher

This chapter is written from the perspective of a solicitor representing **6-1** players' interests in negotiations for professional rugby contracts as an agent and as a lawyer. The principles involved, however, can be extended to many other sports that generally involve teams and the employer–employee relationship. Many of the references to rugby throughout the paper could therefore be read equally in the context of other sports of interest to the reader such as football, hockey, volleyball, basketball, ice hockey, etc. The object here is to provide an overview of players' contracts and the main issues surrounding them that commonly arise. The commercial and legal issues are inextricably linked in this area. The emphasis is therefore very firmly on the various practical aspects of dealing with such contracts rather than simply matters of black letter law. Following some background to this area of sport, particularly in a rugby context, this chapter considers negotiation and then the contents of the player contract.

The good news for sports lawyers is that the law in this area is relatively straightforward. All player contracts involve basic contract law, employment law and, depending on the degree of media and sponsor interest in the relevant sport, aspects of intellectual property law.[1] Issues of taxation also need to be borne in mind. The more complex European dimension is becoming increasingly important in relation to free movement, the *Bosman* ruling and the jurisdiction of international sports organisations.[2] The challenge lies in this mixture of legal issues in combination with commercial factors; particular requirements include having an in-depth knowledge of the sport and, when acting as an agent, an effective negotiation technique. The latter will be dealt with more fully later in the chapter.

Knowledge of the sport

Knowledge of and genuine enthusiasm for the sport is vital. Often the **6-2** negotiator will deal with ex-sportsmen who are now administrators or coaches and who have intimate knowledge of and great interest in their clubs. A strong technical knowledge of the particular sport is often required

---

[1] Special rules relating to the sport in question may restrict the theoretical freedom to contract. See Chapter 2.

[2] See Chapter 5 of this text for a fuller discussion of the European dimension.

in order to debate the merits of particular players with prospective or current employers and sound convincing. Sporting circles are traditionally fairly narrow and conservative in outlook. Therefore familiarity with particular coaches, personalities and traditions is a highly prized attribute. In difficult negotiations or disputes the ability to draw the sides together is highly dependent on being perceived as sympathetic and aware of the needs of the other party. Credibility with clubs and players will follow from being recognised as broadly supporting their objectives and from having a shared interest in the sport. Knowledge of the technicalities and rules of the sport is extremely useful and must be backed up with an awareness of its current trends, business developments, structures and personalities. Networking and information gathering in a sport becomes progressively easier when the interest in the sport is an extension of an agent's/lawyer's lifestyle, with leisure time devoted to it.

Rugby professionalism

6-3   The advent of professionalism in rugby union in recent years has led to a revolution in the way clubs are run and the creation of a vibrant new market in players which has overturned the old club loyalty and lack of player mobility.[3] Increasingly clubs are run as businesses, with new business professionals brought in for key activities. Determined efforts are being made to create a brand image and marketing opportunities for clubs and their star players to maximise revenue and boost crowds. The focus is on off field activities to a far greater extent, thereby involving the players in more challenging roles. Some English clubs have embraced marketing techniques and strategies from the United States to great effect.[4] Many clubs set up limited companies to run their affairs and, in the scramble to get the best players, wages escalated dangerously. After the initial euphoria clubs have attempted to reduce the wage bills, and aim to set more realistic pay norms in the future.[5] The effect on some clubs of rapid change and increased costs has been disastrous; several have gone into administration or receivership and have released some of their players or cut salaries. Disputes continue over lucrative television rights and the structure of the game, with crowd levels generally insufficient to sustain the cost base of many clubs. Players are increasingly viewed as assets of the clubs who can ultimately be traded and the transfer market is gradually taking shape. In Scotland dissatisfaction with the domestic structure lead to speculation that many players would seek contracts in other countries to further their rugby careers following the World Cup in 1999.

---

[3] For a lively discussion of the background to and early stages of the professional revolution in rugby, see the entertaining accounts in I Malin, *Mud, Blood and Money* (Mainstream Publishing, 1997) and S Barnes, *Rugby's New-Age Travellers* (Mainstream Publishing, 1997).

[4] Saracens plc have been at the forefront of such activities under the guidance of their former Marketing Manager, Michael Deakin, who had worked in the United States sports industry before Saracens and his eventual return to Rugby League.

[5] Such an approach has potential pitfalls from a legal perspective, aside from the reduced expectations of individual players. For a discussion of them in relation to sport in Australia, see R Farrell, "Salary Caps and Restraint of Trade", 1997 (5) 1 SLJ 53.

Key participants

In any particular sport there are various bodies, individuals and organisa- **6-4** tions that may impact on issues concerning player contracts at different times. Likely interaction with them should be identified as far as possible in advance and necessary protections built into the contracts. For example, the following have been some of the key participants in rugby union:

"IRB": The International Rugby Board is the international body that regulates the sport.[6] It stepped into the long-running dispute between English clubs and the Rugby Football Union ("RFU") by eventually threatening to expel the latter. It is dominated by certain countries and sets rules and standards for the sport; it is currently based in Dublin.

"Country unions": there is a distinction in style between the Northern and Southern Hemisphere unions.[7] Many unions tend to be resistant to change and conservative. There is a tendency towards an amateur ethos with vast committee structures and bureaucracy. The size of the RFU causes problems although the other home unions are smaller and hence more tightly controlled. They control the international destiny of players who actually wish to represent their counties and do well, as it affects their market value. They have mainly pursued strategies to keep their best players playing within their own domestic systems; the latter have been subject to frequent review and alteration as a result.

"Club groupings": bodies such as English First Division Rugby Limited **6-5** have had a series of battles with the RFU over the right to control players and restructure leagues and fixtures.[8] This has involved a European court action against the unions and the IRB over alleged restraint of trade. A boycott of the European Cups took place in 1998 with no English clubs taking part. Clubs in England range from very traditional to extremely dynamic modern plcs which are at the heart of various initiatives aimed at wresting control of rugby decision making from the RFU.

"Club backers and owners": a new breed of businessman has emerged in English rugby attempting to impose modern business techniques into the running of clubs.[9] Massive cash injections by such entrepreneurs have led

---

[6] Further information on the work of the IRB is available on their website at www.irb.ie.

[7] The main Northern Hemisphere Unions were the participants in the former "Five Nations" competition, namely Scotland, England, Ireland, Wales and France. From 2000 onwards the new competition is the "Six Nations" with the addition of Italy. The Unions' websites are as follows: Scotland—www.sru.org.uk; England—www.rfu.com.uk; Ireland—www.irfu.ie; Wales—www.wru.co.uk; France—www.frfu.fra; and Italy—www.rugbyitalia.com. The primary Southern Hemisphere Unions are Australia, New Zealand and South Africa, who annually contest the Bledisloe Cup. Their websites are as follows: Australia— www.rugby.com.au; New Zealand—www.nzrugby.co.nz; and South Africa—www.sarfu.org.za.

[8] Various organisations have been set up in English rugby, which have parallels in Scotland and also counterparts in the football world, to collectively represent the interests of the clubs and other interests in the game more effectively (the clubs and their backers feel) than the Unions. They include the England Rugby Partnership Limited, English First Division Rugby Limited and England Second Division Rugby Limited.

[9] This new breed of businessmen entered the world of club rugby when it turned professional, bringing with them commercial approaches and attitudes from the world of finance and business. Amongst the best known in recent years have been Nigel Wray at Saracens and Sir John Hall at Newcastle.

them to seek greater control of the game to achieve the efficiencies that they feel are necessary to make returns on their capital.

"Sponsors": sponsorship plays an increasingly important role in allowing clubs to make returns on investments given the high profile that the game is currently enjoying.[10] As rugby has become highly marketable, sponsors increasingly have influence in the way clubs conduct themselves, which impacts on players in various ways.

"Players and representatives": greater demands are increasingly placed on players as they now have to be capable of being ambassadors off the pitch as well as good rugby players on it. In the search for lucrative short-term contracts players increasingly make use of representatives such as agents who act on their behalf in seeking opportunities and conducting negotiations. A relatively new development has been the creation of player unions to create a collective voice for the players in various discussions about the structure of the game and also to provide individual representational services with a greater orientation towards the players' interests.[11]

THE NEGOTIATION

6-6 The negotiation is crucial to securing the best deal for the player in financial, lifestyle and sporting terms. A successful outcome will be a workable contract giving legal effect to the negotiated commercial goals and which creates an employment relationship. The discussions that precede the signing of the contract will shape the relationship thereafter. As a background element the contract will set the scene for the treatment of a variety of issues throughout its duration and problems can result or be magnified by inadequate negotiation of its original terms. The parameters of the player's relationship with the club are set out at that point but also whether the current arrangement acts as a springboard or millstone for their next career move. Consequently, the rigid separation of the commercial and legal tasks during such negotiations is an unduly restrictive and artificial one that can result at best in protracted talks and at worst in a wholly inadequate contract. The negotiation phase is a dynamic one that should be ongoing, even after the contract is signed as the employment relationship develops and flourishes.[12] The best scenario is a three-way dialogue between agent/

---

[10] Guinness, Coca-Cola and BT all had high profile associations with the Rugby World Cup in 1999, although various sponsors of the event reportedly had mixed feelings on the ultimate worth of their investment. For a discussion of the legal issues underlying sports marketing and sponsorship (albeit from an English law perspective), including sample styles of agreement see Verow, Laurence and McCormick, *Sport, Business and the Law* (Jordans, 1999), Chapter 6. See also C Steele, "Sponsorship Contracts – The Full Monty" (1997) 5 (3) SLJ 25.

[11] There are currently two player unions operating in England, run by former players; in Scotland there has been much discussion on the topic amongst current and former players but no equivalent has been formed as yet. The longer running player associations in football in both countries have enjoyed considerable success and a high profile over the years.

[12] There are many useful books and courses available on the topic of negotiation, representing many differing approaches from the rational scientific to the innate and instinctive "gut feel" school. A good practical primer which encourages negotiators to think about their own methods is T Boyce, *Successful Contract Negotiation* (Hawksmere, 1993).

lawyer, club and player during the course of which approaches are refined and ultimately harmonised as knowledge of the other parties' positions develops. A number of critical success factors influencing the process can be identified as outlined below.

Agents

Wherever possible an agent should act for a player in his negotiations and **6-7** dealings with clubs. Reasons for this include: distancing the player from colleagues and employers/prospective employers for salary negotiations and difficult issues; provision of objective advice; and specialist knowledge such as familiarity with key contract terms or negotiation skills. The ideal solution would be an agent who can combine legal and commercial roles.[13] This should result in a contract that is negotiated with a view to its final form, with significant non-financial considerations receiving appropriate attention in negotiations prior to the drafting of the final contract.[14] Where this is impossible a very close working relationship between lawyer and agent is required at an early stage rather than a mere documenting of the transaction. Currently there are no bonding requirements nor registration of any type necessary for rugby agents and in theory anyone could attempt it. The position in football is, of course, very different with FIFA policing activities—for example, by requiring bonds etc.[15] The rewards for players are considerably lower in rugby than in football and agents seek their own remuneration in different ways. Some operate on the basis of a percentage of the first year's (and occasionally subsequent year's) salary with an addition for outlays and legal fees.[16] Others operate on the basis of time spent in acting, even where unsuccessful. Further methods seek to make the club pay for the work done on behalf of the player as part of the agreed contract.

Agents obviously operate under the law of agency and the scope of their authority from the player is a key element.[17] Often players are approached by agents with the prospect of interested clubs in the background rather than the player going out to seek an agent to represent him generally. It is

---

[13] Support for this view can be found in M Goldberg, "Football Contracts etc." (1996) 4 (3) SLJ 101. Another article explores the additional skills a lawyer can bring to such a role: "The Interview: Blair Morgan" (1999) 44 JLSS 30.

[14] The perils of failure to properly document an agreement between a player and a club together with the somewhat *"laissez faire"* approach of the parties in construing what they have agreed are amply illustrated in M Nash, "The Footballer Who Wouldn't Play" (1998) 6 (2) SLJ 28.

[15] FIFA, the football world governing body, administers a licensing system whereby agents are required to lodge a bond (currently £105,000) and undergo a brief interview as to their fitness by the relevant football association.

[16] Further thoughts on feeing methodology can be found in M Goldberg, "Football Contracts etc." (1996) 4 (3) SLJ 101 at 107.

[17] The Scots law on agency is summarised in the *Stair Memorial Encyclopaedia*, Vol. I. Further discussion of the principles in a sports context (based on English law) is contained in Verow *et al.*, *Sport, Business and the Law*, Chapter 7.

crucial to have effective controls on the activities of the agent and to be wary of arrangements that can grant exclusive agency rights, with fees being due even where the contract was not actually concluded with a club directly as a result of the efforts of the agent. Clearly the agent, to justify his role, must add value for the player. Possible roles here include: provision of negotiation services; effecting introductions to clubs; giving advice; drafting, reviewing and concluding contracts. The relationship between the agent and the player must be a close and frank one as clubs often seek to avoid agents, preferring to deal direct with players in an attempt to cut costs. Normally the tactic leads to more difficulties than it resolves but players can often inadvertently weaken their bargaining position and options in these circumstances.

Client knowledge

6-8   No matter how skilled a negotiator is his technique will not achieve the desired results without proper preparation in this area. Many agents spend insufficient time finding out exactly what their clients want and their opinions, together with the various factors that influence their decision making. Obviously, the better the knowledge of the client then the greater the contribution that can be made in advocating his cause and interests. There is no magic formula for success in negotiating player contracts. Each player is different and being aware of and highlighting such differences at the appropriate time can be a powerful tool for an agent. Before discussions develop in earnest with target clubs the agent should seek to find out as much as possible about his client. This "interrogation" will often reveal hidden doubts a player has, contradictions in his expressed views and the real drive which fuels his current ambition in the sport. The following key areas should emerge from discussions with the player (who should regularly be revisited and reassessed):

"Key objectives": What are the player's key objectives? Are they clear and consistent? Some players may be wholly financially driven whilst others have longer-term plans, seeking particular stepping stones along the way. The agent must continually challenge the player's articulated goals to ensure he understands them and is alive to changes in them. A proper "fit" between such objectives and the agreement of particular contracts is the end point of successful negotiations.

"Sport person's view": This is undoubtedly a singular view. Successful sports people are by definition unusual and extraordinary people. They have extremely highly developed motivational and competitive instincts, usually combined with a very strong work ethic and a highly disciplined approach to achieving certain sporting goals. The agent's role here is to understand how the sportsman views the world but to remain objective and detached from such views. Clear and pertinent professional advice must remain paramount for the agent/adviser. This area can lead to some unavoidable tension, with the agent/adviser often playing "devil's advocate" to encourage the sports person to understand a different analysis that may achieve the furthering of their interests.

"Stage of career": This will be discussed more fully in the next section on types of players. Clearly, the development phase that a player has reached will have a major impact on the presentation of his attributes and future potential in any negotiation situation.

"Relationships": As can be seen from many recent examples in the foot- **6-9** ball world, this major factor is often given insufficient attention. A player is not generally an isolated individual who has total autonomy, free from any other influences. The player is likely to have various relationships with family, friends, wife or girlfriends, husband or boyfriends, other players, club members, etc. There may be significant comfort zones that will be badly disrupted by a move to another area or a club with a different ethos and atmosphere. Issues such as a spouse's career, schooling and children, the position of overseas players, housing and social activities may all need to be considered. The web of relationships surrounding a player will need to be addressed in addition to the player's individual views.

"USPs": These are the unique selling points which distinguish particular players from others and allow the agent to develop a case for the signing of a player and to justify the particular package arrived at. Any features about the client that can be enhanced and maximised are relevant for these purposes. They might include experience, international record, exemplary disciplinary record, settled family life, leadership qualities, flexibility, and roles they can perform, etc. Part of the skill in negotiation is identifying the player's key attributes and relating these to the needs of the target club. Careful choice of these features is necessary as nothing is more likely to weaken a negotiating position than highlighting the wrong areas or those where no evidence can be produced to back up the claims made.

Types of players

The appropriate approach to be adopted will vary depending on the type **6-10** of player involved and the stage he has reached in his career. Whilst each individual case is unique there are four broad typologies that may assist in making a rough preliminary assessment on strategy as follows.

"Young players": There may be much promise for the future to trade on but as yet little in the way of a proven track record. The attitude of a club to youth development should be explored to see how much support will be given and to ensure that an inexperienced young player will not be pushed too hard too quickly. The opportunity to learn and study at this stage is especially significant for future careers outside the chosen sport. In rugby clashes between clubs' match requirements and players' examination commitments have already occurred in the English league.[18] Mobility, though, may be easier for younger players with few commitments or dependants.

"Prime players": This category comprises those who are the most sought after by clubs. Such a player has an established reputation and track record, with the potential for future development and success. The choice of club is particularly significant for ambitious players to ensure they can maximise their impact and gain opportunities for the further development of their game whilst they are playing the best sport of their careers. Often such players will have a network of contacts and family commitments.

---

[18] The highly publicised contractual wrangle between Josh Lewsney and Bristol is an example.

"Older players": Generally such players have had a long career and have established a strong reputation. Their best playing days are generally behind them and they may be looking to guarantee one last payday by trading on their reputation. They may also be seeking an opportunity to move into a coaching or a management role in the sport. Actual appearances can be very important here in remuneration formulae as at this stage the player may be more injury prone or less likely to be automatically a first choice selection for the team.

"Key players": They may be individuals who have achieved a "star" status in the game through a combination of outstanding performances and/or their force of personality. They may also be players who operate in a particular position which is in short supply or vital to a team's dynamics, such as fly half or scrum half in rugby, or a goal-scoring striker or central defender in football. Particular attributes such as leadership skills or marketing potential may mark out the player. Requirements will fluctuate over time but some players will always command premium rates. An agent should always test just how keenly a club wants a particular player.

Club's perspective

6-11 The other side in any negotiation is naturally critical to its outcome. There are aspects of clubs' attitudes and perspectives that should be factored into the strategy of any agent or player to assist in interactions with them. Sources of information in this area include information gleaned from other players, past dealings with the club and published information about particular clubs' plans and attitudes.[19] It is essential to discover at the outset why the club are interested in a player and what his future prospects might be. Is he to be part of a large squad providing cover? What is the age profile of team members in his position? Various matters can be more fully explored as follows.

Needs/aspirations: Are the club hoping to play in Europe? Do they have good prospects in their league? Are the coaches well respected and what is their approach? What goals does the club have for the coming season and thereafter? In negotiation with various clubs, the treatment of player and agent will indicate how the player may be treated in the future. Find out as much as possible about the club's financial backing and development plans.

Style/character: Historically clubs have developed in very different ways and have differing characters and forms as a result. The commercial plans of the club may lead to the implementation of a particular ethos and approach designed to increase revenue, to which the players will have to contribute. Different playing styles and personalities may find a better "fit" in some clubs than others and in the long run boost their future prospects. The player must be satisfied with the technical side of the club and that its training and playing regime will suit him and improve his game, but the club's public relations demands and general atmosphere will also play a part. An agent should always be aware of the particular expertise and

---

[19] The various rugby/football annuals, specialist sports magazines, and information held by Companies House are all useful sources.

power base of the other negotiating party within the club. Some clubs have not yet fully integrated the playing and commercial roles, and further information on a decision may be required from a different part of the club.

Availability and fitness: Clubs want the best players to suit their game plan, who will be available for the majority of the time, as they wish to field their strongest possible team and have as many alternative options as they can. Therefore the availability and fitness of their players are amongst their top concerns. The number of games played nowadays in rugby, football and other sports has increased dramatically, which puts greater strain on players. When injuries occur the consequence often is that less salary is earned. It is therefore necessary to ascertain the attitude of the club towards playing its personnel when they are already injured and the expected number of games. So-called "club versus country" issues raise a new dimension and the views of a club on this are vital. In rugby, for example, clubs and international rugby unions will seek primacy of control of the player and such disputes within the game still persist. Other rugby activities will be restricted and subordinated to the interests of the club. Accordingly, if a player wishes to engage in other activities, such as sevens or representative games such as for the Barbarians,[20] advance notification and negotiation is essential.

Discipline/drugs: Clubs generally wish to maintain good wholesome images for their commercial interests and to boost crowds. They also wish to maintain good relationships with the sports governing bodies and to avoid lengthy suspensions and damaging fines. These areas are strongly policed as a result, with clubs having very strict disciplinary regimes that they seek to enforce. The positive attributes of a player can be maximised in negotiations to sell, for example, their excellent disciplinary record, settled family life, etc.

Promotional activities: Sponsors will have particular requirements and demands, and players will be a key element in this commercial strategy.[21] Care must be taken to find out what the player wishes to do in this area and how it impacts on the club's plans. "Star" players have greater scope and potential in this area, which will give a degree of independence and freedom to control how they exploit their own opportunities. Focus on the attributes of the player that may attract clubs in this regard and be aware of any off-putting features.

Salaries: Naturally clubs wish to keep their costs down as much as possible and this will be the biggest element. There was a big push by English Clubs in 1998 to get wages reduced. Displaying sympathy for such goals without downgrading your own client is important. It is usually possible to get an individual deal nonetheless. One approach is always to talk about the "value" of the player to the club in terms of ability, commercial opportunities, publicity, etc and relate those to the "needs" of the club. It is crucial

---

[20] An amateur and highly respected invitation representative team run by Mickey Steele-Bodger. Their website is at www.barbarianfc.co.uk.

[21] See Verow *et al*, *Sport, Business and the Law*, Chapter 6 and C Steele, "Sponsorship Contracts – The Full Monty" (1997) 5 (3) SLJ 25.

to be flexible and to take the initiative where possible rather than succumbing to a rigid "bottom line" argument. There may be tax-efficient methods adopted by the club that an agent can accept if they result in a better package. A sporting career is fairly short and this may be the only opportunity the player has to get a large salary from the game; it will certainly affect future negotiating opportunities. It is useful to look continually at the trends developing in the sport and whether new finance is coming in. The right timing for a negotiation will often coincide with a fresh cash injection. Some pruning of the playing staff usually occurs in the close season. If a player can cover more than one position this may be an attraction to a club, as it will then carry fewer players in total on its salary bill.

Negotiation technique

6-12 The first key point is to define the role. Lawyer, agent or both? The negotiator must ensure that his role in the commercial negotiations is adequate and understood by all participants. There are many styles of negotiation techniques and every individual over time develops their own favoured methods.[22] The best approach is to retain the maximum flexibility. An over-rigid technique prevents the negotiator being able to adapt when things do not go according to plan: the negotiator then becomes easy to outmanoeuvre or impossible to deal with. Classic negotiating ploys can be useful but it is crucial to have a "plan B" and to keep as many options as possible with other clubs open to the player until a contract is signed. It is far easier for a professional agent to do this than a player, as a club is usually a close-knit community who work intimately together. The commercial and practical drivers must be kept separate, where appropriate, from emotion and club loyalties. The agent must simultaneously develop rapport and keep his distance from the clubs. Honesty is necessary to avoid misunderstandings. Negotiations over the telephone can be useful as they will often be more direct than in face to face meetings; this helps to clarify the parties' objectives. Always establish the parameters of the negotiation with the player in advance and develop a range of acceptable results. It is what the player "needs" which is important rather than what other players are rumoured to be receiving. There is a great deal of misinformation on players' salaries in the rugby world. All the factors that motivate the player other than the purely financial should be developed and displayed. The club should be encouraged to talk freely to find out what they want and to get more ammunition for advancing the player's interests. Indeed, it is unhelpful to be overly commercial in the early phases of negotiations in this sphere. A commonality of interests and commitment to the goals of the club and the sport must be demonstrated first. All assumptions and statements need to be challenged as a case is built to justify the player's package. Introducing new ideas and approaches during the discussions is useful to keep things moving and to facilitate constructive discussions with the other side. On the salary side, a price should never be mentioned too soon. Instead, the focus should be on the player's value and unique selling points.

---

[22] See n 12 above.

Markets

The market in players and the financial fortunes of clubs will invariably **6-13** shape the transactions that occur. Monitoring trends is vital to avoid badly timed moves, and devices such as break clauses and contract options are useful to take advantage of market changes. Players talk amongst themselves about salaries and clubs and this is a source of richer information. A new opening will usually be apparent to the players at the relevant club before anyone else. In English rugby when pay freezes, cuts and redundancies occurred, the markets in France and Ireland became more buoyant. Supply and demand in key positions, though, will often go against market trends given the specialised nature of some player roles.

CONTRACTUAL ISSUES

The early rugby contracts were models produced by the RFU in England **6-14** which some clubs adopted.[23] There are various issues and boilerplate clauses common to most players' contracts, with several of the major variables such as remuneration and disciplinary procedures appearing in schedules.[24] In practice the clubs and their legal advisers have adapted such models to their own circumstances. The process of negotiation with players and agents also leads to new clauses being integrated into the clubs' standard approaches. Most of the contracts now develop incrementally as new negotiations take place and major changes in bargaining power occur. Normally the club will produce a contract for the player's agent to revise, although considerable flexibility can be achieved before ultimate signature. As the contract is the foundation document that will shape the whole relationship between player and club, it is crucial that it is user friendly and reliable as well as covering the key issue areas. The best approach is a schematic one that proceeds from an analysis of the main issues the particular sport raises. Rather than adopting pro forma clauses, which are often inappropriate to a particular environment, this approach will enable the major themes from the negotiation phase to be comprehensively addressed. The following represent a selection of the main themes that arise in rugby contracts; they may well be mirrored in other sports.

Health and fitness

Rugby being a highly physical contact sport, the risk of injury is ever pres- **6-15** ent. This can affect availability from the club's perspective and threaten the present and future livelihood of the player, both within and outwith the sport. An initial concern is with emergency medical facilities and treatment being available at the locations where the players train and play. This must

---

[23] This was an early attempt to standardise contracts in a way similar to the models that were used by the English Football League and also those utilised by FIFA, with most of the variable terms appearing in schedules to the contracts. See, generally, M Goldberg, "Footballers' Contracts" (1997) 5 (3) SLJ 19 and M Goldberg, "Football Contracts etc." (1996) 4 (3) SLJ 101.

[24] See also P McInerney and S Rush, "Rugby Union Players' Contracts: The Standard Provisions" (1998) 6 (2) SLJ 19.

be adequate and sufficient for the types of injuries that could arise and the grade at which the sport is being played. Dealing with the financial consequences of injuries is most frequently dealt with through insurance. Adequate policies must be in place and the interface between them has to be harmonised given the differing interests that clubs and countries have in players. The insuring obligations of players and warranties that they have to make should be carefully considered. Closely related to this are the provisions made for sick pay and termination of the contract following serious injury. The time periods are critical, as a player must have sufficient time to recover and be able to draw some form of salary during these periods. One area to watch is cumulative time periods for periods of illness/injury during the whole term of the contract. Clubs are increasingly concerned with fitness standards and some players have been dismissed for failing to meet them. Wherever possible these testing procedures should be made objective and an opportunity given to retake the tests within certain time periods to ensure they are not used inappropriately. Generally there are clauses governing involvement in other activities or sports which are deemed to be "dangerous". The context of these should always be reviewed carefully and wherever necessary excessive and unworkable restrictions avoided.

Employment and discipline

6-16   In the mass media and information age the focus of clubs on conduct has become even stronger. Marketing plans can be thrown into disarray by one incident. Clauses governing conduct both on the field and off it are invariably present.[25] The relationship between such clauses, the club rules and elaborate disciplinary procedures needs to be carefully drafted. Lawyers have become greatly involved in this area of sport in recent years, seeking to ensure that natural justice is observed and proper processes are in place. Players must be fully conversant with the substance abuse policies of their governing bodies and the club's approach to such matters. The duration of the contract is usually fixed with possible options for extension and renewal. Clubs seek to avoid the creation of employment rights and continuity of employment wherever possible, which is a consideration if an extension of a contract occurs.[26] The termination events must be carefully defined and wherever possible should be made mutual. Material breach of the contract by a club or its financial insolvency should always be termination events that the player can enforce. There are often restrictions on other work or for whom the individual can play in sporting events. Care must be taken with those outside activities that players do not consider important or where the player wishes to "keep their hand in" with a particular vocation or training options.

---

[25] For a useful discussion of the nature and purpose of "disrepute" clauses, see David Ligertwood, "Sports Sponsorship – The Role of the Disrepute Clause", (1999) 6 (2) *Sports Law Administration & Practice* 29.

[26] General issues of employment law from an English perspective are addressed in Verow *et al*, *Sport, Business and the Law*, Chapter 5.

Remuneration

Market forces are critical and clubs have learned from their mistakes, but **6-17** there is still money to be made.[27] Salaries comprise many different elements and the overall composition should be carefully balanced. The basic salary is the key. This should be the main sum, which players should receive regardless of whether they are selected or injured as it may be the only income they may have coming in. Ring fencing is crucial also in relation to disciplinary procedures. Incentive payments are now becoming the norm, with clear benefits and drawbacks. One common type is appearance fees, which the player receives when he plays or is selected as a substitute. Definition of the particular circumstances which qualify the player for eligibility for these payments is necessary. These can also extend to the international sphere. Another is the "win bonus" payment which may be based on a straight win or league placement basis. In practice, the worst case and optimum scenarios for appearances must be calculated for players before agreeing to such clauses. Highly individual arrangements have arisen—for example, it was rumoured that an English international player received shares in his club as part of a package. Further arrangements include cars and advantageous pension arrangements that attract tax breaks and can be accessed much earlier than other pension schemes. Always tie down such arrangements very carefully and watch the tax consequences. Taxation itself is a key element and financial advice is required to assess the overall package.

Availability and releases

Many disputes have occurred in the last few years due to the competing **6-18** demands on players from clubs and the countries they are eligible to play for. The primacy provisions relating to who has first call on a player's services must be consistent in club and country contracts. Naturally when consents are required they should not be unreasonably withheld. Matches are not the only source of conflict as assembly periods prior to matches and squad-training sessions are also required. Global agreements such as the "Mayfair Agreement" and the rules of international bodies such as the IRB will often be relevant.[28] The player should be protected as far as possible from these tug-of-war situations. Registration requirements for playing in particular countries are usually made the responsibility of the player. Overseas players may find themselves subject to domestic and EC law on work

---

[27] See also the discussion of remuneration in M Goldberg, "Football Contracts etc." (1996) 4 (3) SLJ 101.

[28] In 1998 the RFU, English First Division Rugby Limited, England Second Division Rugby Limited and the England Rugby Partnership Limited after protracted negotiations arrived at an agreement to govern future relations on various key matters affecting the game, known as the "Mayfair Agreement". One area covered was the release of players for international matches, which had become a power struggle between the clubs and Unions. Quotas were arrived at for matches and training sessions, with player contracts to contain an addendum narrating the Agreement's main terms. These arrangements were applied in most clubs also to internationals from Unions other than England.

permits and residence requirements. The time periods involved in these and how they affect remuneration (such as incentives) should be reflected in the contract.

Commercial activities

6-19 These are of increasing significance to clubs and players. Special events such as the Rugby World Cup and tours of overseas countries by representative teams increase the profile of the sport and the players involved. A player must maximise his own potential but at the same time meet the club's promotional requirements. The scope of commitments made for the club will necessarily restrict what the player can do on his own. International teams add a further layer of restriction. Information exchange on sponsorship obligations by players and clubs needs to be readily provided at the appropriate time. The player must seek to keep as much ownership and flexibility in his own image rights as possible. One method is to license certain rights to the club for a limited duration. The extent to which a club can require the player to undertake promotional appearances and activities should be carefully regulated in the contract and kept within "reasonable" bounds. Intellectual property rights should only be assigned to the minimum degree necessary to enable clubs and players to participate in further commercial opportunities. Limitations on the player's use of club playing gear and imagery in his own endorsements are often imposed. Where the player has a strongly identifiable image already, special provisions are required to ensure that existing commitments are not jeopardised and future projects can be exploited.

Club structures

6-20 The financial problems of leading clubs, coupled with bouts of takeover speculation and activity, have drawn attention to this area. Who exactly is the player contracting with? In the future the player may find his salary affected or find himself contracted to a wholly different club than the one he thought he had joined. Assignation clauses should be approached with these factors in mind. A clause which allows a player a "get out" at his option where an insolvency or takeover type event occurs gives the player greater flexibility. Information discussed in the negotiation phase should be utilised to structure the clauses on transfers and termination in the contract.

Miscellaneous

6-21 The issue of confidentiality is difficult, particularly where it impacts on details of players' salaries and promotional activities. The player should seek protection for his financial arrangements and further details concerning his obligations. International Unions and clubs often have divergent aims but making their contractual regimes consistent is vital. This can be very difficult in the light of confidentiality requirements. Clubs strictly control their media statements but the media often has direct and immediate access to players. Issues to consider are getting clearance for comments and articles, writing regular newspaper columns and possible allegations of bringing the game or the club into disrepute. The player and the club may warrant a variety of matters in the contract. Each should ensure that they can give the requisite warranties, particularly in relation to issues such as fitness and registration. An area which is highly subjective, but often included, is the standard of play of the sportsman. This should be made as objective and limited as possible. Choice of law clauses and methods of dispute resolution are still fairly underdeveloped. Most issues are settled through compromise and agreement but there is scope for developing more sophisticated provision.

7   DRUGS IN SPORT

Alan Grosset

This has become one of the most frustrating and difficult areas in sport and **7-1**
the law and many issues remain unresolved.[1] Both as lawyers and sportsmen, Scots people have taken a pride in the standards which they set and
also in the ethical standards to which they adhere. Unfortunately it seems
that the "win at all costs" attitude of some competitors in sport, which is
now much more professional than it was even 10 years ago, has meant that
there is a continuing battle going on between sports bodies and administrators, and those who wish to win at any cost and who misuse drugs for
the purpose of gaining unfair advantage in sport. The battle is still raging;
this chapter aims to identify the sources of some of the issues and some of
the problems, and also to explain the doping control process.

The ethical basis and international conventions

There are those who have recently offered the view that the battle against **7-2**
drug taking in sport is lost and that we would be better to redirect the
resources involved in the doping control environment elsewhere. However, if that were done sport would then become a contest between
chemists and not between athletes (in the broadest sense). There is a belief
in fair play in sport and to that end control mechanisms should be introduced and implemented. Much of the current debate centres around who
should do that and how, but it is generally recognised within the United
Kingdom, and in particular in Scotland, that sport in general and sports in
particular should adopt rules forbidding the misuse of drugs and procedures which amount to cheating. There should thereafter be mechanisms
which allow the sport to find out who is breaking the rules and then provide for appropriate sanctions for the breaking of the rules. There are therefore three objectives for the doping control process: (a) to protect those
who don't cheat; (b) to deter those who might; and (c) to catch those who
do.

In order to provide a background to the current position, it is necessary
to appreciate that the UK Government is a signatory not only to the
European Sports Charter which calls for countries to unite to combat the

---

[1] See, *eg*, C Moore, *Sports Law and Litigation* (CLT, 1997), Chapter 9; E Grayson, *Sport and the Law*,
Chapter 7; Gardiner *et al*, *Sports Law* (Cavendish, 1998), Chapter 3.

evils of drug taking in sport, but has further been a party (since its incep-
tion in 1990) to a Council of Europe Convention on Anti-Doping, which
now has 41 signatory countries. It has also entered into a Memorandum of
Understanding in relation to doping control with Australia, Canada, New
Zealand and Norway; this arrangement has been extended to include
Sweden and the Netherlands. There is wide recognition that the abuse of
drugs in sport needs to be tackled, not simply because of the concept of fair
play but also because these drugs are indeed damaging and in large doses
can in some cases be life threatening to individuals.

The Government of the United Kingdom has appointed the UK Sports
Council (now UK Sport) to fulfil its public policy obligations on drugs in
sport, including the obligations under the Council of Europe Convention
on Anti-doping. In 1997 UK Sport achieved ISO 9002 certification for the
management of drug testing programmes in sport. In each of the last few
years there have been over 4,500 tests carried out with public money at a
total cost in 1998/99 of over £1.2 million. Most of that money is issued
through the governing bodies of sport in the United Kingdom in that the
governing bodies have an obligation imposed on them consonant with
their receipt of grant aid from one of the UK's Sports Councils to implement such a doping control programme. It is fair to say that the Scottish
governing bodies reacted very positively to a request to enter into this obligation voluntarily and were the first in the United Kingdom to take such
steps.

The IOC List

7-3   This title is shorthand for the International Olympic Committee's List of
Doping Classes and Methods, which is widely used as the basis for anti-
doping rules by the International Federations of Sport and, therefore, the
governing bodies of sport who form the membership of the International
Federations; it is used as the reference point for the identification of the
banned drugs, substances and methods. This list is reviewed from time to
time by the International Olympic Committee but it is felt by sports
lawyers, doctors and scientists that the list is not always as up-to-date as
many would like.

The main classes of drugs prohibited in sport are divided in the IOC List
into a number of classes. Class 1 substances include anabolic agents such as
methandienone, nandrolone, stanozolol, testosterone and clenbuterol (an
anti-asthma medication which is also a powerful anabolic agent that promotes muscle growth and is therefore prohibited as an anabolic agent).
Stanozolol is the substance which was found in Ben Johnson's sample after
the 100 metres race at the Seoul Olympics and nandrolone has been the
subject of much recent press comment which as yet has not been conclusive. Also included in this category is the testosterone/epitestosterone
ratio and there is a sub-definition here which states:

> "the presence of a testosterone/epitestosterone ratio greater than 6:1 in
> the urine of a competitor constitutes an offence unless there is evi-
> dence that this ratio is due to a physiological or pathological condition
> eg low epitestosterone excretion, androgen producing tumour,
> enzyme deficiencies. In the case of T/E greater than 6 it is mandatory

that the relevant medical authority conduct an investigation before the sample is declared positive. A full report will be written and will include a review of previous tests, subsequent tests and any results of endocrine investigations. In the event that previous tests are not available the athlete should be tested unannounced at least once per month for three months. The result of these investigations should be included in the report. Failure to cooperate in the investigations will result in declaring the same positive."

It will be apparent at this stage that there is a need for appropriate medical and scientific interaction with lawyers.

Also included as Class 1 substances are diuretics (although these are not **7-4** prohibited in all sports), peptide and glycoprotein hormones and analogues such as human growth hormone and erythropoietein (EPO); also prohibited are the use or attempted use of substances, equipment or methods which alter the integrity and validity of urine samples currently in use in the doping control process. These include catheterisation and urine substitution and/or tampering.

The list of Class 2 substances includes stimulants such as bromontan, cocaine and strychnine. Also in this category are narcotics such as diamorphine (heroin), morphine, opium and pethidine. There is even a Class 3 list of substances which includes caffeine in levels greater than 12 micrograms per millilitre. There are, in addition, a number of classes of drugs which are subject to certain restrictions such as alcohol, marijuana, corticosteroids and betablockers. There are also situations in which local anaesthetics and the like can be restricted.

However, while this List has the benefit of being an international and basically uniform standard, many of the prohibited and restricted substances and techniques might extend well beyond those which are considered primarily to have performance enhancing effects. It is also necessary to consider for each particular sport just what drugs are relevant to that sport in the context of performance enhancement and the anti-doping regulations. There is a need, therefore, when seeking to draft disciplinary rules, for governing bodies to be careful about the way in which the IOC List is referred to and indeed published. It is believed that it should not itself form part of the rules of the governing body but should be dealt with and referred to by way of an appendix to reflect the fact that the IOC List will change and also that there may be a need for the sport to review what should be a prohibited substance or technique under its own rules.

The actual drug testing process

In the majority of sports the testing process relies upon the collection of **7-5** urine samples although blood testing—which it is believed will be a much more secure, certain and possibly cheaper way of testing for drugs—was introduced for the first time at the Sydney Olympics.

On the assumption that the governing body of sport has the appropriate powers and requirements in its constitution and rules, the arrangements for testing will be the subject of an agreement in Scotland between the Scottish Sports Council (which now operates as SportScotland), as the agent of UK Sport carrying out testing on its behalf, and the individual governing bodies of each sport. Whether the testing process is in or out of competition the ultimate procedure is more or less the same. If the athlete is selected for out of competition testing they will be given short or no notice and they may initially be notified over the telephone. At a competition or squad training session notification will be given in writing that an individual has been selected for a drug test. The competitor is often selected by a random draw or sometimes mandatorily by reason of attaining a certain position where medals are at stake. At that same time (as the athlete is notified) he or she will be given an explanation of his or her rights and responsibilities in the notice. The athletes are entitled to have a representative present throughout the drug testing procedures, except in the toilet cubicle during the actual passing of the sample. The athlete is chaperoned to the doping control station waiting room in the competitive environment; and, where out of competition testing is involved but no official doping station is available, a suitable compromise is found to ensure the privacy and integrity of the procedures.

7-6   The athlete is asked to select a sealed sample collection vessel and go to the toilet with the independent sampling officer (ISO). They must provide a sample under supervision and they will then be asked to select from a minimum of three kits a sealed urine sampling kit. The kit is stored in tamper-evident packaging and the athlete will personally be asked to divide the sample between the A and the B bottles. The sample is intended to be a minimum of 75mls, with a minimum of 30mls being poured into the B bottle. The athlete is then invited to seal the bottles and, after the residue in the collection vessel has been tested to verify the suitability of the sample for testing, the sample numbers will be inserted by the ISO in the sample collection form, with the athlete being invited to check that all of the information is correct. It is important that while this information is being recorded the athlete is invited to declare any medications taken, for instance on prescription, during the past seven days. This declaration will be helpful if there is an unusual finding. The information is certified, the sealed samples are placed in the security sealed transfer bag and then sent by signature-required courier to the International Olympic Committee accredited laboratory by a secure chain of custody. It should be noted that the identifying information in so far as the laboratory is concerned is by number only and not by name. The identified and accredited laboratory in the United Kingdom at the time of writing is at the Kings College Hospital in London, headed by Dr David Cowan. It should be mentioned that if the athlete refuses or fails to comply with the request to submit to testing this is also recorded on the information transmitted to UK Sport, in the same way as the result of the test by the laboratory. The results of the test will be reported by UK Sport to the governing body or International Sports Federation which has asked for the testing to be carried out. It is obviously important, if the programme is to receive effect, that failure to submit to a test be treated as an admission of liability by the athlete; the governing body's procedure should then deal with that failure as if it were a positive test, not unlike the drinking and driving regime.

The chain of custody

The foregoing description of the chain of custody from the passing of the **7-7**
sample through to its final analysis lays stress on the anonymity of the
sample, and the laboratory concerned provides accurate and unequivocal
analysis to the highest technical standards and according to agreed principles.

The *Daily Mail* of 10 February 1999, however, threw some part of the
chain of custody into some doubt. It was reported that a physical chemist,
Dr David Brown, had proved that the security packs in which the urine
samples were transported to laboratories for testing could be opened and
resealed without detection. The company, Versapak, which made the containers is believed to have admitted that an earlier model of its product
used until the middle of 1998 could indeed be opened given the right tools
and a window of opportunity. In light of this, there may still be cases which
could be the subject of appeal.

Other forms of testing

Reference has already been made to the way in which blood testing might **7-8**
provide more satisfactory evidence and high resolution mass spectrometry
has been reported as identifying substances that might not be identified
through the urine test. The resolution of these issues remains in the future
and the current arrangements within the United Kingdom revolve around
the series of contracts between the Kings College Laboratory, the UK Sports
Council, the home countries' sports councils and the bodies to whom they
in turn give grant aid as a part of the programme. At the beginning of
January 2000 the Sydney Olympic Games Committee was reported as having advertised for volunteers to test the testing process they were trying to
devise for EPO; at the time of writing there remains no effective test. The
problem, of course, is that EPO in large doses can be fatal.

The positive test and the review panel

If there is a positive test (*ie* one showing a banned drug for instance), it is **7-9**
reported by the laboratory, in the first case to the Ethics and Doping
Control Directorate of UK Sport. Within 24 hours of receiving that report
they will check the documentary evidence in their possession; then,
customarily where there is a positive test to report, they will telephone the
governing body contact to advise them of the fact that there is a positive
test and to check where they would like the report sent. It is, of course,
important that the report does not arrive unannounced, and particularly
not into the hands of someone who is not authorised to deal with it.
Governing bodies have found this a difficult situation in the past and current thinking is that where the governing body has a medical officer
appointed it should be that person or the governing body Doping Control
Officer who deals with the report. It is important at this stage for the governing body to have the information reviewed, not only by their Medical
and Doping Control Officers but probably also by their legal adviser or
someone who is familiar with their constitution and rules. This is usually
known as "the Review Panel".

The critical issues that need to be dealt with by the Review Panel are:

(a) Is this person a member of our governing body and therefore bound directly or indirectly by our rules?

(b) Is the evidence before us adequate to identify the individual and provide initial evidence of a potential doping offence?

(c) Is it the report of a finding that is clearly prohibited by our rules and regulations?

If the answers to these questions are such as to lead the Review Panel on behalf of the governing body to believe that there has been a breach of its rules, consideration will have to be given to a disciplinary hearing, an area which has proved difficult for governing bodies on many occasions, but it is necessary to consider the issues which will concern the governing body as it tries to deal with the three questions set out above.

Constitutional issues for the governing body

7-10   Each of the governing bodies of sport in this country seeks to a greater or lesser degree to make rules to regulate the administration of its own sport, its constitution and activities. Plainly, therefore, the constitution must have within it the appropriate power to regulate the conduct of the sport and the authority to make the rules. A prudent governing body should also recognise that the rules will only be enforceable if the person who is intended to be subject to the rules agrees to be bound by them. This envisages each person registering with the governing body either as an individual signing a membership application or competition entry form or agreeing to be bound by the rules of a governing body through, for instance, a club which applies on behalf of him and others for membership of the governing body.

The enforceability of these rules against those subject to doping control is therefore based upon the contractual consent of the person concerned and the capacity to consent is a vital precondition to the enforceability of these rules, as discussed later.

7-11   The principle of consent, whereby an athlete becomes a member of a sports body and is therefore deemed to accept and be bound by the rules of that sports body, is thus the legal root in this area of law. Before one can be satisfied that the governing body of sport is indeed in a position to deal with the whole range of disciplinary issues, of which doping control is unfortunately nearest to a headline issue, a review of the appropriate membership structure is critical since much that will follow will evolve from that. One needs to be sure whether the governing body is composed of individuals, clubs, teams, leagues, geographical groupings or sports discipline groupings (ie sports such as swimming, where different disciplines within the sport such as competitive swimming itself, diving, synchronised swimming, water polo, etc are all in membership of the swimming governing body). Once that is dealt with by appropriate wording in the constitution of the governing body, correct disciplinary measures must be in place to ensure that an individual who commits a doping offence can still be disciplined by the governing body, whether they are an individual member or, for instance, a member of a club, affiliated to a league playing in a geographical grouping within the governing body but still all subject to the overall "umbrella" jurisdiction of the rules of the governing body.

One of the issues which is still current and in large measure remains unresolved is the position of coaches working with athletes within the governing bodies, since the coaches themselves might not be in membership of the governing body. Many governing bodies are now looking to register coaches and satisfy themselves as to their qualifications, if need be by examination, which should begin to solve that problem. A clear example of the problem occurred in the former East Germany, where coaches for very young athletes had in fact been those responsible for the administration of banned substances to the young athletes under their care, as is emerging in cases being reported at the time of writing.

There is, of course, an issue all on its own here in that drug testing takes **7-12** place in international junior competitions worldwide and there is a need to ensure that consents have been obtained by or on behalf of all of those thus being subject to testing who at law might not have the capacity to give that consent. From a management point of view, even although in strict terms the law of Scotland will only require a parental consent from a youngster under the age of 16, if there is a junior team that may well contain youngsters of a number of ages up to 18 it would be sensible to obtain parental consent for everyone under the age of 18. Equally, the consent form should put the team manager or other such official *in loco parentis* for reasons of accompanying the youngster to the actual doping control station. There is a need also to consider carefully, when dealing with disability sport, the extent to which consent can be given or obtained by or from such athletes.

Provided, therefore, that the governing body membership clause and the basic discipline clauses are correctly structured and interrelated, it should be possible to answer the question "Is this person a member of our governing body and therefore bound directly or indirectly by our rules?" in the affirmative. One would like to think that the latter two questions are related to the definitions of doping control and disciplinary offences in the constitution of the governing body and, on the assumption that they are all correctly bound together as has been suggested above, and that the individual members are thus obligated to observe these rules, it is possible then to proceed to the next area which sport has found difficult; once again, there have been examples in the past of bad and very bad practice.

The disciplinary hearing

This is the way in which the governing body itself deals with disciplinary **7-13** matters and the need to ensure that there is either an ad hoc appointment of a small disciplinary panel or a disciplinary panel of various office bearers or former office bearers to be the panel before whom the first hearing would take place. There have been numerous examples in sport where the panel of the first hearing failed to observe the rules of natural justice. These may be simply stated for this hearing as follows.

(a) Proper procedures should be followed, giving the person charged proper notice of the charge, a reasonable opportunity of answering it, confirming that they understand the nature of the charge, letting them have an opportunity to state their case, and being given adequate notice of the meeting at which the disciplinary panel will investigate the issue with the person. The person charged must be given the right to be assisted at the hearing by someone of their choosing; while the customary rules of natural justice do not require representation, there is no reason not to permit it if the person charged so wishes, given some of the potentially serious sanctions.

(b) All the parties should be given equal opportunity to hear and deal with any evidence, and the person charged has the entitlement not only to know the name of the person giving the evidence but to challenge the evidence and expect that the evidence will be presented systematically and thoroughly.

(c) The panel has an obligation to be fair and reasonable in conducting the affairs of the sport in line with its own rules and must act in good faith, deal consistently and equitably, make the decision on the relevant evidence and use standards of care which are reasonable and appropriate to the specific case. It follows that members of the panel must be seen to perform their responsibilities without hostility and act in a non-discriminatory manner. They should spend a reasonable time considering the evidence and arguments and not simply just vote.

(d) While the person charged has no right of access to the deliberations of the panel, the findings, and any specific reasons for the judgment, should be stated in writing and the punishment should fit the case. Previous conduct and a record of good behaviour should be taken into consideration.

7-14   One of the other situations, which varies from sport to sport at this stage in the process, is the question of whether or not to suspend the athlete before the hearing has been arranged when what may have been reported is the outcome of the test of the A sample. The idea behind the testing process is that the athlete can ask for the B sample to be examined either in their presence or in the presence of a representative nominated by them. The B sample in the United Kingdom has universally confirmed the A sample finding and, of course, it is only competent to suspend the athlete if the rules of the governing body allow for such a suspension; there are governing bodies who take the view that it is fairer to the majority of the athletes to have a temporary suspension, although that in itself might fall foul of the rules of natural justice. The view, however, has been expressed that the immediate suspension on a positive A sample is not contrary to natural justice provided that the decision is not stated to be final. A difficult issue arises here also if the person who is suspended is part of a team. Here the rules must be clear as to what happens to the team in such circumstances. The whole question of whether or not to suspend on the outcome of the A sample is very close to the concept of "strict liability" in a legal sense and this is still not resolved across all sports.

Internationally within sport this remains one of the most difficult areas since the way many of the rules have been written imposes strict liability giving rise to an obligation on the athlete to explain in a subsequent hearing how the banned substance came to be in their sample. In 1999 the lengthy problem for Scottish sprinter Douglas Walker in his situation with UK Athletics was that for some considerable time he did not know in sufficient detail what the charge was against him in order to outline a defence. The Walker case highlights a particular difficulty at the international level, considered below.

On the assumption, however, that an initial hearing, after observing the rules of natural justice, proceeds to determine that the athlete has been guilty of an offence, there is a need to ensure (as suggested above in relation to the rules of natural justice) that the sanction is fair. There should also be an appeal process, whether internally or externally, as suggested below.

International issues and sanctions

The variety of different ways in which doping control has been approached **7-15** internationally has been indicated above. There is definitely a "conflict of laws" situation between the rules of international sport and the normally recognised international legal jurisdictions. In February 1999 the International Olympic Committee hosted a world conference on doping in sport in Lausanne and sought to put in place a declaration to take forward an international review of doping control in sport, although many countries including the United Kingdom expressed the view that the final declaration was insufficiently strong. Of particular interest is the fact that two sports—football and cycling—through their international federations refused to agree to a minimum two-year ban in their sport on a positive test. It may be that this springs partly from the successful appeal brought by the German sprinter Katrina Krabbe before the German courts that a ban in excess of two years was disproportionate and unlawful under German law for a first offence, but it is still difficult to see how near sport at international level is to adopting an approach to this area which will regain the necessary respect. In this context, it is strange that professional cycling has intimated in the press in the second week of January 2000 that it will require its competitors in the year 2000 to submit to urine and blood testing to demonstrate that the sport is "clean". It will be interesting to see what happens to the major cycling events and their competitors following that announcement.

It is certainly the case that international sports federations are running scared of the level and expense of litigation. One of the significant features in the demise of the British Athletics Federation was the Diane Modahl case which is still ongoing at the time of writing. Indeed, the former international British hurdler, John Ridgeon, after the Lausanne conference stated: "Top class athletes make their living from their sport and are willing to do almost anything to salvage that livelihood. They employ expensive barristers who then look for loopholes and because there is no international body able to test across all sports and all countries there are plenty of those." The basis for looking for such loopholes is indeed, as John Ridgeon said, to try to salvage the livelihood of such athletes. Sandra Gasser was a Swiss athlete who was suspended for failing a dope test after coming third in the women's 1500 metres at the world championships in Rome in 1987. She complained that the regulations under which she was suspended were an unreasonable restraint of trade and in an unreported case heard in London in 1988—*Gasser v Stinson*—Scott J indicated that while rules providing for suspension were by definition *prima facie* in restraint of trade even where the athlete was not paid, the lawfulness of restraint then depended upon the reasonableness of the rules in question. In athletics these rules went so far as to create an absolute offence and to impose a mandatory two-year sentence of suspension. He held that, against the background of the problem of drugs in sport and the public interest in seeing fair sport, the rules in question were not unreasonable and found against the athlete.

7-16   The latter part of John Ridgeon's assertion, about the need to put in place an international body to test across all sports and all countries, and the need to apply sensible sanctions, has been described as "the horizontal integration issue". It is hoped that the IOC is indeed beginning to address this issue and there are suggestions that such a body will be in place before the Sydney Olympics in 2000. Indeed, in November 1999 the IOC and the European Union reached agreement on the draft Articles of the World Anti-Doping Agency, which was accordingly established on 10 November in Lausanne, Switzerland. The Board will have between 10 and 35 members, with the Olympic movement and the public authorities each being able to appoint up to 16 members. Members will be appointed for a three-year term which is renewable on two occasions.

There is, however, a further element of involvement with international issues to which reference should be made. Most Scottish governing bodies will be affiliated to the international federation of their sport directly or indirectly through a British body, and it will be that body through which the sport competes internationally. There is therefore a need to ensure that in so far as each sport is concerned within the United Kingdom vertical integration should be in place. The suggestion has been made by Frank Dick that an adjunct to the new Scottish Institute of Sport might be an ethics body which would seek to have an influence on the way in which sports are set up and managed from the whole disciplinary point of view, not just doping control.

7-17   The international issues therefore continue to abound but it is plain that there is work to be done in Scotland by Scottish lawyers to ensure that the rules of our governing bodies and clubs are such that appropriate sanctions can be brought into play against those who are guilty of drug abuse in sport. That involves, of course, both the whole disciplinary process and membership issues being subjects of review.

At this stage the other international issue should be mentioned, namely European involvement. Most Scottish governing bodies will be affiliated either directly to an international federation or possibly indirectly through a European federation. There is a significant number of sports where the international representation is British and not directly Scottish, and there may be a European overlay before one arrives at the international level. In terms of the rules of each sport which would have to impact on the Scottish governing body's own rules there is, therefore, a need to ensure vertical integration of these rules throughout the sport. Plainly, in football and cycling at least, that will be difficult to achieve.

7-18   Of considerable interest to Scots sports persons and enthusiasts at the time of writing is the apparent impassé between UK Athletics, which has decided on appeal to accept that Douglas Walker has no case to answer relating to the nandrolone metabolites found in his sample taken in 1998, and the International Amateur Athletic Federation, which has refused to accept this decision and called for the papers to be put before them. Subsequently the IAAF hearing in Switzerland despite evidence from a research project led by Professor Maughan of Aberdeen University suggesting that the amount of nandrolone found in Douglas Walker's body could have been produced in certain circumstances without his taking a banned substance, confirmed his ban from international athletics. That was because in the light of their strict liability rule the IAAF held that the study from Aberdeen University was not such compelling evidence in Douglas Walker's favour as to persuade them to overturn their original ban.

It does seem, therefore, as if the threat of legal action by Douglas Walker reported at the end of November 1999 is still in place where he may issue writs against the IAAF and UK Athletics on the basis of lack of jurisdiction and breach of contract. This may bring about public addressing of the strict liability issue. It is fair to say there are also emerging inconsistencies in the way in which the IAAF has dealt with other nandrolone issues in particular with Merlene Ottey, the Jamaican sprinter, who was reinstated on grounds which are not entirely clear.

Procedures and appeals

It is important that for each sport there should be a procedure in place **7-19** whereby an athlete who is dissatisfied with the finding of the disciplinary panel or committee at first instance is in a position to make an appeal; this has proved troublesome in the past. Not only is there the need to make sure that the governing body observes its own rules throughout the entire process, but these rules themselves must be seen to be fair. While the rules of natural justice must still apply, the separation of the appellate body from the first level of disciplinary panel or committee is critical. There is plainly a need to update the constitution and rules of the governing bodies regularly to ensure that they remain entirely appropriate in this difficult legal area.

Scotland has played its part in the establishment of a company limited by guarantee called the Sports Dispute Resolution Panel which seeks to offer an entirely independent and hopefully streamlined way of dealing with arbitration and mediation if both parties (normally the governing body and an athlete) wish to make use of such a service. A panel of five Scottish solicitors, three members of the Bar, an experienced chartered accountant and an experienced internationally respected lay official have indicated their readiness to be available to serve on such panels, all of whom have appropriate sporting and legal or accountancy backgrounds. The expense of taking some of these issues to court has had a challenging impact on many of the smaller governing bodies and indeed Government support had to be obtained by the Scottish Sports Council a few years ago to assist in the staging of a form of independent arbitration to deal successfully with a positive drug test in a sport with a prize money circuit. The international athlete involved had a sponsor and was encouraged to go to court to attempt to obtain resolution. Common sense eventually prevailed, with the help of legal colleagues in Scotland; the learning process in that instance was part of the work leading to the establishment of the Sports Dispute Resolution Panel, which has now appointed a former London Barrister with considerable sports administration experience as its paid director. He will be responsible for the administration of the processes.

Conclusions

7-20 This unfortunately remains law at its most nebulous in so far as Scotland is concerned. Nevertheless, there have been issues in Scotland which demonstrate that there is a readiness to resolve the legal issues in so far as Scots lawyers can and also to provide an input at UK and international level, where appropriate, to ensure that neither sport nor the law are held up to ridicule and disrepute in this extremely difficult area.

8   FOOTBALL

Alistair Duff

This chapter restricts itself to the consideration of the law as it applies to **8-1** football in Scotland only in so far as it can be found in decisions of the courts and then principally those after 1994. European aspects are not dealt with in this chapter, being treated above.[1]

The courts' involvement in football in Scotland is not as recent as most people think. Indeed, in 1424 the Parliament of James I forbade the playing of football, passing an Act on 26 May 1424. It was possibly because, in the early fifteenth century, it seems that the youth of the nation were more interested in playing football than in practising more important skills such as archery.[2] It is only in recent times, however, that cases have seemed to achieve a huge amount of media interest, running to editorial comments in quality newspapers.[3] The editorial published[4] following the sentencing of Duncan Ferguson stated that nobody is above the law of the land; yet it remains a fact that various groups of individuals appear to be perceived as less culpable in their wrongdoing than others. Towards the end of the editorial it commented:

> "All of this raises serious questions for the game of rugby, which is substantially more violent than football will ever be. The exchange of punches, head butts and stamping are much more prevalent in rugby than they ever will be in football, and if the rule of law finds Mr Ferguson guilty of assault, it must be prepared to do the same to rugby players all over the country. This thought should not paralyse sportsmen and their administrators, but simply make them more responsible."

This chapter principally deals with post-1994 material, but to illustrate the point made in the opening sentence, other cases will be considered.[5]

---

[1] See Chapter 5.

[2] G MacKay and A McConnell, "Ancient Legal Bar on Football in Scotland" 1994 SLT (News) 282.

[3] See in particular *The Scotsman* of 11 May 1995 under the Editorial heading "Paying the penalty": this was commenting on the prosecution of Duncan Ferguson for an assault on John McStay. Thereafter, in *The Herald* of 26 May 1995, following his custodial sentence of three months, the Editorial was "Sportsmen and violence".

[4] *The Herald*, 26 May 1995.

[5] For an illuminating trail through potential football criminal cases, see J B Stewart, "Football: Criminal Aspects" 1980 SLT (News) 49–56 (and an addendum at 77) and his complementary article on potential civil cases, J B Stewart, "Football: Civil Aspects" 1981 SLT (News) 157.

In 1926, the Sheriff Court of Edinburgh, in the case of *Petershill Football Club v St Bernards Football Club Ltd*[6] heard how the football club brought an action against another club for payment of £50 for damages. The ground of action was that the defenders induced and procured one of their registered players to break an agreement between him and the pursuers. So the involvement of the courts in protecting clubs' contractual rights to players is nothing new, although of course the sums of money involved nowadays are considerably higher!

8-2   In a recent article Robert Shiels comments on the death of John Thomson during a football match.[7] On 5 September 1931, Thomson was playing in goal for Celtic in an old firm match against Rangers; about five minutes into the second half, the ball went to Sam English, a Rangers player who was then clear and with only Thomson to beat. As they approached, English and Thomson collided and English's knee struck the goalkeeper's head. Thomson fell to the ground and lay still. Thomson was taken to hospital and died at 9.25 pm. Dr Daly certified death as "Depressed Fracture of Skull". A fatal accident inquiry was held in terms of the Fatal Accidents Inquiry (Scotland) Act 1895, as amended by the Fatal Accidents and Sudden Deaths Inquiry (Scotland) Act 1906, the Fiscal having formed the view that a professional footballer was in industrial employment or occupation. The inquiry was held on 15 October 1931 and, as reported in *The Glasgow Herald* of 16 October 1931:

> "Many well known Scottish footballers were present when the FAI was held yesterday ... Mr William Holborn said that he was the referee at the match. Describing the accident, he said the centre forward was in the act of shooting when the Celtic goalkeeper came from his goal and made a dive on the centre forward's feet for the ball. Both men fell, but Thomson was unable to arise and, seeing that he was badly injured, he was removed to the pavilion. Asked by the Fiscal if he thought there was any indication of foul play, the witness replied that there was not. 'It was a pure accident' he said."

Sheriff Wilton, in addressing the jury, said that this was a very distressing occurrence in the football field and he supposed they were satisfied from the evidence that it was an accident. The jury thereafter returned a verdict to the effect that Thomson was engaged in his employment as a professional footballer by the Celtic club, and acting as goalkeeper in a football match with Rangers at Ibrox Park, Glasgow, on 5 September, that in the course of the match he sustained an injury to his head accidentally coming into contact with the body of Samuel English, playing centre forward for the Rangers, in an attempt to save a goal by diving towards Samuel English when in the act of kicking the ball, and that he sustained a fracture to the skull, from which he died in the Victoria Infirmary.

Robert Shiels, in his article, states that this was the third occasion in which a player had been fatally injured in Scottish football. He cites the

---

[6] 1926 SLT (Sh Ct) 42.

[7] 1997 SLG 7.

example of a Dunbartonshire goalkeeper named Wilkinson who received a fatal knock when playing against Rangers at Ibrox and a further example at Firhill Park, Glasgow, in 1909 when James Main (a Hibernian back) had received fatal injuries.

In England, the case of *R v Moore*[8] in 1898 was a criminal prosecution in respect of injury to a goalkeeper. The goalkeeper was in the process of clearing the ball when the defendant jumped, with his knees up against the back of the victim, which threw him violently forward against the knee of the goalkeeper. The victim died a few days later from internal injuries. In summing up the judge said that the rules of the game were quite immaterial and it did not matter whether the defendant broke the rules of the game or not. Football was a lawful game, but it was a rough one and persons who played it must be careful not to do bodily harm to any other person. No one had a right to use force which was likely to injure another and, if he did use such force and death resulted, the crime of manslaughter had been committed. A verdict of guilty was returned. The vicar of Enderby gave the convicted young man a most excellent character reference and the judge postponed sentence.[9]

In 1952, the Criminal Appeal Court in Edinburgh, in the case of *Joseph McCudden v Her Majesty's Advocate*,[10] considered an appeal against conviction by McCudden. McCudden had been convicted on indictment of two separate contraventions of section 1(1) of the Prevention of Corruption Act 1906, namely "By corruptly offering money to a professional football player, who in each case was a centre half, as an inducement to forbear from exercising his skills during a specified league match so to cause his team to be defeated." The appeal was really to do with a technical legal point, but two players, namely Simon Waldie of Queen of the South Football Club and William Telfer of St Mirren Football Club, were offered £250 and £200 respectively, which were not insubstantial sums of money. Waldie was offered the money on or about 26 October 1951 and his team were due to play East Fife Football Club on or about 27 October 1951; Telfer was offered his sum of money on 15 November 1951 and his team were due to play Partick Thistle Football Club on 17 November 1951. Lord Justice-General Cooper stated: "In both cases the same or similar advice was tendered by the accused to the player as to how best to achieve the desired result, namely in particular both players were offered the peculiarly sinister advice to give a bad pass-back to his own goalkeeper, which could be intercepted by an opposing forward." McCudden's appeal failed at the end of the day and, as most readers will be aware, recently this has arisen in England in the Grobbelaar/Fashanu/Segears match-fixing trial, when all the accused were acquitted of corruption charges.

In 1956, the Sheriff Court of Lanark at Airdrie heard a case *Shankland v Airdrieonians Football and Athletic Society*[11] in which there was a contractual

8-3

8-4

---

[8] (1898) 14 TLR 229.

[9] Reference is also made to an unsuccessful prosecution in the case of *R v Bradshaw* (1878) 14 Cox CC 83.

[10] 1952 JC 86.

[11] 1956 SLT (Sh Ct) 69.

dispute between a player and his club about whether he was entitled to a benefit arising after completing five years' service with the club. The player had played between 4 November 1949 and 30 April 1954 on separate annual contracts. The player claimed the benefit on or about 7 May 1954 and the club contended that no sum was due because the player had not completed five calendar years' service. The court held that the club's obligation arose at the end of the fifth playing season and decree was granted for £500.

In recent years there have been more and more sporting judicial reviews (not confined to football), and these are dealt with more fully in Chapter 3. As early as 1965, in the case of *St Johnstone Football Club Ltd v Scottish Football Association Ltd*,[12] Lord Kilbrandon said: "The courts would entertain actions arising out of judgments of the governing bodies of private associations, whether or not the civil rights and patrimonial interests of their members had been interfered with by the proceedings complained of, when a gross irregularity, such as a departure from the rules of natural justice, had been demonstrated." This case is still cited both in England and Scotland in the context of administrative law and judicial reviews.[13]

Another area which might be thought to be new is crowd safety. However, the lack of safety is well known to Scots law: for example, the Ibrox disaster on 2 January 1971 in which 66 people died on stairway 13. A Home Office inquiry was set up under Lord Wheatley with terms of reference relating to crowd safety at sports grounds in Great Britain.[14] The report was of great significance as it was the first report to lead directly to an Act of Parliament, namely the Safety of Sports Grounds Act 1975. In terms of the actual Act, it was stated that it was "An Act to make provision for safety at sports stadia and other sports grounds".[15] There was also litigation arising out of the Ibrox disaster.[16] This was some twenty years before the Hillsborough disaster on 20 March 1989, which led to what is known as "Taylor's Reports": these had far-reaching consequences for football clubs in that in the final report, namely *The Hillsborough Stadium Disaster (Final Report)* (Cm 962), the most important recommendation was that of all-seater football stadiums.[17]

8-5   In 1977, in the case of *Hosie v Arbroath Football Club Ltd*[18] Lord Stewart dealt with a damages action raised by a man who sustained severe injuries

---

[12] 1965 SLT 34 at 35.

[13] As recently as 28 May 1999 it was quoted in Lord Eassie's Opinion in the judicial review of Colin Fraser against a decision of the Professional Golfers Association.

[14] The Wheatley Report (Cmnd 4952, 1982).

[15] In terms of the general note it is stated: "This Act represents the third attempt to put the provisions for safety at sports stadia and other sports grounds on to the Statute Book. The first two Bills were lost in the dissolution of a Parliament."

[16] See *Dougan v Rangers Football Club Ltd* 1974 SLT (Sh Ct) 34; *McGhee v Rangers Football Club Ltd* 1977 SLT (Sh Ct) 15.

[17] See Chapter 2.

[18] 1978 SLT 122.

when knocked down and trampled by a crowd at a football ground. The action was brought in terms of the Occupiers' Liability (Scotland) Act 1960. The occupiers of the football ground were blamed on the grounds that they knew, or ought to have known, that the gate could be lifted off its runners by the pressure of a crowd and that someone could thereby be injured. It was established that no one inspected the part of the gate that gave way prior to the accident and that no one had applied his mind to problems of crowd safety resulting from the gate being broken down either accidentally or deliberately. It was held that it was reasonably foreseeable by the occupiers that there might be an attempt by an unruly crowd to force the gate, that the behaviour of the crowd did not amount to a *novus actus interveniens* breaking the causal link, and that accordingly the occupiers were liable since they had failed reasonably to maintain the gate. Mr Hosie was awarded damages totalling £76,260.

In 1983, in the case of *Celtic Football and Athletic Club Ltd v Customs and Excise Commissioners*[19] which was dealing purely with VAT, the taxpayer, Celtic, was a member of the Union of European Football Association (UEFA) which took part in knockout competitions in which pairs of clubs played each other twice, once at home and once away. By Article 18 of the UEFA Rules, each home club was obliged to pay for its visiting opponents' board and lodgings as well as for the travelling and accommodation expenses of the match officials. Celtic was assessed to VAT on the footing that the accommodation provided to the visiting clubs and match officials constituted "business entertainment" within article 2(2) of Value Added Tax (Special Provisions) Order 1977. Accordingly, and by virtue of article 9 of the 1977 Order, they were not entitled to credit in respect of input tax for services used by them for that purpose. It was held that "entertainment" for the purposes of article 9 of the 1977 Order meant "hospitality" which was provided free to the recipient. Since Celtic's visiting opponents had reciprocal obligations under the UEFA Rules to meet Celtic's accommodation expenses when they played their away matches, the entertainment was not free to them. Accordingly the services supplied to Celtic were not for the purposes of business entertainment within the 1977 Order and Celtic was entitled to credit for input tax in respect of tax paid on the supply of these services. The appeal was allowed.

Dealing with a more recent case, involving an assault on the pitch, **8-6** Andrew Brannigan (of Arbroath) broke an opponent's leg in three places (J Deakin of Albion Rovers) after a tackle. Brannigan was convicted at Airdrie Sheriff Court on or about 1 October 1987. This is believed to be the first prosecution of an assault involving a professional footballer. In *The Scotsman* of 2 October 1987 it was reported: "Footballer fined £150 for assault on opponent". Announcing the verdict Sheriff Cameron said: "What started out as a run changed in character and the intent crept in of causing injury. It changed to a deliberate attack on Mr Deakin. It wasn't a mere transgression of the rules. The accused must have known that the ball was away." It was reported that one of the witnesses was a rugby player,

---

[19] [1983] STC 470.

Mr James Smith, a spectator at the game, who described Brannigan's assault on Mr Deakin as "A ferocious deliberate act". During questioning from the Fiscal Mr Smith said "As tackles go this could not be described as a tackle. I can't imagine for the life of me what he was trying to kick, but it certainly wasn't the ball."

A much more high profile case—which is probably erroneously thought to be the criminal court's first involvement in dealing with actions of professional footballers on the pitch—concerned Terry Butcher, Graham Roberts, Francis McAvennie and Christopher Woods, who were charged that on 17 October 1987 within Ibrox Stadium, during an Old Firm match, whilst participating in a football match, they did conduct themselves in a disorderly manner and commit a breach of the peace. In the appeal, *Butcher and Woods v Jessop*[20] against their convictions they were unsuccessful. In the context of Christopher Woods' appeal, reference was made to an interesting part of the original sheriff's notes and was in the following terms:

> "The immediate circumstances of the incident were that the appellant was taking part in a vigorous 'contact sport'. I take into account that circumstance even though it is not a contact sport to the same degree as rugby and some other sports. Violent tackles, as long as they conform to the rules of the game, are not only permissible but are an integral part of the game itself. The rules provide for over-enthusiastic tackles and for other infringements and specify appropriate penalties to be imposed by the referee. That does not mean to say, however, as appeared to be argued on behalf of the appellant, that on the field of play all infringements of the rules must be left to the referee. It was conceded that if an assault took place, then that might properly be prosecuted in the criminal courts. I see no difference in principle between that crime and the crime of breach of the peace."[21]

8-7 It can be clearly seen from the above that prior to 1994 the courts have taken quite an active interest in all areas of football; the cases mentioned are illustrative only and are certainly not exhaustive. It is perhaps worth remembering J McCluskey QC's words (as he then was) in May of 1974 at the opening of the Biennial Congress of the European Union of Football Associations in Edinburgh, reported in *The Scotsman* of 22 April 1978. He commented that wearing a football jersey did not put a person above the law; steps might have to be taken to curb football violence both on and off the field. He said that if there was an incident witnessed by thousands, or even millions, through television, unless the football authorities took effective steps to discipline the players to prevent such incidents, the time could come when those responsible for administering criminal law might have to step in. These have turned out to be prophetic words indeed.

---

[20] 1989 SLT 593; 1989 SCLR 119.

[21] For cases involving custodial sentences in football and rugby, see A M Duff, "Summary of Criminal Prosecutions for Football and Rugby Violence", 1994 SLT (News) 281 and for cases involving civil actions concerning sporting injuries, see A M Duff, "Civil Actions and Sporting Injuries Sustained by Professional Footballers" 1994 SLT (News) 175.

Some recent cases from 1994 to date, will now be considered, based on the writer's own regular reports in "Scottish Update", appearing in most issues of *Sport and the Law Journal*.[22] The sources are arranged into three categories, namely criminal cases; civil cases concerning injury; and all other civil cases.

CRIMINAL CASES

In a report in *The Herald* of 3 August 1994 it was stated that a footballer who **8-8** was banned for 50 years for punching a referee, fracturing his cheek bone, was jailed for four months at Kirkcaldy Sheriff Court on 2 August 1994. Graham Harper, who was playing for Covenanters against Tokeim, in a Sunday AFL match, with about 10 minutes to go, was about to be booked by the referee and he thereafter punched the referee in the left side of his face knocking him to the ground.

There was a report in *The Scotsman* of Tuesday 6 December 1994 that a former professional footballer assaulted the opposing team's manager during a West of Scotland Amateur Cup Tie. The incident led to the game being abandoned. James Grant was playing for an Uddingston amateur team, Oakside, on 26 March 1994 when he punched Robert Neil, the manager of the opposing side and host club Galston United. Mr Neil lost a tooth and suffered neck injuries when he was felled by Grant's punch to the jaw after he came on to the Barrmill pitch to protect the referee. The court heard that Grant had been banned from playing for 18 months by the football authorities in connection with the incident and his club had been barred from cup competition for 10 years. Sheriff Thomas Croan told him, "This is another example of the unacceptable face of sport." He deferred sentence for two weeks for background reports.

On 5 January 1995 *The Herald* reported that Norman Lawson admitted assaulting Neil Hardie of Saughton Park, Edinburgh, in July 1994 by butting him in the face in a match between Gyle Centre Staff and Safeway Shop Staff. Sheriff Shiach said it was a fairly serious assault and deferred sentence until 25 January 1995. Lawson's victim had two chipped teeth, a cut inside his mouth and a bleeding nose. The sheriff also advised him to get legal representation as he had a conviction for culpable homicide (manslaughter) from 1988. It was further reported in *The Herald* on 26 January 1995 that the player was fined £250 and ordered to pay his victim £100 compensation.

A report in *The Herald* on 11 May 1995 stated that Duncan Ferguson, after a two-day trial, was found guilty of deliberately head-butting another player during a premier league game between Rangers and Raith Rovers at Ibrox on 16 April 1994 (see the following appeal court judgment).

In the case of *Richard Anderson v Hamilton*[23] Richard Anderson pled guilty **8-9** to assaulting a referee on 25 September 1994 at a football pitch in Lochgelly.

---

[22] Fourteen Updates appearing in *Sport and the Law Journal* (SLJ) spanning from Volume 3, Issue One, 1995 up to and including Volume 8, Issue One, 2000.

[23] Unreported decision of Lord Allanbridge dated 18 May 1995.

The assault was by kicking the referee on the legs to his injury. He was sentenced to 90 days' imprisonment and he appealed against that sentence. The appellant was playing as a member of the local public house team and sometime during the match the referee decided that the time had come to bring the match to a halt; when he did so the appellant objected and kicked the referee once on the back of the legs. The referee had stopped the match because several players were drunk and carrying out dangerous tackles. Although Anderson had been banned from playing football for 50 years, he was single, unemployed and willing to pay a monetary fine and, as Anderson had now addressed his drinking problem, it was suggested that reports be obtained on a possible non-custodial sentence. However, the appeal court held that 90 days' imprisonment was not excessive where Anderson had a four-page record of previous convictions including eight crimes of violence with sentences up to six months' imprisonment.

8-10　　We now turn to the most high profile case which is that of Duncan Ferguson. His appeal against sentence was heard on 11 October 1995.[24] The Lord Justice-General summarised the charge: on 16 April 1994 at Ibrox, while participating in a football match, he assaulted John McStay and did lunge at him, seize hold of his clothing, butt him on the head and knock him to the ground, to his injury. On 25 May 1995 he was sentenced to three months' imprisonment. The minute stated that the sheriff decided to impose that sentence in view of the gravity and nature of the offence and the appellant's previous convictions. The Lord Justice-General stated:

> "The court has no wish to intervene in physical contact sport such as professional football. It is well aware that contest and physical fitness, strength and agility and some measure of aggression are part of the game, both for player and spectator. But when acts are done which go well beyond what can be regarded as normal physical contact and an assault is committed, the court has a duty to condemn and punish such conduct. It has to be made clear both to players and to the public that such criminal acts cannot be tolerated on the field of play any more than they can be tolerated in any other place in the country. A footballer who assaults another player on the football field is not entitled to expect leniency from the court just because the incident occurred in the course of a football match."

Later on the Lord Justice-General said:

> "on the contrary, one of the factors which may indicate the gravity of the offence is the fact that the assault has been committed in public before so many spectators. This fact becomes all the more important where the player is a public figure and the incident occurs during a game which has such a high profile as a league match in the Scottish Premier Division. These are fixtures which set the standard of conduct throughout the country and any sentence for an assault committed in these circumstances must reflect the need to deter others from engaging in similar acts of criminal violence."

---

[24] *Ferguson v Normand* 1995 SCCR 770.

The Lord Justice-General accepted that the sheriff had overstated the matter in describing the appellant's record as a quite appalling one of previous violent offences.

> "We would not put the matter in that way. On the other hand the sheriff did have before him three previous convictions which we have described. To our mind the most important factor is that on the last occasion the appellant was ordered to serve a period of probation, which he was still serving at the time when the offence, with which we are now dealing, was committed. For a person who has been dealt with leniently in that way to commit an offence of the same kind while on probation is a serious matter."

The Lord Justice-General ended by saying: "In our opinion, in all the circumstances, the sentence of three months' imprisonment which was intended to be an effective punishment and a deterrent to others, cannot be described as excessive and we have no alternative in this unfortunate case but to refuse the appeal." Readers may be aware that around the same time Eric Cantona was originally sentenced to a period of imprisonment in England, but this was reduced on appeal to community service. It should be remembered that it is not appropriate to treat this case as like with like. Eric Cantona appeared before the court as a first offender. It would be fair to say that Duncan Ferguson suffered unprecedented media attention and, in one respect, it brought to a head the general feeling that there was no consistency in dealing with violence on the sporting field. It was felt that it was really a legal lottery as to whether a player was prosecuted or not and the Lord Advocate, on 10 July 1996, issued instructions to Scotland's chief constables which consisted of a five-page document with 11 points.[25] However, it is respectfully submitted that the guidelines do not clarify matters sufficiently and it appears to be business as usual.[26] For instance, the Lord Advocate, in paragraph six, states that experienced police officers should be well able to identify incidents where the conduct involved could be viewed as criminal. For that reason these guidelines do not seek to define in detail the circumstances in which police officers should take action. However, the Lord Advocate wishes the police to investigate and, where appropriate, report incidents where the violence involved goes well beyond that which would be expected to occur during the normal run of play and that which the rules of the sport are designed to regulate. In deciding which incidents to investigate, the police should pay particular regard to incidents where the violence or disorderly behaviour has occurred after the whistle has been blown and whilst the ball is dead and to incidents where the violence or disorderly behaviour has occurred in circumstances liable to provoke a disorderly or violent response from spectators. The guidelines are concluded by the Lord Advocate saying:

> "Chief Constables will understand that it is always open to a Procurator Fiscal to call for a report on an incident which has come to

---

[25] See S Miller, "The Lord Advocate's Instructions of 10 July 1996 to Chief Constables", (1996) 4 (2) SLJ 40.

[26] See A Duff's "Scottish Update" (1996) 4 (2) SLJ 28.

his attention, whether or not such incident has been reported to him by the police. However, the Lord Advocate considers that provided these guidelines are followed, it will only be on rare occasions that a Procurator Fiscal will find it necessary to take the initiative and instruct a report."

8-11   In *The Scotsman* of 2 April 1997 there was a report that a footballer was cleared of breaking an Icelander's jaw with a head butt. It said that Scotland Junior International centre half, Ian Ashcroft, was cleared of breaking an Icelandic player's jaw during a friendly game. A jury took only 20 minutes to find the head-butt charge against the Pollock Junior footballer not proven. The referee, an Anthony Smith, said that he blew his whistle and, as he lectured two players, including the Icelander, he saw Ashcroft run up and head-butt the Icelander. The referee immediately sent off Ashcroft and later reported the matter to the junior authorities. The accused had denied assaulting the Icelander, but agreed his arm might have come into contact with him whilst he was separating the two players. Ashcroft was suspended for six matches by the football authorities after the incident and he declined to comment after the hearing because of the civil case against him.

A report in the *Edinburgh Evening News* of 15 October 1998 stated that the referee attacked by goalkeeper Peter Davies claimed justice had been done after the player was banned from football for five years. Former Celtic signing, Davies, aged 19, raised his hands to referee, Robert Ormond, after being sent off whilst playing for Armadale Thistle against Bonnyrigg Rose. The West Lothian club immediately expelled him, and the disciplinary committee of the East Region Junior FA handed out a "monster ban".

8-12   In *The Herald* of 6 November 1998 it was reported that an amateur player who head-butted another player was banned by a sheriff from attending football matches and prevented from watching them on television on Saturdays. Sean McAulay butted Philip Rose, a police officer, and left him permanently disfigured after an amateur match broke into violence. McAulay was a striker with California whilst Mr Rose was playing for Glenvale at a game in Falkirk under the Stirling and District Amateur Football Association. Mr Rose had legitimately taken possession of the ball when McAulay barged into him, kicking. Mr Rose fell to the ground. The referee stopped the game and awarded a free kick to Glenvale. The Procurator Fiscal said: "At that point the accused took a few running steps towards the victim and head-butted him. There was an audible crack and the referee intervened. He issued a red card and the accused was sent off." Sheriff Albert Sheehan placed 27-year-old McAulay on probation and ordered him to do 240 hours' community service. He banned him from attending any football matches for three years and recommended that the community service should be carried out between 3 pm and 5 pm on Saturdays. In a letter to the court the referee said that the head-butt was the worst he had ever seen. Sheriff Sheehan ordered McAulay to pay his victim £1,000 compensation. He also added conditions to stop him enjoying football, ordering him to hand over passport photographs of himself to be sent by the court to the Scottish Football Association, and banned him from attending football matches as a player, spectator or in any capacity for three years. McAulay was banned by the Scottish Football Association for 10 years after the attack, which took place in November 1997.

From the above, it should be abundantly clear that sportsmen are not immune from the law and any notion that the law of the land stops on the touchline is wrong.

CIVIL CASES CONCERNING INJURY

Civil actions between professional footballers as a result of injuries received **8-13** on the playing field are still relatively scarce and up to and including 1994 only three Scottish cases had reached the courts. In 1982 Jim Brown of Hearts issued proceedings against J Pelosi and St Johnstone Football Club, and thereafter, in 1993, proceedings were raised by Ian Durrant of Rangers against Neil Simpson of Aberdeen Football Club and Steven Murray of Celtic against Jamie Dolan and Motherwell Football Club. None of these actions ran their full course and it is believed that Brown settled after the issuing of a summons, Durrant settled on the morning of a civil proof and Murray (for whom the writer was acting) settled on the morning of a jury trial scheduled to last six days. Consequently, no Scottish judge has yet applied his mind to the standard of care to be exercised by footballers towards each other. Steven Murray received a substantial award of damages, but the actual terms of the settlement are confidential. The Murray case was pled in the closed record as follows:

> "The said accident was caused by fault on the part of the first defender for whose actings and omissions in the course of his employment with them the second defenders are liable. It was the first defender's duty to take reasonable care for the safety of other players in the said match, including the pursuer. It was his duty to take reasonable care in tackling opposing players such as the pursuer and to do so within the rules and conventions of the game. It was his duty to take reasonable care to avoid striking the pursuer after the pursuer had played the ball. He knew or ought to have known that there was a likelihood of causing injury to the pursuer if he lunged at the pursuer with his foot high and the studs of his boot visible. It was his duty to take reasonable care, to avoid striking the pursuer with his foot. In the exercise of the aforesaid duties, the first defender failed and thus caused the accident. He failed to take reasonable care for the pursuer. He failed to tackle the pursuer within the rules and convention of the game. He failed to attempt to gain possession of the ball or to dispossess the pursuer of the ball. He struck the pursuer after the pursuer had played the ball, and with his foot high. But for the first defender's failures in duty, the accident would have been avoided."

The above cases have shown that nowadays players do not appear as **8-14** reluctant to sue other players for bad tackles and since every professional football club is required to carry indemnity insurance—indeed, it is the insurers who would have to settle any claim if the club were vicariously liable—if players can satisfy the courts as to liability, then there will be no problem with enforcing the damages claims. Nowadays, most top league matches are recorded on videotape; thus, evidence of the tackle or challenge would not be difficult to obtain even although interpretation may vary. Given the huge sums of money that are at stake, it is not surprising that, on the face of it, more actions are being raised. The cost of funding any such action will still probably stop a lot of potential claimants.

The first time the English courts dealt with an action between two professional footballers was in the case of *Elliott v Saunders and Liverpool Football Club*.[27] In this case the plaintiff, Paul Elliott, was ultimately unsuccessful as the judge held that he had failed to prove that there was any intent by the defendant to jump on or at him rather than at the ball. The judge found that Saunders was not guilty of dangerous or reckless play and that the plaintiff had failed to prove that the defendant was in breach of the duty of care that he owed to the plaintiff in all the circumstances of this case. The judge went on to say: "However, I think it is right to add that although I have rejected his claim, I do not, by any means, think that it was a hopeless one. His case was supported by a very large number of eminent witnesses and, on paper, appeared to have reasonable prospects of success." The judge made further comments about why video recordings in this case had been accepted by both the parties and the court as a proper aid to try to discover the true facts, but the judge stated:

> "Video recordings, like photographs, have their limitations. More than one witness gave the view, which I accept, that what is seen on a video recording may be affected by the height and angle from which the pictures were taken, and may give a distorted impression. The pictures are two dimensional and not three dimensional and there is always the possibility with modern techniques of editing the video material by selecting parts most favourable to one party. For these reasons video recordings, like still photographs, are by no means decisive to show the true facts. They are an aid, and in this case I found them a good aid, but they are no more than that. The evidence of eye witnesses, particularly that of the plaintiff and the defendant, are at least of equal importance."

This case did nothing to put an end to the debate as to whether the standard of care should be that of reasonable care or reckless disregard and this debate is still ongoing.[28]

8-15   Towards the end of May 1994, Michael Hendry, who played for Alloa, raised court proceedings against Steven Cody and Stranraer Football Club for an allegedly reckless tackle. Cody was sent off for the tackle and eventually this case, again, settled during 1996 without the matter going to a full hearing, with the pursuer being awarded an undisclosed sum of compensation.

8-16   There have been more recent cases in England over the past few years including *O'Neill v Fashanu and Wimbledon Football Club*, which was an unreported decision of the High Court in 1994, *McCord v Cornforth and Swansea City*, an unreported decision of the High Court in 1996, McCord receiving

---

[27] QB, 10 June 1994, unreported.

[28] See A Duff, "Reasonable Care v. Reckless Disregard" (1999) 7 (1) SLJ 44.

£250,000 damages for an injury that brought his career to a premature end (and believed to be the first time in England that a plaintiff's claim was successful), and culminating in the case of *Watson v Gray and Another.*[29] In this case it was held that a professional footballer injured in a tackle by another professional player established negligence against that player if he proved, on the balance of probabilities, that a reasonable professional player would have known that there was a significant risk that what the second player did would result in serious injury. The judge said that "such a forceful, high challenge, particularly when carried out when there is a good chance that the ball had been moved on, was one that a reasonable professional player would have known carried with it a significant risk of serious injury" and thus he found in favour of Watson. The writer understands that this case was appealed but in *The Scotsman* of 8 May 1999, it was reported with regard to Gordon Watson that "Footballer wins one million pound award for wrecked career". It stated: "A footballer, whose career was wrecked when he was injured in a tackle was awarded almost one million pounds in damages yesterday. The compensation payout, believed to be the highest awarded to a player injured in a game, could now open the floodgates for similar claims from injured footballers."

Footballers and their advisers should be aware that in the context of off the ball incidents, if the matter is reported to the police, applications could be made to the Criminal Injuries Compensation Authorities. Certainly the writer has done this successfully for rugby players but is not aware of this having been done for any footballer.[30]

The above cases highlight how important it is for, especially, professional footballers to have in place the appropriate insurance to cover them for career-ending injuries, as to pursue the matter through the courts is expensive and, except in the clearest of incidents, is somewhat of a lottery.

ALL OTHER CIVIL CASES

The following Court of Session cases will illustrate how there appears to be **8-17** many more cases now being dealt with by the courts; one of the reasons is probably that the amounts of money involved now are very considerable as compared with previous amounts. In 1995, in the case of *Boyd v Motherwell Football and Athletic Club Ltd,*[31] Boyd, a professional footballer, sought payment from Motherwell, his former employers, of the sum of £50,000, as representing the unpaid balance on the sum of £75,000 that Motherwell had allegedly agreed to pay Boyd as a condition of his agreeing to transfer to another club. Lord Cameron, hearing the case, accepted the evidence that, generally speaking, if a player's transfer was negotiated whilst the player was still under contract, a higher fee could be obtained than at the end of a player's contract. In the present case, two clubs, namely Chelsea

---

[29] QB, 29 October 1998, unreported.

[30] See A Duff, "Scottish Update" (1997) 5 (3) SLJ 43.

[31] Unreported decision of Lord Cameron, 17 February 1995.

and Nottingham Forest, were interested in signing the player prior to the end of his existing contract on 30 June 1991 and accordingly, since Motherwell would have obtained a higher sum, they would be prepared to make certain payments to Boyd. Most of the evidence concerned the evidence of the footballer himself, the representatives of Motherwell and the pursuer's agent. Towards the end of the judgment, Lord Cameron said: "I hold on the evidence that, at the meeting on 27 March 1991, the defenders have established that the sum of £50,000, which was then offered to the pursuer, was clearly and specifically related to the proposal that he should agree to transfer to play for Nottingham Forest Football Club and extended no further." Later on Lord Cameron said: "Further, I am satisfied that the subsequent reference to £25,000 by Mr Chapman, upon which figure the parties agreed at the conclusion of that meeting, was reasonably to be understood and could only be understood as being the figure which the defenders, on their own account, would pay to the pursuer as a condition of his agreement to transfer to Chelsea Football Club." The said Mr Boyd did of course end up transferring to Chelsea.

In 1996, Lord Hamilton dealt with the case of *Irons v Partick Thistle Football Club Ltd*[32] in which there was a dispute about two footballers agreeing to join a football club and signing pre-printed contract forms which contained blanks. The blanks were subsequently completed as the footballers understood they would be, although they did not record accurately the terms agreed. The footballers averred, and at a proof the court held, that they had been verbally offered and had verbally accepted certain signing on fees and promotion bonuses as part of the terms of their engagement. These were not recorded in the written contracts as they were subsequently completed, which instead recorded a lower signing on fee and no promotion bonus. The club did agree that promotion bonuses were due but at a lower level than the footballers alleged. The footballers sought reduction of the written agreements and payment of the outstanding signing on fees and promotion bonuses. The court held that although the written contracts were not reducible since, on the evidence (the pursuers not anticipating that they would be completed in terms different from those used) the contracts had not been entered into as a result of misrepresentations made, it was nonetheless possible to rely on the oral evidence to add to their terms, since both parties agreed that the written contracts were incomplete, and, on the evidence, decree was pronounced in respect of the promotion bonuses.

8-18   Again in 1996, the case of *Gillon v Chief Constable, Strathclyde Police and Airdrieonians Football Club*[33] was, in short about duties of care, a safe system of working and the liability of the occupier of a football ground. The pursuer was a police officer engaged in crowd control duties at a football match; she was injured when a football player ran off the pitch and collided with her. The issue was whether the police force and football club were liable in damages. The parties were basically agreed, following *Bolton v Stone*,[34] that,

---

[32] 1997 SLT 983.

[33] 1997 SLT 1218.

[34] [1951] AC 850.

as a matter of law liability depended on whether or not the risk of injury was such as to warrant precautions being taken. As part of her case against the football club, the pursuer led the evidence of a professor of mechanical engineering, a Professor Maunder, who was of the view that it was necessary and practicable to install a barrier somewhere between the pitch and the enclosure to separate the police from the pitch. Both defenders, however, founded on evidence from a police inspector and from the secretary of the football club that in their experience such collisions were unknown. The police force argued that, given the lack of previous collisions, the risk of injury to a police officer was so small as to justify them ignoring it. They also argued that even if they had given instructions to police officers to have regard to their own safety, this would not have prevented the accident as it would not have been possible for her to watch the pitch and the crowd at the same time. The football club argued that there was no real duty to take care for the safety of police officers who were present in the ground in a different capacity from other persons. Counsel for the second defenders, amongst other cases, referred to *Simms v Leigh Rugby Football Club*,[35] which basically applied the test in *Bolton*. In the *Simms* case a rugby league footballer was alleged to have sustained injury as a result of being propelled off the pitch and against a wall some seven feet away from it. The trial judge found that allegation not proved but went on in any event to hold that he thought, from the evidence, the risk of such an event happening was so minimal as not to warrant or require any precautions to be taken. Lord Johnston held in the Scottish case, *Gillon*: (1) that the risk of injury to police officers from football players coming off the pitch with sufficient force to cause injury was so minimal that it could be ignored by the police force and the football club; (2) that even if this was wrong, any negligence did not cause the accident as any instructions by the police force to the pursuer would have been unlikely to have prevented it; (3) that the pursuer had not proved that the erection of a barrier by the football club was a practicable safety measure.

Lord Johnston, at the end of his opinion, said: "On the whole matter **8-19** accordingly the pursuer's case fails against both defenders, a conclusion I reach with considerable regret, since I have no doubt that the pursuer sustained a genuine injury while carrying out conscientiously her duties in accordance with her instructions, but at the end of the day this accident, unfortunate and tragic as it was, must be regarded as such and no more."[36] In essence, the pursuer was not successful on the basis that the risks of injury were so small as to justify their being ignored, and it is rare nowadays for an accident to be regarded as just that.[37]

In 1996, in the case of *Ferguson v Littlewoods Pools Ltd*[38] Lord Coulsfield dealt with the enforceability of betting and gaming agreements, namely football pools. Members of a football pools syndicate sued for the payment of prize money from the pools company. The pursuers had delivered

---

[35] [1962] All ER 923.

[36] 1997 SLT 1218 at 1222.

[37] The footballer, incidentally, was Tony Cascarino of Celtic.

[38] 1997 SLT 309.

completed coupons and their stake money to an agent, who subsequently failed to deliver them to the pools company. One of the coupons contained a winning line which would have entitled the pursuers to share in a sum in the region of £2.3 million. The coupon completed by the syndicate indicated that they accepted that, with the exception of certain provisions, the transaction was binding in honour only. The defenders contended that the transaction was a *sponsio ludicra* and, as such, was not recognisable in law and, furthermore, that the terms of the agreement excluded any legal liability on their part. The pursuers countered that the agreement was not a *sponsio ludicra*, that gambling was now an important part of public life and enforcement of gambling debts was consequently a matter of considerable public interest; and that the honour clause in the agreement, in seeking to exclude legal liability, constituted an unreasonable term to which effect ought not to be given. Lord Coulsfield held that there was authority, binding in the court, that gaming transactions were unenforceable in Scots law; and that a football pool did not fall within the limited exception, giving effect to proprietorial rights; and the action was dismissed. Readers will be aware from current newspaper reports of the increasing number of disputes regarding pools wins and lottery wins.[39]

8-20   Most readers will be aware that there were various court cases and court actions concerning the setting up of the new Premier League. In 1997, in the case of *Scottish Football League v Smith*,[40] Lord Hamilton dealt with an action in which the Scottish Football League sought interdict against the holding of a Special General Meeting of the League to consider applications by six members of the League to retire from it, and moved for interim interdict. In terms of the League's constitution, the decision to convene the Special General Meeting had been taken by its management committee—six of the members were connected with clubs which had applied to retire from the League. The League argued that the six members were disabled from participating in the committee's decision in view of their interest in the outcome of the Special General Meeting. Lord Hamilton held: (1) that there was a material distinction between an administrative decision of the committee, such as the convening of a meeting, and an executive decision where the committee decided a matter of substance committed to it; (2) that the fact that the subject-matter proposed to be brought before the Special General Meeting was one in which a committee member had an interest did not disable that committee member from taking part in the decision to convene the Special General Meeting; (3) that where the defenders were very likely to succeed at the end of the day, the balance of convenience favoured them and the motion for interim interdict was refused.

In 1998, in the case of *Macari v Celtic Football and Athletic Company Ltd*,[41]

---

[39] Scots law is sympathetic to actions between parties who enter into joint ventures to gamble and so it should not be thought that anything said herein prevents actions between the gamblers as opposed to actions by gamblers against the bookmaker: see *Forsyth v Czartowski*, 1961 SLT (Sh Ct) 22 and cases therein cited.

[40] 1998 SLT 606.

[41] 1999 SLT 138.

Lady Cosgrove dealt with the former manager of a football club suing the football club for wrongfully dismissing him in breach of his contract. The pursuer in the action, Luigi (known as Lou) Macari, commenced employment with the defenders on 27 October 1993 and, on 8 November 1993, the parties contracted in terms of a service agreement whereby the defenders confirmed the employment of the pursuer as the football team manager of the company. Clause 2.2 thereof provided: "The period of notice required to be given, by either party, to terminate the employment of the manager, shall be not less than 2 years, such notice not to be given during the first year of the employment of the manager. The Company may elect to make pay in lieu of notice."

Macari's employment with the defenders was terminated on 14 June **8-21** 1994, that is to say on a date within his first year as manager. In the present action the pursuer averred that by terminating his said employment the defenders were in breach of their contract with him, and thus sought payment of damages for the loss he had sustained as a result of the breach. In their counterclaim the defenders averred that they had suffered loss and damage as a result of the pursuer being in material breach of the service agreement and sought payment of the sum paid by them to obtain the player's release from his employment with Stoke Football Club. The case raised short but sharp questions of law upon which the decision ultimately depended. Celtic averred that Macari was, at common law, in breach of his contract of employment, namely that an employee must obey the instructions of his employer, provided those instructions did not require him to carry out anything which was illegal and provided, having regard to all the circumstances, those instructions did not fall to be regarded as wholly unreasonable. It is of the essence of the relationship of employer and employee that the employer is in charge and can expect the employee to carry out his lawful instructions. The duty of the employee to obey his employer is at common law regarded as of such importance to the relationship that a single act of refusal or disobedience to carry out a legitimate instruction will entitle the employer to dismiss the employee summarily. Celtic's position was that it was not a matter of one single act of disobedience but of a significant number of such actions persisting over a period of time disclosing an attitude by Macari, whatever his reason or motive might have been, that he did not intend to be bound by the essential terms of his contract that he would obey all lawful instructions, and that accordingly his dismissal was justified in the circumstances. Macari's counsel disagreed with the basic proposition advanced on behalf of Celtic, namely that an employer can give instructions to an employee provided these are neither illegal nor immoral and the employee is required to obey them. It was submitted in particular that an employee was only required to obey the instructions of his employer if these were given in good faith and as a part of the employee's employment. Macari's position was that, in the circumstances of the present case, the important question was whether the instructions given to Macari by Celtic's then managing director were given in good faith or whether they were motivated by a desire to be rid of Macari, in which case they would evince an intention no longer to be bound by the contract.

8-22   The judge was of the view that the legal principle which applies in the circumstances of this case is that where an employee's dismissal is justified, then averments about malice on the part of his employer are irrelevant. The judge held that Macari had failed to establish that he was wrongfully dismissed by Celtic and found that he was, by his actings and conduct, in material breach of his contract with them. Celtic's counterclaim was to seek payment from Macari of the sum of £250,000 which was paid by them to Stoke City Football Club to secure Macari's release and acquire his services. It was submitted that if Macari was found to be in material breach of his contract with Celtic, they were entitled to damages for any loss flowing directly and naturally therefrom and that, in the circumstances, the payment by Celtic to Stoke had been largely a wasted expenditure. Macari's counsel submitted that this claim was not sound in law in that Macari was not involved in or privy to the negotiations which led to him being acquired from Stoke; the object of the bargain entered into between Celtic and Stoke was achieved in that Celtic received what they paid for, namely the release of Macari. In the event of Celtic deciding to sack Macari during the course of his contract—hence the expenditure incurred was the price Celtic paid to achieve what they did in fact achieve—there had been no wasted expenditure and no loss or damage. The judge held that the expenditure already incurred by Celtic for Macari's release was not a loss which flowed naturally and directly from his subsequent breach of contract, nor would it have been within the reasonable contemplation of the parties in that event.

Macari reclaimed and failed in the Appeal Court.[42] Lord Caplan, in considering the appeal, said:

> "The approach taken by the Lord Ordinary in deciding the case was basically very straightforward. The pursuer was in fundamental breach of contract. He had wilfully refused to carry out the employer's instructions. Moreover, after the employer had brought to his attention that they were expecting him to observe the residential provision in his contract, he breached his contract by failing to remove within a reasonable time (indeed a time which he himself had suggested). The pursuer's breaches of contract clearly go to the root of a contract of employment and the defenders were entitled to treat his conduct as a repudiation of the contract. They were thus entitled to accept the repudiation as terminating the contract provided that they indicated that acceptance in clear and unequivocal terms. This is what they did. They brought the contract to an end by dismissing the pursuer and obviously he was well aware of what they had done."

In the original case, Macari had tried to make much of Mr McCann's motivation in wanting to be rid of him from the outset, and Lord Marnoch said: "It is no doubt correct that the motive of an employer in dismissing an employee is, as such, irrelevant, but in my opinion this cannot mean that in

---

[42] Unreported decision of the Lord President, Lord Caplan and Lord Marnoch in the reclaiming motion for the pursuer in the cause of *Luigi Macari v Celtic Football and Athletic Company Ltd* 2000 SLT 80.

assessing the evidence anent the validity of that dismissal—both as regards reasonableness of instructions and materiality of breach—the judge should put out of his or her mind any relevant background circumstances, including, in this instance, the underlying motivation attributed by the Lord Ordinary to Mr McCann.

There have been other cases beyond the scope of this article.[43]

CONCLUSIONS

It is hoped that this chapter has shown that the courts' involvement in foot- **8-23** ball in Scotland is not new and, furthermore, that since the 1990s there appears to have been more and more cases reaching court, probably as a result of the sums of money now involved in football and the fact that the sport is big business. The writer should remind readers that cases listed in this chapter are not exhaustive; merely the better-known ones or those that have come to the writer's attention which have been reported.

---

[43] Lord Macfadyen issued an opinion in 1996 in the judicial review of Duncan Ferguson (*Judicial Review of Duncan Ferguson*, 1 February 1996, unreported); and see A Duff, "Own Goal" (1996) 4 (1) SLJ 12. This was tied up with the criminal case previously mentioned. Lord Bonomy issued an Opinion in 1998 in the judicial review of *Dundee United Football Club v SFA* 1998 SLT 1244. This case is under appeal and the hearing of the appeal is set down for 6 and 7 January 2000.

9 RUGBY AND THE LAW

Professor Lorne D Crerar

The game of "Rugby Union" ("rugby") is a popular sport in Scotland and is **9-1** one of the most physical team sports played in this country. In a normal match, players will tackle, ruck and maul their opponents in a bid to out-score them and win the game. What could otherwise be considered crimi-nal actings happen as a matter of course, as the court heard in *Lord Advo-cate's Reference No 2 of 1992*: "to bring another person down by means of a rugby tackle would not constitute assault in the course of a game of rugby, but ... it would be criminal if the person tackled was a stranger in a public street".[1] Rugby as a sport should be of interest to every sports lawyer, for such is the nature of the game that any deviation from the laws of the game may expose a player to the risk of legal action in the criminal or civil courts. Akin to any professional sport, the legal issues in rugby are many and com-plex. An appropriate starting point is to consider the governing body, the Scottish Rugby Union[2] and the pivotal role of the referee.

Virtually all matters associated with rugby are within the jurisdiction of the SRU. SRU rules and bye-laws govern the playing clubs, the amateur players, and the professional players who are contracted to the SRU, and most schools fixtures are within the ambit of the authority of the SRU. The membership of the SRU is categorised, with full and affiliated members subdivided into groups. Full members comprise the Clubs and District Unions who are, for the time being, full members. Affiliate members com-prise the registered holders of debentures issued by the SRU, registered holders of interest-free loan certificates issued by the Union, and also any rugby playing school which has successfully applied to join as an affiliated member. *Ex officio* members will comprise past Presidents of the Union, Trustees for the Union, and Members of the Committee of the Union dur-ing their terms of office. There is also the category of Honorary Member: Members of Unions who have been invited to play rugby whilst on their visit to Scotland, or any past player or person of distinction who has been honoured by the Committee with either permanent or temporary member-ship.

---

[1] 1993 SLT 460.

[2] Hereafter referred to as the "SRU". The structure of management of the game of rugby in Scotland has been subject to considerable review (the *Mackay Report*).

9-2   Various rules and bye-laws exist as to the constitution of the SRU, election thereto and the powers and procedures involved in running its business. Of utmost essence are the three overall objectives of the governing body that it must bear in mind in the carrying out of its functions. These are[3]: to promote, encourage and extend the game of rugby football throughout Scotland; to arrange trial, representative, international and other matches which may be for the good of rugby football; and to assist clubs that are members of the district unions and schools so far as is possible to play rugby football and in the provision of playing facilities including *inter alia* playing fields and accommodation.

As the governing body, the SRU promulgates the laws of the game, that is, the rules of play to which players must adhere and referees enforce. The laws and rules are in the main part adopted from those as issued by the International Rugby Board. The SRU do, however, have a Laws Committee consisting of not more than six representatives (on annual appointment) who have as their administrative functions: to consider and report on any proposed changes to laws; to recommend alterations to proposals; not to propose changes that would depart from the principles of specific proposals submitted by unions; and to investigate and report on matters that the Union may direct.

9-3   The rules and laws of the game are provided for in a uniform framework. Amendments are also laid out for matches involving age groups of under-19 or less and teams of less than 15 players (for example seven-a-side matches). The general rules of play and the laws of the game are not of importance for our purposes, but at the outset it should be understood that the squad size of team must include a number of players capable of playing "front row". Front row players are generally considered to have the need for special scrummage skills and without them there is a danger of injury.

Squad size:	Front row players requirement:
15–18	4
19–22	5
22	6[4]
23	6 (+3 locks)[5]

Normally, there should be 15 players in each team on the playing area at any given time. There are circumstances in which fewer players will be on the playing area. First, a player may be injured in some manner, and have to leave the field of play. Further, if a player suffers an injury that creates a bleeding or open wound, he must not be allowed to remain on the field of

---

[3] SRU bye-law 2 (a)–(c).

[4] This requirement is only mandatory at under-19 level

[5] This also is only mandatory at under-19 level. "Locks" are otherwise known as second row players.

play for grounds of health and safety, and it is the referee's duty to enforce this provision.[6] Teams have the option of fielding a substitute to provide temporary replacement, which will become permanent if the injured player does not resume play. Further, a player should not be permitted to remain on the pitch if a doctor advises his replacement. A player replaced by permanent substitution cannot re-enter the field of play. Players may be substituted for any reason, with up to two front-row substitutes and five of other positions, when the ball is dead (that is, out of play) and with the specific permission of the referee. Importantly, where a team is rendered short of players to properly constitute a scrummage, the referee is under an obligation to ensure that scrummages follow SRU rules which seek to minimise the likely risk of injury.[7]

The referee during the game of rugby is, in terms of law 6(5) of the game, **9-4** "the sole judge of fact and law. All his decisions are binding on the players." It is a complex task interpreting the laws of the game and dissention from his decision may lead to penalty with the ultimate sanction of sending from the field of play ("sending off"). It is interesting to note the difficulties caused in reviewing a referee's decision for sanction of a player that is to be considered by a disciplinary panel or tribunal of the governing body regarding the player's conduct. For example, the Rugby World Cup 1999 discipline procedures provide by way of assistance and explanation for circumstances considered by a referee but not sanctioned by him during a game (Regulations 16.7.2 and 16.7.3 of the World Cup Procedures):

> The Regulations relating to burden of proof have been prepared with Law 6(5) of the Laws of the Game of Rugby Football clearly in mind. It is essential to preserve the integrity of this Law and the referee's position as sole judge of fact and law during a Match. Any decision by a referee during a Match cannot be affected by a ruling of a Disciplinary Committee. It has been recognised, however, that a referee may make an error when deciding, for example, that a Player be ordered from the field. In such a case the ordering off cannot be reversed, but it would be unjust to impose a further penalty on the Player. In order to overcome this type of situation Regulation 16.7.3 makes a distinction between the referee's decision on the field of play and the reasons for the decision. This means that when after a Match a Disciplinary Committee comes to consider the disciplinary consequences of an incident where the referee has already made a decision on the field in relation to that incident, the Disciplinary Committee may, nevertheless, enquire into the referee's reasons for that decision and the circumstances surrounding it. In order to comply with the spirit of Law 6(5), Regulations 16.7.2 and 16.7.3 provide that the Disciplinary Committee shall not find a referee's reasons for making a decision to be wrong unless: in the case of an ordering off the Player concerned proves, or in any case where there has been a citing in relation to an incident where the referee has made a decision on the field of play the evidence demonstrates that, on the balance of probabilities, the referee's reasons for his decision were wrong."

---

[6] *SRU Handbook*, B:2 Laws of the Game, r 3(6)(a).

[7] See *SRU Handbook,* r 3(12) and, for more, para 9-13.

SPECIAL FEATURES OF RUGBY THAT RAISE ISSUES OF LIABILITY

9-5 One of the most apparent features of the sport of rugby is the fact that rugby is a game based on robust physical strength and a plethora of physical contact. Unlike many other sports commonly played, rugby is one of the few team sports where competition is carried out in some apsects of play by means of physical superiority over the opposition. Few if any players would have consideration for the physical wellbeing of the 16-stone centre charging at them; their only thought being to tackle the player and stop their team advancing further up the pitch. Likewise, the centre has no thought for his opposite number and would gladly "hand-off" the defender in order to pass him and move further toward the try-line.

It follows that the working culture of the game is unlike most others and many aspects create potential liability. Tackling the ball carrier involves actions that found elsewhere would likely constitute assault and if not executed properly could conceivably give rise to liability—such as the high tackle (a tackle around the head or neck area). In some circumstances, the most common being a "ruck" situation where some players are on the ground in proximity of the ball, it is not uncommon to witness players' boots coming into contact with the bodies of players of the opposition and indeed their own team. The difficulty in considering whether such action raises issues of liability is to consider whether the act is merely a breach of the laws of the game and outwith the working culture of the match. A common example of a perceived criminal act is fighting and, particularly, punching. Some regard punching to be part of the game[8]; however, the SRU are clearly committed to eradicating this feature from the game's environment.[9] This commitment has been mirrored by members of the judiciary, who have often imposed rigorous sentences "in the public interest".[10]

9-6   Furthermore, scrummaging, rucking, tackling and mauling all provide situations in which serious injury has been caused. Two recent unfortunate cases, *Smoldon v Whitworth*[11] and *Van Oppen v Clerk and Board of Bedford Charity Trustees*,[12] have highlighted such injuries and the fact that when

---

[8] See *R v Billinghurst* [1978] Crim LR 553 where Welsh internationalist Mervyn Davies was called as a defence witness. He stated punching was the rule rather than the exception in rugby. Recently, when a Mr Feyers was charged with assault after punching a player on the field of play, Scottish internationalists David Sole and Jeremy Richardson wrote letters in Feyer's defence claiming punching was the norm. The response from the procurator fiscal was damning: "The letters from Mr Sole and Mr Richardson reveal an element of cynicism concerning the laws of rugby and the laws of the land. It is rather worrying that it seems acceptable to carry out this sort of attack".

[9] See "No protest over Johnson failure", *The Herald*, 26 February 1999, where Alan Hosie, Five Nations Chairman, stated: "It is a culture we have all been brought up with in rugby. Dare I say that it is an accepted norm that sometimes punches will be thrown because of the physical nature of the sport. I won't hide from that. There is no place for it in rugby football. It may well be that culture has to change".

[10] See para 9-8 below and the cases of *Henderson* and *McMillan* therein.

[11] [1997] PIQR 133; [1997] ELR 249; *The Times*, 18 December 1996 (CA), p 30.

[12] [1989] 1 All ER 273.

injury is caused, participants attract liability with either criminal and/or civil consequences.

LIABILITY OF PARTICIPANTS

Criminal liability

In Scotland the public criminal authorities have intervened in the sport of **9-7** rugby, in instances considered appropriate, to seek to impose criminal sanction upon a participant. Such a situation will normally arise where it is considered that it is in the public interest and/or the governing body has not taken appropriate action. Whilst the reports of cases that have seen trial provide an adequate forum for examination of the subject, discussion of the Lord Advocate's Instructions of 1996 to Chief Constables regarding criminal law and sport provides a helpful insight into when an act will be deemed to be criminal and thus attract liability.[13] In opening, the Lord Advocate states that any matter arising on the sports field should be handled by those involved in the administration, refereeing and playing of sports. Whilst asserting the fact that many sports involve "deliberate physical contact and a measure of aggression as essential elements" the instructions recognise the need to identify the situation "where the violence goes well beyond what can be regarded as normal physical contact for the sport concerned". In such a circumstance, and although the governing body may have acted, the instructions provide "no question of consent arises and an assault may have been committed". It is in such a case that the criminal law may become involved; however, it is clear that the Lord Advocate's instructions see the role of criminal law as a matter of last resort.

There have been several well-publicised cases whereby the Procurator Fiscal Office has instructed police to investigate allegations of criminal conduct. Clearly the Lord Advocate's instructions have been of use.[14] One of the most recently publicised, at the time of writing, is the case of Jason Feyers, which involved an investigation by police on the instruction of the Procurator Fiscal of Jedburgh, and which led to prosecution and subsequent conviction meriting a fine of £1,000 and a compensation order of £500.

There are a number of principles that should be remembered in con- **9-8** sidering the criminal liability of a player. First, consent is no defence to actions of assault or other such crimes,[15] and so it follows that if a procurator fiscal instigates proceedings following from an on-field fight, it is of no relevance to claim that your opponent consented to the risk of being struck. Secondly, it is established that *mens rea* need not be an issue for a successful prosecution. Charges along the lines of "reckless conduct causing injury" could be brought and this would negate the need to prove intent.

---

[13] For a more detailed discussion, see S Miller, "Criminal Law and Sport in Scotland: The Lord Advocate's Instructions of 10th July 1996 to Chief Constables" (1996) 4 (2) SLJ 40.

[14] The Lord Advocate gave corresponding instructions to Procurators Fiscal and whilst these are private, unlike the instructions to the chief constables, one presumes they must be similar in substance.

[15] *Smart v HM Advocate* 1975 SLT 65.

The consequences of criminal proceedings should not be considered lightly by players. What is generally considered to be the first case of prosecution in Scotland, that of Francis Vernall, resulted from a charge of assault to severe injury after Vernall, of St Mungo's Academicals, had punched a member of the opposing side, Glasgow University. After complaints from the University team were met with an internal investigation and no further action from St Mungo's, a complaint was made to the police and prosecution ensued resulting in a fine of £50 for Vernall.[16] In many respects Mr Vernall may consider himself as fortunate, for, had his case occurred more recently, he might have incurred a custodial sentence. One player, Scott Henderson, for example, had his 60-day sentence upheld by appeal judges who did not view it as an excessive sentence for an assault.[17] Similarly, player Scott McMillan was jailed for nine months for a head-butt when he pled guilty at Haddington Sheriff Court on an indictment of "assault to severe injury". His sentence was upheld on appeal, with Lord Allanbridge ruling:

> "We are quite satisfied that this was a case where the appellant ran forward in a rugby game and took a calculated and deliberate aim at another player whom he then head-butted in the face causing that player to suffer from the severe injuries which we have described. Such an assault is a very serious matter indeed whether or not it occurs in a rugby pitch or during any other such game".

9-9   One issue that often arises is the difficulty of witnessing such assaults, as Ken Macauley of North Berwick RFC discovered[18]: due to the nature of the game there is more opportunity for the discreet committal of offences. During a match against Duns, Macauley alleged that he had his head "stamped on" by one of the many opposition players involved in the ruck—Macauley being on the ground and out of the clear sight of those surrounding him. Stitches were required and Macauley was anxious to have the police press charges against the opposing player whom he believed to be his assailant. However, with no other witnesses, as the police informed him, a prosecution could not be raised. Indeed such issues arise at all levels. For example, Jason Leonard, the English internationalist, was cited for punching Rob Wainwright in the Calcutta Cup match of 1996. After close examination of the video evidence and listening to the oral evidence presented by the player, who pled not guilty, the Five Nations Match Commissioner decided that the evidence was not conclusive enough to find a verdict of guilty.[19]

Any player involved in the game of rugby in Scotland should be aware that if he perpetrates an assault or other criminal act upon an opponent he is liable to prosecution at the hands of the criminal authorities.

---

[16] As reported in *The Scotsman*, 31 January 1980.

[17] *Henderson v Carmichael* 1995 SCCR 126. The player's actions also merited him a six-week ban from the SRU.

[18] See *The Herald*, 16 March 1995.

[19] See *The Herald*, 7 March 1996.

Civil liability

The liability of players has become of increasing import and subject to   **9-10**
litigation. With rugby growing evermore commercial many consider it is
likely that civil court actions will increase—especially with the advent of
the professional game. An example of such a view is that of former England
stand-off and commentator Stuart Barnes, who wrote:

> "Players know themselves what aggression is permissible or otherwise
> and if someone oversteps the mark the victim should consider legal
> action as a serious option. A crime deliberately committed on a sports
> field belongs more in a courtroom than on a rugby pitch. No fair-mind-
> ed players would object to such action and it is certainly more likely to
> eradicate the odd psychopath who will always graze on the rugby
> pitch, than the hot air that currently fills our winter reading".[20]

The principles which apply to the game of rugby as to whether or not a
player may be liable in damages to another do not differ from other contact
sports in Scotland. Such issues of liability and loss have been considered in
full elsewhere in this text. Suffice to say that the threat of such actions
amongst players seems to be on the increase, perhaps principally because
there is a growing group of players who depend upon the game for their
livelihood.

Liability of player to others

The professionally contracted player has a number of obligations and   **9-11**
duties that he requires to observe, arising from his contract of employment
with the SRU, or, where appropriate, his club. Issues will therefore be, in
the main, contractual. With contracts at the highest level likely to be
tailored to each player's needs, it is difficult to provide comment other than
by reference to the terms of the contract style found in the *SRU Handbook*,[21]
which it is anticipated is likely to be indicative of those agreements.

Duties may include: to play for his club as the club specifies, report
promptly at and fully participate in training sessions and to do likewise in
social functions and promotional activities when given reasonable notice.[22]
A player will usually be free to further his interests in business or employment where that participation does not affect his ability to carry out his
obligations under the agreement to the club, and where this does occur the
player should obtain the written agreement of the club.[23] The player should
obey the reasonable instructions of the team manager or his nominated
representative, conduct himself in a manner of the highest standards and
not bring the game into disrepute.[24] Further, the player should use all
reasonable endeavours to maintain his form of health and level of fitness

---

[20] See E Grayson, *Sport and the Law*, p xxxvi (introduction)—quote from an article in the *Daily
Telegraph* by Stuart Barnes (once England international stand-off half).

[21] *SRU Handbook*, A:5 Employment of Staff.

[22] *SRU Handbook*, A:5 Employment of Staff, Specimen Service Agreement, r 3.1–3.1.3.

[23] *SRU Handbook*, r 3.2.

[24] *SRU Handbook*, r 7.1–7.2.

and, in participating in promotional matters, conduct himself suitably and maintain a tidy appearance.[25] The player must abide by the rules and regulations of the IRB and the SRU.[26]

9-12   Two well-publicised examples of breach of contract were the fines imposed upon international players Bryan Redpath and Peter Wright. Redpath incurred a fine amounting to £1,000 for breach of contract after an unauthorised article appeared in a Sunday newspaper in the player's name. Wright was fined £2,000 for alleged foul play and he, too, was considered to be in breach of his contract according to his employers.

Liability of the referee

9-13   It is established that a referee owes a duty of care to those involved in the match and so he must not breach this obligation. It follows generally that if it is foreseeable that injury will occur due to the referee failing in this duty, he may be found liable to a participant suffering loss. Much concern was expressed by referees following the recent English court decision of *Smoldon v Whitworth*.[27] The court established that, as evidenced by the unusually and unacceptably high number of collapsed scrums during the match, the referee had failed to ensure the proper procedure was followed for the formation of scrummages. He had failed in his duty to the players as it was foreseeable that a player could suffer serious injury due to this breach of duty. Although this case was distinguished on certain merits, such as the difference in rules—it being an under-19s match[28]—the principle is clear. Following from *Condon v Basi*,[29] the duty of care imposed was that which was appropriate in all the circumstances of the case, taking full account of the factual context. Although there was concern voiced that judgment in favour of the plaintiff would "emasculate and enmesh in unwelcome legal toils a game which gave pleasure to millions",[30] it is important to note that, as the presiding justices ruled, the case had very special facts and any future cases would have to be decided on their own circumstances. Further, the court dictated it would be of tremendous difficulty for any plaintiff to establish that a referee had failed to exercise the appropriate level of skill and care required in a "hotly contested game of rugby football". That said, it is likely that given these similar and highly unusual circumstances the courts would consider a referee to be in breach of his duty of care. The referee will not be held liable for oversights or errors

---

[25] *SRU Handbook,* r 7.3–7.6.

[26] *SRU Handbook,* r 7.7.

[27] [1997] PIQR 133; [1997] ELR 249; [1996] TLR 731.

[28] See para 9-3 above for an explanation of the difference in rules regarding different levels of play.

[29] [1985] 1 WLR 866.

[30] [1996] TLR 731 at 732.

of judgment that would be easily made during a competitive and fast-moving game.[31]

Some more controversial commentators hold the opinion that it will not be long before referees are taken to court for professional negligence for a matter such as not enforcing a mandatory red card for a player who punches an opponent who cannot defend himself.[32] Certainly, authority suggests that an injured player in Scotland is more likely to have success in a civil action against his playing opponent.

DISCIPLINARY ISSUES

The disciplinary panel

As in every sport, situations may occur in which rules are broken, resulting **9-14** in the need for sanctions to be imposed in the interests of the game and those involved in it. The necessity of disciplinary rules and fair procedures is to preserve the spirit and uphold the laws of the game. It is generally considered of utmost importance that decisions of disciplinary bodies are made in a "fair, consistent, independent and expeditious manner".[33] It is appropriate to examine, first, the SRU disciplinary rules and procedures, and then cases of interest that have attracted the public eye.[34] Indeed, two recent cases have highlighted the significance of procedure in disciplinary issues.[35]

When an appropriate matter is brought to the attention of the SRU, they will establish a disciplinary panel, which shall have the delegated power to act in the name of the Union in the hearing and determining of disciplinary issues.[36] The SRU do in fact have a standing disciplinary panel, with election to the panel having one notable requirement—namely a person may not sit on the panel if he is a member of the same club that the player,

---

[31] Worth noting is the court's consideration of *volenti non fit injuria* in *Smoldon v Whitworth*. It was not open to argument that the player had consented to the risk of injury by participating voluntarily in the scrum for, although the player might have consented to the ordinary risks of the game, he could not be said to have agreed to the referee's breach of duty in failing to apply the rules intended to protect players from injury.

[32] See Philip Lehain, "A yellow card for the ref", *The Times*, 9 August 1994, p 33. The author is a barrister who, apart from specialising in personal injuries and professional negligence, is a rugby referee. Coincidentally, Lehain acted for the applicant in the above case, *Smoldon v Whitworth*.

[33] *SRU Handbook*, B:3 Discipline, "Objective of Disciplinary Rules".

[34] See 1999 (7) 1 SLJ 33.

[35] Massimo Giovanelli, the Italian sent off for stamping at Murrayfield, had his eight-week ban quashed after it was found that the hearing for his sending off was technically incorrect. Also, there was the failure by Edinburgh Reivers to submit citing forms with the appropriate signatories in relation to the assault on Matthew Proudfoot by the Toulouse lock Hughes Miorin.

[36] *SRU Handbook*, B:3 Discipline, r 1.1.

subject to potential sanction, is from.[37] The declared areas within the juris-diction of the panel are[38]: players ordered from the field of play for an offence; players who are cited as having committed an offence which would have resulted in a sending off if detected by the referee; misconduct by the player other than on the field of play; and misconduct other than by players.

The Union must appoint a secretary to the panel and he is responsible for the implementation of the rules and procedures.[39] The Union have a stand-ing disciplinary secretary who administers all disciplinary matters on behalf of the Union.

Players ordered off

9-15 From the moment a player is ordered from the field of play he is not per-mitted to play, coach, referee or take any active participation in any game of rugby until his case has been determined by the panel.[40] The referee should complete a written report and send it to the disciplinary secretary within 48 hours of completion of the match or such further time as is per-mitted by the panel.[41] The report should contain the following particulars[42]: the date, venue and teams participating in the match; the name of the player and his team; the circumstances of the ordering off; the reason for the ordering off; and any other information that the referee considers rele-vant.

If a player is ordered from the field as a result of intervention from a touch judge, then the touch judge also requires to submit a report.[43] Upon receipt of the reports, the disciplinary secretary notifies the player and supplies him with a copy of the report of the referee and, where applicable, the reports of the touch judges.[44] Notification of the impending hearing does not require to be in writing, although it invariably is. As for the reports, they can be sent to the player's address as last known by the disciplinary secretary, handed to him, or directed to his club.

On notification, three options present themselves to the player. The disciplinary panel hearing may proceed either on the basis of (1) the referee's report alone; (2) the referee's report accompanied by the player's submissions in writing; or (3) the referee's report and the player's verbal submissions to the panel, along with witnesses who were present at the game in question.[45] If the player has not notified the disciplinary secretary with an elected procedure within seven days, the hearing may proceed on

---

[37] *ibid* r 1.2.

[38] *ibid* r 1.1.1–1.1.4.

[39] *ibid* r 1.3.

[40] *ibid* r 22.1.

[41] *ibid* r 2.1.

[42] *ibid* r 2.1(a)–(e).

[43] *ibid* r 2.3.

[44] *ibid* r 2.5.

[45] *ibid* r 2.6(a)–(c).

the basis of the report alone.[46] Where a player elects option (3), the disciplinary secretary advises the player of[47]: the date, place and time of the meeting of the panel at which the disciplinary proceedings will be heard; the requirement for him to attend; and if he is unable to appear, he must notify the secretary immediately.

Although the panel must afford the player a reasonable opportunity to attend and be heard, there is nothing in the disciplinary rules and procedures which prevents a decision being made in the absence of the player where that player is unable, fails or declines to attend within a reasonable period. The panel determines what is reasonable in these circumstances. Likewise, the referee who submitted the report concerned should attend the hearing, although there is nothing to prevent the panel deciding in his absence.[48]   **9-16**

The rules provide that the panel shall have the power to regulate its own procedure, but of course this must be in accordance with natural justice, otherwise grounds for appeal will be established.[49]Although the disciplinary committee has complete discretion, one recent English case highlighted that it is imperative the player be afforded the right to defend himself properly.[50] Procedures require to be just and fair and reasons should be given for refusals to requests. The normal procedure for a hearing will depend upon which option was selected by the player, be it option (1), (2) or (3) (see above). In the case of options (1) or (2) the panel considers the report or reports and the player's responses (if any) and such other information as known to the panel, if appropriate.

Where the player attends, the procedure differs.[51] The referee and player(s) are in attendance throughout the hearing, and the player may choose to have representation in any form (including legal representation).[52] The chairman introduces the panel members and then outlines the procedure that will be followed during the course of the hearing. The referee must attest to the player's identity and is informed that he can make supplementary comments to his report at the end of the hearing. The chairman then reads the report(s) of the referee (and touch judge(s), where applicable) and may have any points clarified by the referee (or touch judge(s)). The player can give evidence if he elects to do so, along with any witnesses he may have brought. The referee can then make comment with regard to the evidence of the player and witnesses. The player is offered an opportunity to sum up his position and as a matter of course he is given the "last word" in the proceedings.   **9-17**

---

[46] *ibid* r 2.7.

[47] *ibid* r 2.8(a)–(c).

[48] *ibid* r 4.1.

[49] See para 9-24 below.

[50] See *R v Marsh* [1994] Crim LR 52. Much care should be taken to consider the views expressed in *Jones v Welsh Rugby Union, The Times*, 28 February 1997.

[51] *SRU Handbook*, B:3 Discipline, r 5.

[52] *ibid* r 9.1. The SRU has always taken the view that the disciplinary hearing is critical to allowing the player a full opportunity to explain his conduct; legal representation was considered a means of ensuring that full opportunity.

When witnesses are heard, including the player and referee, there is no cross-examination except by members of the panel. Questions may be addressed to the witnesses by persons present at the hearing, through the chairman.[53] Any and all evidence is available to the panel, who may receive and consider such evidence as they consider appropriate including writing, videotape and photography.[54] Video evidence is considered only after all oral evidence has been heard. Further, if a panel requests the attendance of a witness and they fail to attend, or refuse to do so, then the panel may refuse to allow the admittance of evidence from that witness if received in any other form.[55]

9-18   Once the panel members have heard all the evidence and witnesses concerned, they deliberate in private[56] and then notify all interested parties in writing as soon as reasonably practicable.[57] Where they deem it appropriate, the panel may notify those concerned orally after the hearing. It is accepted practice that the player should be the first person to know the decision once made. Where the decision is adverse to the interests of the player, he is notified by the disciplinary secretary of his right to appeal.[58] If the player then does so, his suspension may be lifted in very exceptional circumstances and this may allow him to resume playing notwithstanding the pending appeal.[59] The suspension will lift if the appeals committee receives a written request from the appellant and they decide to grant a stay of suspension.[60]

Citing of players

9-19   The purpose of citing is to bring to the attention of the SRU acts of foul play undetected by the match officials which, if detected, would have resulted in sending off the player concerned. Citing a player to the SRU should be made in writing and within three days of the match or within such time as the panel may determine reasonable.[61] A complaint will be deemed to have been sent at the earliest of (1) when it is posted, (2) when it is transmitted by fax or other medium, or (3) when it is received by the disciplinary secretary or chief executive of the Union.[62] The complaint should contain the date, place, player and team to which the alleged offence relates and the name of the opposing team, the name of the referee, and the exact

---

[53] *ibid* r 6.1.

[54] *ibid* r 7.1.

[55] *ibid* r 8.2.

[56] *ibid* r 10.1.

[57] *ibid* r 11.1.

[58] *ibid* r 11.2.

[59] *ibid* r 22.2.

[60] *ibid* r 22.3. To date it is understood no such suspension has been granted by an appeals committee.

[61] *ibid* r 12.1.

[62] *ibid* r 12.1(a)–(c).

nature of the foul play should also be included in as much detail as possible.[63] The disciplinary secretary then seeks to obtain reports from the appropriate officials and any obtained shall be copied to the player along with a date, time and place for a meeting of the panel to determine the complaint.[64] The complainant must also be notified.[65]

Unless otherwise directed, the procedure for the hearing follows a similar line to that of hearings for sendings off. The player and his club, the complainant and referee should all be present. The substantive differences occur due to the reason that it is a third party who is citing the offence, and accordingly once the chairman has introduced the panel and established that the player fully understands the procedure to be followed, the complainant must explain his reasons for citing an alleged breach of the laws of the game of rugby.[66] If the complainant or his representative is a witness to the incident, the panel may ask him questions.[67] Indeed, each witness for the citing club may be questioned by the panel on giving evidence. The cited player must be heard and he may give evidence in mitigation of his actings where appropriate.[68] He is entitled to lead witnesses who also may be questioned by the panel after giving evidence.[69] Cross-examination is only permissible from the complainant club or cited player by questions posed through the chairman.

Once all parties have led evidence, both the complainant and player are **9-20** afforded the opportunity to sum up their submissions. At this stage, the panel will close the proceedings and then deliberate as to a decision and, if applicable, what penalty is to be imposed. To return a verdict that upholds the citing, the panel must be satisfied the alleged foul act of play did in fact take place and, in all the circumstances, would have merited the player being sent off.[70] The panel gives written notification of the decision (or where appropriate orally), at the end of the meeting. The practice is to notify the player of the decision, before any other party.

Other alleged misconduct by players

Where there is alleged misconduct by a player, but not on the field of play, **9-21** and it is brought to the attention of the panel, the procedures to be followed mirror the process involved when a player is cited by a complainant other than the referee. The complaint is determined at a hearing in the same procedure as described for hearings of players sent off, with amendments where appropriate. For the avoidance of doubt, drug abuse constitutes other alleged misconduct by players and is dealt with

---

[63] *ibid* r 12.2(a)–(e).

[64] *ibid* r 12.3.

[65] *ibid*. The complainant must be a member of the Union or club.

[66] *ibid* r 12.4(d).

[67] *ibid*.

[68] *ibid* r 12.4(g).

[69] *ibid* r 12.4(h).

[70] *ibid* r 12.4(m).

accordingly. "Drug abuse" will be constituted if a player is detected as having taken any substance in contravention of the IRB rules on doping. The penalties, as recommended by the IRB, for drug offences are severe.

Alleged misconduct other than by players

9-22 If misconduct other than by a player is cited to the panel, the procedure follows that as outlined for players ordered off the field of play,[71] with minor amendments where applicable.

Penalties to be applied

9-23 If the disciplinary panel find against the cited person in terms of a complaint under other alleged misconduct by players, or misconduct other than by players, the panel shall have at their complete discretion the option of what penalty to impose. For an offence established either due to a sending off or citing by another person, the penalties to be imposed are found in guidelines issued from time to time by the SRU. For a doping offence, penalties applied mirror the IRB sanctions, but the panel does of course have the option of exercising its discretion in sentencing. It is the practice to follow the IRB's guidelines on sentencing.

Appeals

9-24 Where a person wishes to raise an appeal from the decision of the panel, he must do so within seven days of receiving notification of the decision of the panel.[72] An appeals committee, convened by the SRU, has the power to hear and determine appeals against decisions of the panel and any matters arising in the course of the appeal.[73] The appeals committee can adopt such procedure as they consider appropriate in hearing the appeal, but the members cannot be a member of the disciplinary panel and must be wholly impartial and independent of any of the parties involved.[74]

An appeal must be lodged in writing stating the appellant's name, the decision appealed against and the grounds of appeal. The grounds of appeal must include at least one of the following[75]: the decision of the panel was excessively harsh or oppressive; the panel misdirected itself in the application of the laws of the game and/or disciplinary rules; there has been a breach of natural justice; and/or the panel reached a decision that no reasonable panel would have reached.

Where appeal is on the grounds that the decision of the panel was excessively harsh or oppressive, that is an appeal against the length of sentence; if the appellant has accepted the referee's report he can invite the appeals

---

[71] See para 9-15 above.

[72] *SRU Handbook*, B:3 Discipline, r 17.1.

[73] *ibid* r 17.2.

[74] *ibid* r 17.3.

[75] *ibid* r 17.5(a)–(d).

committee to convene without hearing verbal submissions from him. With such an approach, the player is afforded the right to make written representations to the committee for consideration.

The appeals committee can, in exercising its full discretionary powers, **9-25** decline or accept to hear all or any of the evidence sought to be led at the appeal hearing.[76] If a party wishes to introduce new evidence at the appeal hearing stage then that party must, two days prior to the hearing, provide a written outline of the nature of the new evidence to the disciplinary secretary, who shall then inform the other parties to the appeal.[77] Where evidence is given, cross-examination must only take place through the appeal chairman, in so much as the appeals committee, at their discretion, allow. Once all evidence has been led and submissions have been completed, the appeals committee is left with a number of choices[78]: affirm the panel's decision; uphold the appeal, thus setting aside any decision and quashing any penalty imposed; uphold the appeal in part, so setting aside only part of the decision; substitute a lesser offence and/or penalty for the offence and penalty appealed against; substitute a greater offence and/or penalty for the offence and penalty appealed against; uphold the appeal and return the issue to the panel for reconsideration and redetermination by them; defer consideration of the appeal pending receipt of information, evidence or clarification from the panel or a person not in attendance at the hearing; stay a suspension imposed by the panel pending the determination of an appeal; and/or, take any step that, in the exercise of its discretion, the appeals committee feels is appropriate to deal with the appeal in the correct and just manner.

If the committee does not deliver an oral decision at the conclusion of the hearing, as it may do, then once the appeals committee has come to the appropriate decision, the disciplinary secretary shall notify the appellant as soon as reasonably practicable.[79]

Miscellaneous

In all cases and all hearings the standard of proof is the balance of proba- **9-26** bilities.[80] If a complaint, however arising, cites more than one person (and usually concerning the same incident at the same match), then the proceedings may be heard together, provided there is no manifest prejudice to either of the parties.[81] In such a case, the panel may alter their procedure to deal with any idiosyncrasies that may so arise. Where it is alleged that foul play was due to provocation or retaliation, neither can be used as a defence but may only be presented in mitigation of the penalty.[82]

---

[76] *ibid* r 17.9.

[77] *ibid* r 17.10.

[78] *ibid* r 17.12(a)–(i).

[79] *ibid* r 17.13.

[80] *ibid* r 18.1.

[81] *ibid* r 19.1.

[82] *ibid* r 20.1–2.

Character evidence may only be received for the purposes of setting a penalty. A previous penalty may be evidenced during the hearing, but shall only be relevant to the penalty to be imposed in the present proceedings. Also, the previous penalty cannot be used to question the merits or otherwise of the present proceedings. Accordingly, each case should turn on its own merits and the penalties imposed should be fair and equitable in all the circumstances.[83]

It is wholly within the discretion of the panel or appeals committee to decide whether or not they are to publish details of the misconduct, offence and penalty, and the identity of the player(s) concerned.[84]

Other matters

9-27   The SRU's disciplinary procedures govern the playing of participants in domestic games in Scotland. However, Scottish players involved in European Cup games will be governed by that tournament's disciplinary code. The Six Nations Championship (comprising Scotland, England, France, Ireland, Wales and Italy) issue their own code of discipline for the tournament as did Rugby World Cup 1999 for the recent world cup tournament centred in Cardiff. The fundamentals of all of these different procedures are similar, particularly in that their purpose is to dispose of disciplinary matters in a fair and equitable manner. For the first time the World Cup 1999 introduced to Scottish players the concept of "citing commissioners" who could cite players allegedly guilty of foul play for matters undetected by the referee *and* for matters he had seen and penalised. The citing commissioner principle has been carried forward to the Six Nations disciplinary code currently operating.

COACHING, TRAINING AND INSURANCE

Coaching and training

9-28   Coaching at SRU level ranges from certificates of level I–IV, followed by the SRU National Coach. Qualifying in levels I–III is dependent on the successful completion of training courses run by the SRU, which are open to all by application. The position of National Coach is of course by invitation only, as are places on courses for attainment of the level IV certificate. Participants are educated in the proper coaching of rugby, with special provision for the coaching of under 16s, where special attention must be given.

Coaches must be careful not to cause or facilitate injury to their players. For example, in the case of *Van Oppen v Clerk and the Bedford Charity Trustees*,[85] in an action for damages, the plaintiff alleged the school was negligent in, amongst other things, "failing to take reasonable care for the

---

[83] *SRU Handbook*, B:3 Discipline, r 21.3. It is in fact the Union's practice to do so.

[84] *ibid* r 23.1. See *St Johnstone Football Club v Scottish Football Association* 1965 SLT (Notes) 35 and also the recent case of *Jones v Welsh Rugby Union* [1997] TLR 118.

[85] [1989] 1 All ER 273.

plaintiff's safety on the rugby field for failing to coach or instruct the plaintiff in proper tackling techniques and in particular the technique of the head on tackle".[86] The court found that adequate training and instruction was given to the pupils and the injury sustained was not as a result of negligence on behalf of the school but due to an "unfortunate accident". The decision contains extracts that are particularly illustrative in this matter. The court found that a duty of care was present and that if players did not follow correct techniques, injury was more likely to be sustained. Indeed, Boreham J stressed the importance of coaching and instructing, dictating that parties under the duty of care must not only coach "the application of correct techniques" but also "the correction of potentially dangerous errors and lapses".[87] This follows from the case of *Affutu-Nartey v Clarke*,[88] where the court held that it was wrong and a breach of duty of care for a schoolteacher taking part in a game of rugby with 15-year-old boys to have any physical contact with the boys, as any injury arising therefrom would lead to liability and an award of damages.

Insurance

There are two areas to be considered: public liability insurance for the liability of those involved in the game, such as coaches, referees, touch judges, trainers, instructors or voluntary medical attendants; and personal accident insurance for players.   **9-29**

Public liability insurance is an integral part of the SRU's master policy and all member clubs are covered. If injury is sustained by any third party as caused by a coach, referee, touch judge, trainer, instructor or voluntary medical attendant a claim should be directed towards the insurers. This, however, will only cover activities specifically relating to the playing of rugby—such as matches and training. Thus, clubs should be vigilant in ensuring insurance is arranged to cover the many activities of a rugby club, including all business, social and corporate hospitality events. Indeed, it is important that clubs have adequate protection against any claim arising from the Occupiers' Liability (Scotland) Act 1960. Section 2(1) places a duty of reasonable care upon the occupier, that is to say the club, to ensure that the premises are in a fit state, to the extent that they take steps to repair any defects that they knew of or ought to have known of.[89]

The SRU operates a personal accident insurance scheme and insists that the club protect its players. Indeed, this is a compulsory requirement of membership, but the cover does have options to it and can be extended to include further benefits. The compulsory insurance affords protection in the event of accidental death and permanent total disability for all senior, midi and mini teams of each member club. Optional cover, which the SRU "strongly recommend", can include temporary disablement for senior

---

[86] paras h–j.

[87] at 277, para c.

[88] *The Times*, 9 February 1984.

[89] *Wallace v City of Glasgow District Council* 1985 SLT 23.

teams, accidental death and permanent disability for selection and general committee members and even death by natural causes. The compulsory insurance, of course, has an "operative time", that is when and for what cover is provided. Accordingly, the operative time is whilst participating in a club fixture and in official practice matches, coaching or training sessions or whilst travelling to or from these activities.

9-30   As for players outwith the SRU, such as those who play for schools or clubs that are not affiliated, it is prudent to view insurance as an individual matter for each player. This follows from the case of *Van Oppen v Clerk and the Bedford Charity Trustees*,[90] where the court considered questions of whether persons in positions such as *loco parentis* have a duty to provide, or to advise on the provision of, insurance for injury and loss sustained when playing rugby. The case concerned a boy injured during a school's inter-house rugby match, who alleged that, amongst other things, the school was negligent in "(ii) failing to ensure that the plaintiff was insured against accidental injury and (iii) failing to advise the plaintiff's father of [*sic*] (a) of the need for accident insurance or (b) that the school had not arranged such insurance".[91] In finding for the defendants, the court said the school, being in *loco parentis*, "was under a general duty to the plaintiff and to all pupils to exercise reasonable care for his and their safety both in the classroom and on the games field".[92] The court found that the duty of care could not be extended to imposing an obligation to procure insurance for the pupils or advise parents as to insuring, as this would go too far and result in almost absolute liability—opening up the possibility of all sorts of claims.

9-31   It is worth noting, however, as Grayson comments,[93] that the defence argued that the defendants were only under a duty to advise in areas regarding health or physical welfare or perhaps purely educational matters. Yet, as the House of Lords held in *IRC v McMullen*,[94] school sport is "purely educational"—leaving a grey area perhaps?

It is hoped this chapter has helped to clarify some issues and point out some difficult areas.

---

[90] [1989] 1 All ER 273.

[91] at 274.

[92] at 277, para a.

[93] E Grayson, "Breaking new ground in schools" (1988) NLJ 532.

[94] [1981] AC 1.

10   GOLF

David Williamson

Some would say that the King Jameses had it right. Not only is golf a waste **10-1** of a good walk, it may also be seen as the unwarranted expenditure of time which could more usefully be employed in more profitable pursuits, like learning the bow and arrow for the regular international fixture with the English:

> "It is decreeted & ordained, ... and that the Futebol and Golfe be utterly cried down and not to be used; ... and as tuitching the fute-bol and the golfe, to be punished by the Barronis-in law".[1]

> "And that the Fute-bol and the Golfe be abused in time cumming, and that the buttes be made up and schuting used".[2]

> "It is statute and ordained that in na place of the Realme there be used fute-ball, golfe or uther lik unprofitable sports, for the common gude of the Realme & defence thereof".[3]

Until recently, though it could scarcely have conformed to the description of "unprofitable" used in the old Scots Statute, for professional participants, golf—in common with most sports—had largely failed to reward lawyers in the material sense (with the possible exception of Mark McCormack); but, as time progresses and areas of yet untapped profit occur to the legal profession, the increasing litigiousness of society, the increase in leisure time, and the increase in the numbers of people playing sport (golf in particular) may all have contributed to the comparatively recent burgeoning of golf-related litigation, and may be expected to continue to contribute to its further expansion and development.

    In this chapter, aspects of liability for accidentally sustained injury caused by golf and golfers are examined. Though it has been said that "[t]he outcome of any case concerning golf course injuries must depend on its own particular facts",[4] the observation was made in the context of acceptance of negligence as a foundation of possible liability in the action, and there are some general principles which may, arguably, be extracted

---

[1] Wappenschaws Act Scots Parliament 1457 (James II).

[2] Armour Act Scots Parliament 1471 (James III).

[3] Wappenschaws Act Scots Parliament 1491 (James IV).

[4] *Pearson v Lightning* (Court of Appeal), per Sir Christopher Slade [1998] 20 LS Gaz R 33.

from the cases, not least the principal Scottish authority *Lewis v Buckpool Golf Club*.[5]

LIABILITY OF PARTICIPANTS TO EACH OTHER

10-2   In the case of injury sustained by playing participants in golf (but not necessarily, it may be argued, in the case of passers-by or those whose properties abut golf courses who may have potential recourse to the law of nuisance), where one player has been the cause of injury to another, liability has been accepted to be based, potentially, only on negligence. For present purposes, that includes the possible breach of "statutory duty" imposed on occupiers of land, such as golf course operators, by the Occupiers' Liability (Scotland) Act 1960, since the liability which is thus imposed is, for most practical purposes, essentially co-extensive with negligence at common law. There requires to be a duty of care owed by A to B, and a failure by A to conduct himself in a manner consistent with the due performance of that duty, with the result that B is injured. The duty arises, generally, where there is a foreseeable risk of harm—but not infrequently, as will be seen, recognition of the existence of the duty (and on occasion the determination of its ambit) occurs, at least in part, because of the apparent ease by which it is decided that it can be duly performed. And the existence of a duty to act in a particular way may, in appropriate cases where the rules or indeed the etiquette of the game have something to say about the particular situation, be influenced by the terms of those rules or the normal appreciation of the nuances of that etiquette. But, as is very clear, even if nothing else may be, all cases will turn on their own individual facts; whether a duty exists and whether it has been breached, critically depends on the view of the court of the reasonableness of the conduct of A. If what A has done appears to accord with what sensible golfers would have done, paying due regard to the risks inherent in their proposed action (and, it would seem, their *objectively* perceived personal level of ability), then there will be no liability, even if serious injury is caused to B, for it will be just an accident, a rub of the green.

An example of that can be seen in the Australian case of *Woods v Roberts*[6] where an injury which seems to have been eminently foreseeable did not result in the injured golfer recovering damages because the court found that the following golfer, whose drive injured the plaintiff, was entitled to rely on the fact that the plaintiff's playing partner (who was looking for a ball in the rough) had, as course etiquette demanded, waved the following match through, notwithstanding that he and the plaintiff were in range of the drive and even where the defendant apparently could not see from the tee where the plaintiff was when he drove off.

In so far as any general principles can be divined from cases where the result turns on the facts of each individual case, the following may assist in identifying them.

---

[5] 1993 SLT (Sh Ct) 43.

[6] [1997] SASC 6467.

In *Lewis*[7] the question that arose for decision was whether the mis-hit by **10-3**
the second defender was something a reasonable man would have had in
contemplation as a risk that was reasonably likely to happen. That required
there to be more than a mere possibility, but not a greater than even likelihood, and if it was reasonably likely to happen then it was negligent to
neglect such a risk in a situation where it could be avoided without difficulty, disadvantage or expense.[8] Whether, on the facts,

> "there was a real risk of which the defender ought to have been aware,
> that he would hit the ball off the toe of the club and not straight down
> the fairway, the fact that danger was not actually perceived by the
> participants does not mean that it should not have been apparent to a
> reasonable man. The law of negligence is full of cases where an unap-
> preciated risk has been held to have been reasonably foreseeable. In
> addition, the absence of previous accidents does not mean that there
> was no risk: it is consistent also with the recognition of a risk and the
> taking of steps to avoid it.

> "For a golfer like the second defender a mis-hit causing the ball to go
> off at an angle of 30° was not a mere possibility, nor a risk that was so
> small that in the circumstances a reasonable man would have been
> justified in disregarding it and taking no steps to avoid it. On the con-
> trary, it was a real risk and the worse the golfer the greater the risk. It
> was not a risk which required any extraordinary or expensive action to
> eliminate it."

The approach taken, in principle, by the sheriff principal in *Lewis*[9] was **10-4**
cited, with apparent (though tacit) approbation, in the Court of Appeal in
England in *Pearson v Lightning*,[10] where two citations from *Clerk and Lindsell
on Torts*[11] appear to demonstrate the general delictual principles which fall
to be applied in determining whether there may be liability in any given set
of circumstances:

> "(a) the more foreseeable the potential for harm in a particular type of
>   relationship, the more likely it will be that a notional duty will be
>   found to apply to that relationship; and
> (b) the more foreseeable the particular harm in question, the more the
>   defendant will be expected to take precautions against it."

All this is entirely consistent with general negligence principles and indeed
with the approach taken by the Court of Appeal in the football case of
Condon v Basi,[12] where it was held that:

> "Participants in competitive sport owe a duty of care to each other to
> take all reasonable care having regard to the particular circumstances

---

[7] 1993 SLT (Sh Ct) 43.
[8] *Lewis* at 45 (citing Lord Reid in *Overseas Tankships (UK) Ltd v The Miller Steamship Co* [1967]
1 AC 617 at 642).
[9] 1993 SLT (Sh Ct) 43 at 45.
[10] [1998] 20 LS Gaz R 33.
[11] (17th edn), para 7–182.
[12] [1985] 2 All ER 453.

in which the participants are placed. If one participant injures another he will be liable in negligence at the suit of the injured participant if it is shown that he failed to exercise the degree of care appropriate in all the circumstances or that he acted in a manner to which the injured participant cannot be expected to have consented."

The case concerned an allegedly bad, or dangerous, tackle in a Sunday football match and the observations may fall to be seen in that context. It may be argued that "friendly" golf, purely for recreational purposes, cannot be equated with a competitive, or a contact, sport. But, in the final analysis, it does not really matter what the game is: what those participating in it require to observe is reasonable care in the prevailing circumstances.

The issue of "consent" (which may be in some circumstances a component in the principle of *volenti non fit injuria*, which is discussed later in a golfing context) is elusive. Plainly it is applicable in rough or contact sports where a degree of consent to some risk of injury (to the hard but fair tackle, for example) is inevitable; it is rather more difficult, at least as regards participants, to apply consent principles to golf though it may prove a defence in some circumstances to claims by injured, invited, spectators. In the case of golf it may mean no more than that a participant may consent to *some* risk of injury, perhaps, for example, where a perfectly well-hit shot to a clear green bounds forward off a bunker downslope and strikes someone in the preceding match waiting on the next tee. That would, arguably, be "just one of those things" that happen in golf, something to which participants in the game impliedly consent.

10-5   There are difficulties for the adviser in applying these general principles. Not least of these difficulties is the apparent need to examine the competence of the defender. In the second part of the passage quoted in *Lewis* there appears to be what may be a golfing truism dressed up as a curious (or perhaps spurious) legal principle: "the worse the golfer the greater the risk". With respect to the sheriff principal, that, surely, depends on the risk which requires to be foreseen. It may be that it is more likely that a poor golfer will hit someone who is standing 25 yards away to the right and at an acute angle. Incidentally, in *Pearson*[13] the expert evidence, as recorded, was (to this author) wholly remarkable: that a golf ball, however badly stuck, will never deviate more than 30° from its intended destination. That evidence was given by a former English national golf coach. Clearly he moves in golfing circles more elevated than most. But if, as in *Lewis*, the golfer is playing well and has scarcely hit a bad shot all day, why should it be more than a "possibility" that, with other players on the course and in the vicinity, one of them may be struck on this occasion by a thoroughly unexpected appalling shot. And what about the low handicap player who hits the ball a very long way but who has, on the odd occasion when he gets it wrong, a tendency to hit a high slice out to the right (which he himself describes, euphemistically, as a "fade")? Is it more than a remote possibility that he will slice the ball off the tee so that it will drop among the fourball match advancing normally up the adjoining fairway to the right of

---

[13] [1998] 20 LS Gaz R 33, per Simon Brown LJ.

the player 225 yards away? Is the answer to be found in the precise circumstances of the round so far? Or in the defender's normal propensity to bad shots? If the defender has missed five of the last nine fairways to the right, maybe he should not drive off until the adjacent fourball has advanced beyond his possible dropping zone? But what if he waits until they reach the green only a short distance away and then completely "duffs" the ball off the toe of his 3-wood among them, felling one of their number? If the principled approach is taken to its logical conclusion then, if the shot is so inexplicably bad, so completely out of character that it is a possibility only and thus not foreseeable, then the injured party will have no remedy.[14]

The truth of the matter appears to be that, while paying lip service to **10-6** principle, the courts have, as a matter of fact in most of the cases, simply examined the whole circumstances and in light of them have penalised (perhaps as a good golf course should) particularly bad shots, when played at inappropriate times. So the principles are applied retrospectively to produce what is seen to be the proper result; and in the majority of cases, since (as has been seen) they turn on their own facts, that can easily be achieved by the court of first instance without the possibility of interference by the Court of Appeal applying normal appellate principles. In *Pearson v Lightning*[15] the court said: "I do not say that all judges would necessarily have reached the same conclusion. Despite Mr Sterling's [the plaintiff's expert] opinion on the point, it seems to me a good deal less than self-evident that it was absolutely reckless for the defendant to have played this particular shot." Nonetheless, the finding in fact that injury to the plaintiff, who was standing some 80 to 90 yards off line from the defendant's intended line of shot, was foreseeable following a ricochet from a tree, was not disturbed.

The determination that there is liability is easy where the risk is obvious **10-7** and the likelihood of it occurring reasonably high. So a bad golfer, especially one who is in fact playing badly, may well be held to be at fault if he does not defer his shot till all possible casualties are out of all possible lines of fire. Of course he does not believe, or think for a moment, that the nearby player is at risk. The ball will not go anywhere near him. But viewed objectively, in the light of all of the evidence, there is, in all the circumstances, an obvious and foreseeable risk of injury. However, the low handicapper may not be faulted for hitting a very bad shot in identical circumstances of proximity of potential casualties. Perhaps conversely, if the poor golfer hits a shot of such prodigious length (for him) that it is a source of astonishment and wonder to his playing partners, he would escape liability for injuring a golfer in front who would normally be reasonably regarded as well out of the poor golfer's range? So the problem in applying the principles becomes acute at the margins of foreseeability in the particular circumstances of the case. Mr Shipley, the unsuccessful second defender in *Lewis*,[16] had, so it is recorded, been playing particularly well. He had scarcely hit a bad shot all day. So why was it foreseeable that he would do so at

---

[14] See *Brewer v Delo* [1967] 1 Lloyd's Rep 488.

[15] [1998] 20 LS Gaz R 33.

[16] 1993 SLT (Sh Ct) 43.

the spot where Mr Lewis came within the range of a particularly inept blow? The answer is, with respect, not wholly self evident. The finding in *Pearson*[17] is capable of being defended as a matter of logic in that the defendant there was hitting a tricky shot, from a difficult lie, and with obstructions, from which the ball could have ricocheted, between the player and his intended target. The ball could have gone anywhere. So it was not sensible to have had a go at the difficult shot when there was any risk to those around; he should have waited. Mr Shipley was the second defender in the case. It can only be a matter of conjecture whether the pursuer thought that his case against the golf club was the stronger one.

How have the general principles been applied in some of the cases? The following series of examples is not intended to be exhaustive.

10-8   In *Brewer v Delo*[18] the plaintiff's action, as has been seen, failed. He was struck by a hooked tee-shot when playing an adjacent hole 200 yards or so from the tee where the ball was struck by the defendant. Hinchcliffe J decided that either the risk of injury on these facts was not foreseeable or that it was so slight that it could be ignored. So, he found, there was no duty incumbent on the defendant to take any precautions against it. The decision appears to accord with principle. The shot was off line, but it was not a really bad shot and the casualty was distant. So the risk that he might be hit by a poor shot was remote. But what if the defendant was a persistent hooker and had pulled his previous three drives? Arguably, and if viewed objectively, it could be said that the risk of hitting someone on the next fairway was, in these circumstances, foreseeable.

10-9   *Feeney v Lyall*[19] turned on its own facts and on the geography of the golf course in Glasgow where the accident occurred. It was in this case the pursuer's bad shot that was heavily penalised by the court. Playing on the ninth hole he hooked his drive on to, or at least towards, the adjacent sixth fairway. As he was searching for his ball he was struck in the eye by a ball which had been propelled a prodigious distance by the defender, more or less to where he meant to hit it when driving off the sixth tee. The pursuer's contention that he was, or ought to have been, visible to the defender was rejected as a matter of fact, first because the pursuer's evidence of precisely where he was (actually standing in the fairway just where the defender would have wished to hit his drive) was not accepted by the court and, second, because of the sight lines from the tee—the hole was a slight dog-leg with trees down the left hand side—the defender was prevented from seeing the pursuer where he actually was. It was a matter of concession by counsel for the defender that, had the pursuer been visible from the tee, the defender would have been negligent in driving when he did, for the obvious reason that the pursuer contended that he was standing precisely where the defender intended to hit the ball. Further, since the defender was a low handicap golfer of some considerable prowess, it was presumably foreseeable that he would achieve what he intended. The case

---

[17] [1998] 20 LS Gaz R 33.

[18] [1967] 1 Lloyd's Rep 488.

[19] 1991 SLT 156.

is perhaps of most significance because of what the Lord Ordinary (Kirk-wood) said (of course *obiter*) in relation to contributory negligence. Had he found for the pursuer he would have reduced his damages by 25 per cent on account of the pursuer's own fault. His basis for doing so was this:

> "The pursuer admitted that, when playing the ninth hole, he was on the sixth fairway and that he knew that there were golfers on the sixth tee, but that he did not at any stage check to see if these golfers were preparing to drive off the sixth tee, which would have *ex hypothesi* been visible to him, as he assumed that, as he had been on the sixth fairway first, he had a right to carry on playing ... He just assumed that they would have waited. In the circumstances I would have taken the view that the pursuer had failed to take reasonable care for his own safety."

Quite why the pursuer would have been held at fault is not obvious. Perhaps he should have foreseen the impatience of a group of good golfers when they see someone less proficient in a place where he ought not to be and, moreover, holding up their game! But it is surely plain that, on the hypothesis that the pursuer was visible to the party on the sixth tee and was standing in the fairway, just where the drives might land, the pursuer was entitled to expect that the defender's party would not commence to play, without warning, when he was in the way.

Less than proficient golfers are not, of course, a purely Scottish phenom- **10-10** enon. So golfing injuries are sustained in various parts of the world. Tasmania may be one of the less likely locations and the facts in *Crawford v Bonney*[20] were indeed singular. The first hole at Winyard Golf Club is a par 5. Mr Crawford drove about 200 yards down the middle. Mr Bonney, the defendant, managed to hit the ball along the ground about 50 yards into the right rough. Then he hit it sharp left about 100 yards into the left rough. The plaintiff erroneously thought that it had gone into the fairway and was lying ahead of his own ball. He assumed, wrongly, that it was his turn to play, and so he went to his ball in the fairway and hit it. He then turned round and the defendant's third shot, from maybe 40 yards behind, hit him in the eye. The defendant said that he thought that there was no risk that he would hit the plaintiff! Maybe he had a point—for he clearly had some difficulty hitting the ball at all. The trial judge (Wright J) observed wryly: "Having regard to the lack of directional control which he had manifested during the two earlier shots taken that morning, and the angle at which the ball left his club on each of these two occasions, it is surprising that he should have dismissed from his mind the possibility that his third shot may represent a danger to the plaintiff." The trial judge found that the plaintiff had not sanctioned (*ie* consented to, either expressly or impliedly) the play-ing of the third shot by the defendant (notwithstanding that it was in fact his turn!) because he had mistaken where the ball was. He rejected, also, the argument that because the defendant was only 14 years old at the time the standard of care owed by him was reduced, finding that the simple expedient of warning the plaintiff to stand clear because he was going to play would have prevented the accident. It was, he held, both in accor-dance with common sense and the rules of golf that the defendant should

---

[20] Tasmanian Supreme Court, 6 December 1994 (Judgment B1/1995).

not have played when he did, given the plaintiff's position at that time. Contributory negligence was rejected, also, on the basis that the plaintiff had no reason to anticipate the defendant's negligence in the circumstances. The decision clearly accords with principle as regards primary liability. For the defendant to have hit his third shot when he did was clearly a foolish thing to have done with his partner just ahead of him up the fairway. But had the view been taken that, playing with a clearly incompetent novice, the plaintiff had failed to take due note of what that novice was doing, and had played out of turn (in contravention of the rules of golf), without checking that it was safe, the plaintiff had been to an extent the author of his own misfortune, that view would have been, it is suggested, equally sustainable.

10-11   It is important to note that the foundation of negligence in the majority of participant cases does not appear to be the participant's lack of skill in playing the bad shot as such; rather it is the participant's negligent misjudgement in playing the bad shot when he did when (as it appears) his (objectively ascertained) general lack of skill might give rise to a foreseeable risk that any shot played by that player at that time might be a bad shot and thus foreseeably could injure others on the golf course. So it is the simplicity of the precaution that would have been efficacious which appears to feature prominently. That is certainly the case in both *Lewis*[21] and *Pearson*.[22] In both cases the negligence alleged and upheld by the court was simply the failure to wait until it was safe to play. And in *Pearson* the Rules of Golf were cited: "*Safety*: Prior to playing a stroke or making a practice swing, the player should ensure that no one is standing close-by or in a position to be hit by the club, the ball or any stones, pebbles, twigs or the like which may be moved by the stroke or swing." That, of course, begs the obvious question of whether the person is (or may be) in such a position—which leads back to the issue of foreseeability and thus to the objective assessment of the prowess of the particular defender.

10-12   Returning to *Lewis*, its facts were that the pursuer, when putting on a green which was fairly adjacent to a tee, was struck by the second defender's drive from that tee. Among the findings in fact were the following:

> "[The second defender] was aged 32 and had been playing golf since he was 15 or 16. He played once or twice a month in the summer and once every two or three months in the winter. He was not a member of a golf club. For the purposes of the competition, he had been given a handicap of 24, which is a high handicap, indicating a less skilful player ...

> "The second defender intended to drive his ball down the centre of the fairway by striking it with the face of the club; instead he hit the ball with the toe of the club and it went off at an angle of 30° and struck the pursuer who was still putting on the fourth green and injured him."

Put very shortly, it was held that the risk of injury from a shot mis-hit by the particular defender could have been simply averted by his waiting until

---

[21] 1993 SLT (Sh Ct) 43.
[22] [1998] 20 LS Gaz R 33.

the fourth green had cleared, so in consequence of his failure to take that simple precaution he was found liable, even though neither he nor his playing partners anticipated the real risk that the second defender, who had been playing well all day, would hit what was, on any view of the matter, on the day, a wholly uncharacteristically dreadful shot.

And in *Pearson*, the trial judge in the county court found six reasons for **10-13** finding the risk of injury and the defendant having failed to take such care as was appropriate in the circumstances:

> "*Firstly*: There was a real risk that the defendant would mis-hit the ball. That is a real risk because every golfer, from best to worst, does; that should have been very freshly in the mind of the defendant because not moments before he had seriously mis-hit the ball, when it went from the tee and landed off the eighth hole in the rough on the ninth hole. He must have mis-hit the ball on this occasion. Although he says he hit it well, he was using an iron which was perfectly capable of elevating the ball (if properly hit) above the bush in question, he must have seriously miscalculated or failed to hit the ball accurately because the ball hit the bush and that is what caused the deflection.

> "*Secondly*: The risk of mis-hitting the ball was increased because he was in the rough and the lie of the ball would have increased the risk of mis-hitting it. The precise lie of the ball is something that is only known to the defendant but I am satisfied that the risk of a mis-hit is altered and increased when the ball is in the rough.

> "*Thirdly*: The plaintiff was in range of the defendant and the defendant knew that they were there, and in range.

> "*Fourthly*: Not only was he in the rough, which of course affected the lie of the ball, but he was in the rough on the wrong hole. He was on the ninth hole: that is, he was off the eighth hole which was the hole that he was playing. That, of itself, is not a major factor but it was another factor which increased risk and should have put him on guard and made him take extra care as to what he was doing.

> "*Fifthly*: He knew, or he ought to have known, that if the ball hit the bush, it would deflect in an unknown way. Whilst the range of deflection for mis-hitting a ball with a club off the tee is put at 30° (that is a known maximum deviation for a mis-hit ball) as soon as the ball hit the bush it could have deflected in any direction. Where it would go was anybody's guess and that is something that either was known or ought to have been known by the defendant.

> "*Sixthly*: Given that there were a number of factors that increased what risk there was, that risk could very easily have been avoided by a short wait."

Whilst some of these observations may be, arguably, questionable, the sixth is the most significant. As has been previously observed, the defendant was essaying a tricky shot, a shot which could really have gone anywhere. Why it should be at all relevant that he had previously hit into the rough is not obvious. Most golfers, other than the best, know that the success of one shot seldom gives much of a clue about the result of the next one. Nonetheless, it was probably not too much to ask that the defendant should, before trying a shot which, undoubtedly, could have gone anywhere, have ensured that no one was in an area of any danger.

10-14   An older case, *Cleghorn v Oldham*[23] simply confirms what may be seen as self-evident but has a certain amusement value, particularly for aficionados of PG Wodehouse. Somewhere in the Home Counties (the West Runton Golf Club), the defendant, Miss Oldham, was playing golf with her boyfriend, Mr Cleghorn. Miss Cleghorn was her caddie and, so it was suggested, her chaperone. Somewhere about the twelfth or thirteenth hole, the boyfriend hit a dreadful shot. In Wodehouse-speak he "pressed" or "foozled". Miss Oldham decided to show him how it ought to be done, but in swinging at an imaginary ball—a sort of after the event practice swing or demonstration shot—she hit the plaintiff on the head with her club. Not surprisingly, Miss Oldham was found liable, the judge rejecting the defence that her caddie/chaperone had (in some unexplained way) consented to what befell her by going on to the golf course in the first place. The (amusing) note of the exchanges between counsel and the Bench included the suggestion that by going on to the golf course at all the plaintiff had taken upon herself the risk of one of the players hitting her on the head—presumably with a golf club. It is not perhaps surprising that, even in 1927, that proposition did not find favour with the court.

Returning to Australia and to *Wood v Roberts*,[24] the plaintiff's action failed where he was struck by the defendant's drive which he had sliced (he was a left hander) from a tee after being invited to play through by the defendant's playing partner who had lost his ball in the left hand rough. As in *Feeney v Lyall*[25] an issue arose as to whether the plaintiff was at a point where he was visible from the tee. The trial judge found against the plaintiff on that issue, holding that he was out of sight of the defendant when the latter was driving off, and he also rejected the contention that the defendant had a duty, after being waved through, to ascertain the position of all of the preceding group before driving off. Again the case was one dependent on its own special facts as the Appeal Court made clear: "We were referred to a number of cases involving golfing accidents. I find such cases unhelpful as they each depend on their own particular circumstances."

10-15   *Horton v Jackson*[26] as regards the players (though it may be of greater interest in its consideration of the liability of the golf course operator) is a clear case of the liable party having disregarded a notice of a kind commonly found on golf courses prohibiting play until an adjacent green is clear, and causing injury to a person in a position where the notice was intended to protect him.

In *Clark v Welsh*,[27] a South African case, the plaintiff was struck by a ball driven by a playing partner, a novice golfer, at a highly acute angle when

---

[23] (1927) 43 TLR 465.

[24] [1997] SASC 6467.

[25] 1991 SLT 156.

[26] CA, 28 February 1996, unreported.

[27] (1975) 4 SA 484.

the plaintiff was standing close by, and very slightly ahead of the player, in the normal position which might be adopted when waiting for a playing partner to play. The case is interesting from a sports law perspective as it contains a useful conspectus of authority on various aspects of potential liability in the course of playing or watching sport, but in the result the decision turns on the foreseeability of the mechanism of the injury which the plaintiff sustained. The judge determined that the shot was so woeful and that the ball had gone off the club at such an acute angle, that, notwithstanding the general finding that the defendant was a golfer whose skill was, to put it charitably, somewhat lacking, it did not require to be anticipated by the player and that she had no duty to warn the plaintiff to stand in a different position to avoid injury. Evidence from the plaintiff's witness that the defendant would normally hit seven or eight shots (though not necessarily drives which she was better at) per round at right angles (the accident happened on the eleventh tee on a day when it was recorded that the defendant was playing better than usual—which, as her normal prowess was recorded to be, may not have been saying a lot) was rejected by the court as unlikely to be correct.

Both *Pearson*[28] and *Clark*[29] are of particular interest to those presenting **10-16** participants' cases for the apparent reliance upon expert golfing witnesses as to the likely behaviour of golf balls when addressed by the less skilful. In both cases, the result was plainly critically influenced by the view the court reached on the vital issue of foreseeability of the risk of the particular accident which occurred, a risk which was assessed by the court on the basis of (so it seems) general experience of golf and golfers, especially of those less expert, rather than an objective appraisal of the particular prowess, on the particular day, of the particular defender. Whilst that may be a generally legitimate approach, it is suggested that it may work to the disadvantage of a pursuer who is injured by a shot of the type which occurred in *Brewer v Delo*,[30] perhaps in circumstances where the particular defect in stroke-making is one which, on the evidence of the round so far, the defender ought *himself* to have anticipated, even though the objective likelihood of the off-line hook hitting someone quite distant was fairly remote if determined generally, perhaps with the benefit of general expert advice from a professional. But it will be, no doubt, in the majority of cases generally difficult for a pursuer to obtain evidence of the general golfing prowess of a stranger. And so it will remain easier, applying the general principles, to obtain damages from a bad golfer than from a good one.

LIABILITY OF GOLF COURSE OPERATORS

Participants

Many golf courses are operated by members clubs. Difficult issues arise in **10-17** relation to the ability of members to sue clubs of which they are members

---

[28] [1998] 20 LS Gaz R 33.

[29] (1975) 4 SA 484.

[30] [1967] 1 Lloyd's Rep 488.

for injuries sustained while participating in the sport. No reported case has yet succeeded in Britain against a golf course for an accident to a playing golfer. There have been some successful cases elsewhere. The Bar Common Room in Kilmarnock Sheriff Court sports a yellowing press cutting (whether to amuse or to encourage inventiveness in pleading is not immediately apparent) recording the success of an American golfer against a golf course when he was injured by a badly positioned tree from which his ball rebounded. But there is no reason in principle why, on appropriate facts, a case against a golf course operator by a person injured while playing should not succeed. For if there is a foreseeable risk that a mis-hit shot by A will hit B (and such a mis-hit shot is itself foreseeable) when B may be playing nearby in a different match, it may be contended that that foreseeable risk is caused by, or at least materially contributed to by, the necessary proximity of the players as a result of the layout of the golf course. In addition, there may also be a foreseeable risk of injury as a result of the configuration of a "traditional" golf course where blind shots may frequently be encountered. These risks may, in many circumstances, be significantly greater than a mere possibility. Readers will be aware of courses, or holes, where the risks of an accidental injury may be considerable. The writer knows of one holiday course, of fond memory (he won a competition there once), where there are four holes which share a common "fairway", perhaps more accurately described as a sizeable field (and also reachable by a bad hook from yet another tee) and where, when it is busy, players necessarily drive in the general direction of a small crowd! Waiting until the fairway is clear is simply not a practical proposition if anyone is to progress their round.

10-18   The answer lies, it is submitted, in a consideration of the practicability of any precautions which might ameliorate the risk, having regard to the magnitude and seriousness of that risk. It is the balancing exercise familiar to the law of negligence.[31] The greater the risk and the more serious its likely consequences, the more the reasonable person will do to obviate it. But if the risk is remote, there may be no obligation at all to guard against it; and if the risk can only be obviated by measures which are (whether in terms of money or trouble and inconvenience) disproportionately excessive having regard to the likelihood of significant injury, the failure to take these measures will not be a breach of the obligation to take the *reasonable* care which common law and the Occupiers' Liability (Scotland) Act 1960 require.

So, applying those principles, it may well be found to be negligent, in an appropriate case, to omit a simple precaution, such as a bell or a flag to denote when it is safe to play at a blind hole. Signs such as "Do not play until the fourth green is clear" or "Players on the twelfth fairway have priority" (in the case of crossing fairways) will, in many cases, suffice as a reasonable precaution. But where the risk is particularly high, there can be no guarantee that a court would not be persuaded that a more complicated and expensive option—a mesh fence or, in an extreme case, the reconfiguration of the dangerous part of the course—would be required.

---

[31] For examples, see *Bolton v Stone* [1951] AC 850; *Mackintosh v Mackintosh* (1864) 2 M 1357 at 1362–1363.

Modern courses often appear to be designed with built-in safety features, such as trees or wide areas separating fairways and significant distances between greens and adjacent tees, the juxtaposition of which may arguably pose the greatest risk of injury to participants. Questions may turn on the availability of land (and possibly funds) for more complex solutions, even where there is a significant risk. It will be a matter of fact and degree in the particular circumstances of any case but, it is submitted, only extremely serious risks will require major precautions. It is unlikely, for example, that the double greens on the Old Course, which undoubtedly present a foreseeable risk of injury to players putting on them from approach shots from the sharing hole, would be found to be so dangerous that they required to be dug up and moved apart!

In *Lewis v Buckpool Golf Club*[32] the pursuer originally sued both the golf club and the golfer whose shot struck him. The pursuer's case failed at first instance against the club. It was based on the contention that the green and the tee were too close. They had been in that position for many years and there had been no accidents before. The precaution which the pursuer contended was required was held to be in excess of that which was required of a golf course operator in the exercise of reasonable care for the safety of golfers. The finding was not challenged on appeal.

In *Horton v Jackson*[33] a case was made against the golf course operator in **10-19** negligence and under the (English) Occupiers' Liability Act. The plaintiff was playing golf at the Maldon Golf Club, near Liverpool. He was on the sixth green. Jackson, the first defendant, played off the ninth tee and his ball struck and injured the plaintiff. Three complaints were made: that there should have been a longer tree and fence screen than there was; that the sign denoting the priority of the players on the green should have been more clearly worded; and that the priority should have been in some way more rigorously enforced. There was no doubt that the configuration of the course had been appreciated to be dangerous for the green had been moved, on advice, and the screening had been erected. There was evidence of other previous accidents to players. After the accident extra warning signs were erected. The trial judge held that the club had done enough, even having regard to the accepted risk of injury. On appeal the court said:

> "The committee of the club had taken safety measures; they erected the screen and put up the notice giving priority ... the notice was there, it was clear in its terms, it was visible ... There was ... no call for further precautions. There is a limit in reasonableness to the number of steps a golf club can take to protect players. It is not reasonable to require a golf club to erect a sign to tell a golfer that he must not aim a drive at a person standing or walking 25 yards away from him who is in plain view."

Though, as ever, the case turned on its facts, it is noteworthy that, in the (apparent) absence of evidence that players disregarded instruction to give

[32] 1993 SLT (Sh Ct) 43.

[33] CA, 28 February 1996, unreported.

the players on the green priority, the court was prepared to assume, in the club's favour, that golfers would behave in a sensible and generally careful fashion. That must be right in principle. Again the decision relied (at first instance) on expert evidence from golf course architects and those familiar with the risks associated with golf courses. There was reference made to guidelines (presumably for the construction of new courses) which prescribe a 30 m separation of greens and tees, but which might be available to be used by a pursuer to contend for course alteration even in an established setting. But at the end of the day, the impression is left that the factor which influenced the court to the greatest extent was the "folly" of the liable golfer for playing when he did. He clearly ought not to have done so and it was not possible for the club to guard against such activity. But if there was to be evidence that the club was full of foolish, impatient, golfers who routinely disregarded safety instructions as to priority and who were not made subject to any sanction for doing that, the factual background could well, in such a case, require a club to take quite extreme measures to secure safety.

10-20   A proof before answer has, with some hesitation, recently been allowed in *Milne v Duguid*.[34] The case is reported principally on other matters and contains no analysis of the legal issues involved in the pursuer's case against the greenkeeper of Westhill Golf Club, near Aberdeen. The pursuer alleged that the cause of her serious eye injury which occurred when, it was averred, her own ball rebounded off a stone in the rough after she had struck it, was the failure of the greenkeeper to inspect the area of the eighth hole where the incident occurred regularly and to remove or "cover safely" stones there. Though the report does not so say in terms, press coverage of the case indicates that the pursuer contended that the area where the offending stone was located was in a place where many balls struck by lady players came to rest on the particular hole. Though held to be relevant for inquiry—so that the need for and practicability of the desiderated precautions will be a matter for evidence—it is suggested that the pursuer may be asking rather a lot of golf club management if they are to be required to eliminate what are essentially natural hazards present on the course, a requirement which, it may be thought, is grossly in excess of what may be reasonable to protect a player against a remote chance.[35]

Summarising, a successful action by a player against a golf course operator will realistically only have substantial prospects of success, applying normal negligence principles, if (a) there is a high risk of injury; and (b) that risk can be materially reduced or eliminated by a precaution which is relatively simple or is at least in some proportion to the magnitude and severity of the risk, regard being had to the proper conduct of the game, in the absence of actual evidence of regular transgressions of the rules or any specific precautions already installed, such as warning signs.

---

[34] 1999 SCLR 512.

[35] The greenkeeper in fact obtained absolvitor: see 2000 GWD 20–817. (The Supreme Court of New South Wales in *Shorter v Grafton District Golf Club* (23 March 2000) upheld a decision in favour of the plaintiff who was attacked by a kangaroo in the rough. (See 2000 SJ 494.) The case was decided on its facts—there had been previous kangaroo attacks on golfers and no warnings about dangerous kangaroos had been given to golfers!)

Theoretically, at least, it might be possible to sue a golf course designer **10-21**
who had so designed a new course as to be obviously dangerous to those
using it (or indeed to course neighbours). It goes almost without saying
that in modern reparation practice, the court would need to be satisfied,
applying the *"Hunter v Hanley"*[36] test, that the design was so lacking that it
fell short of the standard of safety design to be expected of a competent golf
course designer in designing a modern golf course if acting with care and
skill—and the deviation from the proper standard was of such a magnitude
as to amount to negligence. Golf club operators sued by an injured player
might, in appropriate circumstances, have a right of relief against the
designer, if the fundamental problem which gave rise to the danger was
one of layout.

Neighbours and passers-by

Unlike the position of participants, golf courses have been found liable to **10-22**
make reparation to neighbours and passers-by. In an early case, *Castle v St
Augustine's Links Limited and Chapman*,[37] a taxi driver who had passed a golf
course in his taxi cab was struck by a ball and lost an eye. He sued both the
golfer and the golf course. His case against the golf course was decided in
nuisance. Like all such cases it turned on its facts. A member of the Bar who
apparently played regularly on the course gave "expert" evidence that he
"much oftener than he would have liked" sliced on to the adjacent road
from the thirteenth tee where the offending ball had come from. Sankey LJ
found for the plaintiff, holding that:

> "The directors of the club knew or ought to have known that balls
> driven from the thirteenth tee frequently landed in the road. That the
> tee and the hole are a public nuisance under these conditions and in
> the place where they were situated. The slicing of the ball into the road
> was not only a public danger but a probable consequence from time to
> time of people driving from this tee."

Shortly after that, a court of seven judges held in *McLeod v The Provost,
Magistrates and Councillors of the Burgh of St Andrews*[38] that the pursuer had
presented a relevant case for damages pled in negligence against the local
authority as proprietors of the path on which the pursuer had been walking, a path running parallel to, and, it seems, outwith the course itself,
when she was hit by a golf ball which had ricocheted off a fence following
a sliced drive at the first hole of the Old Course. The pursuer averred that
the path was frequently bombarded by golf balls sliced from the first tee
and that, in consequence, the path was dangerous to use. The pursuer
merely averred that as a result of the existence of that danger, the Burgh
were under an obligation to protect the public against it, though no specification was given as to how that protection was to be afforded other than
"by warning or otherwise". Somewhat surprisingly, perhaps, given the

---

[36] 1955 SC 200.

[37] (1922) 38 TLR 615.

[38] 1924 SC 960.

standard of pleading required in reparation cases at the time the case passed muster to the extent that the sheriff's allowance of proof was not disturbed. It was suggested that the proper view of the pursuer's case was that her complaint was about the location of the path and not the danger of the golf course as such. The pursuer's claim was not, therefore, truly made as a sporting accident at all and no case was pled against the Old Course proprietors, so it can only be a matter of speculation how the court would have approached the issue of layout of an historical world-renowned golf links, where any physical separation of the walking public from flying golf balls would be seen by many as verging on sacrilege, as would be the remodelling of the course if unsafe because of aspects of its configuration.

10-23   It is submitted that, having regard to the approach to golf injury cases, whether pled in negligence or in nuisance, it will be difficult, especially where golf has been played on ancient courses from time immemorial, to make out a case against the golf course. That will be because, it is suggested, if the case is in negligence, the precautions which will be required to obviate the risk will be readily held in such a case to be excessive, beyond that which is reasonable to obviate what may be seen to be a minor risk. If the case is pled in nuisance, and if damages are sought, the court could find it difficult to find an element of "fault", which since *RHM Bakeries (Scotland) Limited v Strathclyde Regional Council*,[39] as explained in *Kennedy v Glenbelle Limited*,[40] is a necessary requirement of a successful nuisance case in Scotland, though what may amount to "fault" in that context may be a more elusive concept than the need to establish it.

Since one of the remedies which may be granted in the case of a nuisance or anticipated nuisance is interdict, the ability of the neighbours of golf clubs to prevent players continuing to trouble them in their enjoyment of their own property may have the effect of forcing golf course operators to take very significant precautions to prevent that trouble, and critically may depend on whether what, colloquially, would be readily accepted as a *de facto* nuisance, conforms to the requirements of a nuisance in law. In England, in a cricketing case, the court refused to grant an injunction where a nuisance was established by the regular striking of cricket balls into a neighbouring garden, upon a basis which bore to balance equitable considerations.[41] It is not obvious that the same result could follow in Scotland, where the ability to refuse an order where rights are found to be infringed seems more restricted.[42] Nor is it obvious precisely how the modern developments in the Scots law of nuisance will operate so as to provide (or not) a remedy where a use is being made of land which does not involve "nuisance-fault" but is nonetheless a use which is unreasonable to the extent that it deprives the neighbour of much of the enjoyment of his property.

---

[39] 1985 SC (HL) 17; 1985 SLT 214.

[40] 1996 SC 95.

[41] *Miller v Jackson* [1977] 3 All ER 338.

[42] *cf Anderson v Bratisanni's* 1978 SLT (Notes) 42.

In *Kennedy*,[43] the Lord President (Hope) identifies the requirement of **10-24** fault in the law of nuisance, and what may amount to such fault, in this way:

> "The essential requirement is that fault or *culpa* must be established. That may be done by demonstrating negligence, in which case the ordinary principles of the law of negligence will provide an equivalent remedy. Or it may be done by demonstrating that the defender was at fault in some other respect. This may be because his action was malicious, or because it was deliberate in the knowledge that his action would cause harm to the other party, or because it was reckless as he had no regard to the question whether his action, if it was of a kind likely to cause harm to the other party, would have that result. Or it may be—and this is perhaps just another example of recklessness— because the defender has indulged in conduct which gives rise to a special risk of abnormal damage, from which fault is implied if damage results from that conduct. In each case personal responsibility rests on the defender because he has conducted himself in a respect which is recognised as inferring *culpa* by our law."

So it can be seen that "nuisance-fault" is not co-extensive with fault as it is viewed in the law of negligence. It is the last passage in the list of ingredients in nuisance-fault which is the most interesting and relevant to the matter of nuisance liability of a golf course operator. The statement was made in the context of a case involving risky engineering operations—but what, it may be asked, is a "special risk of abnormal damage" in other contexts? If the configuration of a golf course is such (and perhaps its clientele so lacking in proficiency) that neighbouring proprietors (or other passers-by) are peppered while enjoying their gardens, or adjacent roads or paths, by golf balls, may it be contended that there is indeed a special risk of abnormal damage? Being blinded in one eye by a wayward golf ball may, it is submitted, amount to abnormal damage; and if golf balls regularly leave the confines of the golf course, may there not be a "special risk"? And if these ingredients are present, the need must be to take efficacious precautions to avoid the damage—so that if damage occurs, there will be nuisance-fault: *Edinburgh Railway Access & Property Co v John Ritchie & Co*,[44] cited without disapproval in *Kennedy*.[45]

Readers will be familiar with the current fashion for golf course develop- **10-25** ment with a (usually expensive) residential element. It is suggested that, in principle, greater obligations may be incumbent upon golf course developers to design projects of that type with the safety of residents in mind. Similarly, where golf clubs sell off surplus land for the express purpose of residential development, it must be arguable that, if the intended house plots are at regular risk of being bombarded by hooked drives off the fifth tee, the club might be expected to have, if acting reasonably or without nuisance-fault, expended some of the money from the sale in taking steps to minimise, if not to eliminate, that risk.

---

[43] *Kennedy v Glenbelle Ltd* 1996 SC 95.

[44] (1903) 5 F 299.

[45] *Kennedy v Glenbelle Ltd* 1996 SC 95.

10-26   Such an approach would be generally in accordance with the decision in
Lamond v Glasgow Corporation.[46] There the facts were that the golfers of the
Littlehill Golf Course in Glasgow, which was operated by the defender
local authority, were prone to hook balls out of bounds at the seventeenth,
where there was an adjacent lane used by pedestrians. Mr Lamond was
struck on the side of the head by such a shot. He sued the Corporation,
alleging that they should have put up a fence, prohibited play at the
offending point, or realigned the hole—the last precaution upon the basis
that its configuration was such that it increased the likelihood of a shot
being hooked out of bounds. The hole and the lane ran roughly parallel to
each other and were separated by a low wire fence and a few trees. The
fence and the trees provided no physical barrier between the course and
the lane (not unlike the position at St Andrews described in *McLeod*[47]). Two
issues arose for determination. The first was whether there was a real risk
of injury. The second was whether the desiderated precautions were
reasonable. The case was pled in negligence. On the first issue, the Lord
Ordinary interestingly appears to have rejected a mathematical approach
to the probability of injury. There had been no previous report of actual
injury to users of the lane, though there was evidence, which the court
accepted, that there had been many near misses in the 40 or so years during which the course had been used. Counsel for the Corporation sought
to argue that there was a mathematical probability of 1.5 million to one
against a passer-by being hit. The Lord Ordinary engaged in what, with
respect, appears to be wholly incomprehensible mathematics before,
apparently, disregarding that scientific method in favour of what he
described as "the day to day practice", a synonym, it seems, for a common-
sense approach to foreseeability. It is respectfully submitted that that must
be right. As the sheriff principal pointedly observed in *Lewis*[48]: "The law of
negligence is full of cases where an unappreciated risk has been held to
have been reasonably foreseeable. In addition, the absence of previous accidents does not mean that there was no risk." If a large number of golf shots
are regularly finding their way into adjacent subjects, especially those to
which the public have regular resort, as the evidence disclosed, it is a matter of good fortune, surely, that injury has not resulted rather than the
absence of a real or foreseeable risk of injury to a passer-by. Someone,
someday, as Mr Lamond was, will be in the wrong place at the wrong time.
The discarding of the mathematical approach, however, can be contrasted
interestingly with what the Court of Appeal did in *Horton*,[49] where (it
appears in the context of considering whether the precautions actually
taken previously were sufficient, rather than whether there was a foreseeable risk) the judge at the trial had regard to the fact that there had only
been two established incidents of golfers being struck in "upwards of
800,000 rounds". It can also be contrasted with the well-known case of

---

[46] 1968 SLT 291.

[47] 1924 SC 960.

[48] 1993 SLT (Sh Ct) 43.

[49] CA, 28 February 1996, unreported.

Bolton v Stone[50] where the unlikelihood (by mathematical analysis of the frequency of the potential event) of what occurred relieved the club of the obligation to guard against it, notwithstanding that the event—the hitting of a six—was to be striven for, rather than, as in the case of a misdirected golf shot, to be avoided if possible.

The second question in *Lamond* was rather less satisfactorily answered. **10-27** That perhaps reflects the broader approach to negligence liability cases 30 years ago, where batteries of experts were the exception and not, as now, the rule. It was held that there were practicable precautions which could have been taken to prevent the injury to the pursuer and that those precautions were reasonable. Astonishingly, the realignment of the part of the course in question was held to be a reasonable and practicable precaution. Though it involved the alteration of four holes and although no evidence appears to have been led (by either side) as to its prospective cost, the Lord Ordinary was able to find that that: "could be achieved without unreasonable disturbance to the course from the players' point of view and without unreasonable expense." The cost of a safety boundary fence was £1,300 which was not a substantial sum, even at 1968 prices, for a large local authority and it is hard to quarrel with that part of the decision which suggests that the erection of such a fence would be reasonable. But given the historical absence of accidents, the probability of injury, though it was foreseeable, could not have been large, and therefore the precautions against it which the reasonable golf course operator would be required to take, would not be so great as those required to guard against a major risk, if the matter is, as it was, viewed as a potentially negligent failure to take precautions. So it is less than obvious that the failure to realign the course could be stigmatised as an omission which a reasonable golf course operator, acting carefully, could not have perpetrated.

Nevertheless, the case does helpfully exemplify, in the case of neighbours **10-28** and passers-by, the same approach in principle as applies in the case of participants: if there is a foreseeable risk of injury to passers-by or neighbours from the use of the golf course (which as *Lamond* suggests does indeed include an assessment of the general competence—or rather incompetence—of its patrons) then the golf course will require to take reasonable precautions to reduce that risk if not to obviate it, and the more likely an accident to a passer-by the more significant (and potentially expensive) the precautions which will be expected of the reasonable golf course operator.

There are even more unsatisfactory features in *Whiteford v Barton and Clydesdale District Council*.[51] A car on a road adjacent to Hollandbush Golf Course, operated by the Council, was struck by the first defender's drive. It was established, as a matter of fact, that when he drove off, the pursuer's car was not in sight, so he was assoilzied. That must be correct, for he thus had no reason to anticipate that he might strike it and no need therefore to defer playing his shot. The course operators were held liable to make reparation to the owner of the damaged car upon the basis that injury to persons and property on the adjacent road was foreseeable—"a real risk

---

[50] [1951] AC 850.

[51] 1986 SCLR 259.

and not a mere possibility". So far that is uncontroversial, in the context of the determination of the *existence* of a duty of care, but when dealing with the issue of the precautions which might have prevented the damage, the sheriff principal said:

> "If, as appeared to be the case, the cost of erecting a wire fence along the length of the fourth fairway would be prohibitive, and it is thought to be too difficult to alter the lay-out of the hole, then I should have thought the second defenders could insure against risk of a similar accident occurring in the future for a comparatively small sum."

10-29   That is coming very close to a case of strict liability for the escape of dangerous things—here golf balls. The case was a summary cause and the legal basis for the action remains unclear from the report (though a case of *res ipsa loquitur* was expressly rejected). There were express findings in fact that the erection of a fence would be very expensive and the layout of the course difficult to alter. The ability to insure against risk (which also, incidentally, figured as a throw-away line in the decision in *Castle*[52]) cannot logically feature in the determination of what may be an omitted reasonable precaution. It may be that what the sheriff principal was truly suggesting was the sort of nuisance-fault liability which the Lord President identifies in *Kennedy v Glenbelle Limited*,[53] that is to say the carrying on of an intrinsically and significantly dangerous activity which necessarily involves a risk of injury or damage to a neighbouring land user. If that is the case, it is submitted that the case goes too far (if it does so) in categorising the playing of golf (as such) as falling within the Lord President's classification of the circumstances which can constitute nuisance-fault. But, as is suggested earlier, it may be possible to argue successfully a nuisance-fault case in appropriate circumstances upon the basis that the playing of golf at that particular place involves a real risk of injury to neighbours or passers-by and where there are no practical precautions which may be taken against it. So the continuation of play there in these circumstances amounts to a nuisance-fault because the golf course operator effectively takes upon himself the risk of damage and liability for it merely by continuing play. But if the sheriff principal is effectively determining that there is strict liability for golf balls escaping out of the golf course, in any circumstances, and that the golf course operator's remedy can only be to insure against that liability, that, it is submitted, is an attempted reintroduction of the principle which can have no place in Scots law—essentially strict liability for the escape of "things", a proposition inconsistent (save perhaps in relation to the interference with watercourses) with the modern Scots law of nuisance. However, as noted, it may be arguable, depending on the particular facts of the case, that a course layout which presents a serious risk of injury or damage to passers-by or their property, which risk cannot be ameliorated to an acceptable degree, does amount to nuisance-fault.

The cases on liability to neighbours or passers-by do not, when examined, appear to present a logically consistent position. All that can be said

---

[52] (1922) 38 TLR 615.

[53] 1996 SC 95.

meantime, in the absence of any determination of the possible applicability of nuisance-fault principles to the playing of golf where effective precautions to prevent damage by the "escape" of golf balls cannot be taken, is that a failure to take such measures as are reasonable may give rise to liability on normal principles of negligence.

Spectators

Accidents to golfing spectators (those watching golf being played), whether **10-30** simply casual onlookers, or invitees to an organised event, have not troubled the courts, so far, in the United Kingdom in any reported case. But the regular watcher of golf, whether in person or on television, cannot have failed to notice the regularity with which members of the spectating public are struck by wayward shots, even by the most notable of golfers. In *Cleghorn*,[54] Ms Cleghorn is described as a "spectator" but, given her proximity to Ms Oldham, the defendant, when she was struck and her participation as a caddie, the case provides no real assistance as to the circumstances in which liability may attach to the promoter of a golf tournament or event to which spectators, whether paying or otherwise, are invited. The issue may turn on "consent" on the part of the spectator. By attending the event, the spectator, it can be argued, subjects himself to the normal risks inherent in the game, so far as these may affect a spectator. It is not quite the same sort of consent as was considered in *Condon v Basi*[55] although it is akin to it. A spectator who attends a sporting event (just like the participant in the sport itself) consents, arguably, to the normal risks of the sport. So the golf spectator requires to take on himself the risk of being struck by a wayward shot. But that consent, applying normal consent principles in the law of negligence, does not extend to the *negligent* management of the event.

Assistance can be obtained as to the principles to be applied from spectator accidents in other sports. In *Wooldridge v Sumner*[56] Diplock LJ (as he then was) said:

"The practical result of this analysis of the application of the common law of negligence to participant and spectator would, I think, be expressed for the common man in some such terms as these:-

'A person attending a game or competition takes the risk of any damage caused to him by any act of a participant during the course of and for the purposes of the game or competition, notwithstanding that such act may involve an error of judgement or a lapse of skill, unless the participant's conduct is such that it is reckless disregard of the spectator's safety.' "

The approach is, it is submitted, equally applicable when considering liability on the part of an event organiser—the spectator takes the risk (in a question with the participant and the event organiser) of at least some of the normal risks of the game.

---

[54] *Cleghorn v Oldham* (1927) 43 TLR 465.

[55] [1985] 2 All ER 453.

[56] [1963] 2 QB 43.

10-31   In *Wilkes v Cheltenham Home Guard Motor Cycle and Light Car Club*[57] a spectator was injured when attending a motor cycle scramble. A rider lost control of his machine and went into the crowd. The organisers had separated the spectators from the racers in a manner approved by the sports governing body, the Auto Cycle Union. The club were not liable, it was held, to the injured watcher. The case is not altogether satisfactory because the first instance decision that the club were not negligent was not challenged in the Court of Appeal.

It may be that the requirement identified by Lord Justice Diplock in *Wooldridge*[58] of reckless disregard or foolhardiness goes too far and that the true modern analysis is that the organiser is liable to spectators if he fails, negligently, to protect spectators from a foreseeable risk of injury against which a careful tournament organiser, acting reasonably, would guard. That, put broadly, is the ratio of the physical safety of sportsgrounds cases such as *Hosie v Arbroath FC*[59] and *Cunningham v Reading FC*.[60] The latter case is interesting to the extent that it involved the need to take reasonable care to guard against the foreseeable behaviour of football hooligans, a matter which may now, since the events of the 1999 Ryder Cup, require to be addressed by certain golf tournament organisers. Whilst spectators' safety may be capable of being advanced by physical separation of the participants from the spectators, on a golf course that can realistically only be achieved by distance, which rather defeats the purpose of going to watch golf. It is suggested that since, despite concessions to the contrary effect in some of the cases, golf is probably not an intrinsically dangerous game (at least to watch and as compared with, say, Formula 1 motor racing), a tournament organiser will not be liable to a spectator who is injured by a mishit golf ball if the organiser takes the normal crowd control precautions found at golf tournaments.

10-32   It may be argued, however, that if an organiser invites less skilful players to participate—say in a charity pro-am tournament—he may require to anticipate serious lack of skill on the part of the amateur participants. That, of course, may be part of the attraction for spectators. Readers may recall the golfing exploits of the former US Vice-President, Spiro T Agnew, whose drives posed a major risk of significant injury to those standing within a few feet of the tee! If a participant whose bad golf is well known plays in a tournament, the sort of issues (of foreseeable real risk) which lead to findings of negligence in the participants' cases which have been cited earlier may arguably come into play and lead to a requirement for greater precautions than would be required of a careful tournament organiser, where the risk to be anticipated is the excessively hooked or faded shot from a tee 300 yards back up the fairway from the viewing point, struck by a tournament professional. So, in an appropriate case, it may be negligent to permit spectators to stand close to and in front of a tee from which golfers of doubtful ability will be playing—and in such a case the careful organiser will be

---

[57] [1971] 1 WLR 668.

[58] [1963] 2 QB 43.

[59] 1978 SLT 122.

[60] [1991] TLR 153.

expected to take precautions which exceed (or at least may differ from) those which may be required to protect spectators from mis-hits at the Open Championship. It cannot, however, be overlooked that, subject to the need to make golf watching worthwhile, precautions for safety (such as physical separation by distance from the golfer or adequate stewarding) are likely to be held to be readily practicable—so that in most spectators' cases, the important fact issue for determination by the court will probably be the foreseeability and the magnitude of the risk which will necessitate the precautions, rather than the reasonableness of the precautions themselves.

CONSENT AND RELATED ISSUES

Interesting and difficult questions may arise, both as regards liability as **10-33** between participants and as between the participants (and/or organisers) and spectators, from "consent" and/or the voluntary assumption of risk— which in some cases may amount to much the same thing but in others may not. It is not the function of this chapter to analyse in depth the principles which underlie the maxim of *volenti non fit injuria* (as to which see *McCaig v Langan*[61]). But it is important to note, as Sheriff Principal Ireland did in *Lewis*,[62] that the consent in issue is the consent to the act complained of, the act involving the lack of reasonable care. The *volenti* defence in *Lewis* was rejected because the act complained of was not the second defender's bad shot (to which it could be argued the pursuer had consented as something which happens, not infrequently, in the game) but rather the fact that he played it when it was unsafe and thus careless of him to do so.

It is difficult to envisage a *volenti* defence succeeding in a spectator's case. **10-34** "Ticket" *volenti* is governed by the Unfair Contract Terms Act 1977, s 16 (3) (f). It provides: "Where under sub-section (1) above a term of a contract for a provision of a notice is void and has no effect, the fact that a person agreed to, or was aware of, the term or provision shall not of itself be sufficient evidence that he knowingly and voluntarily assumed any risk." So a warning on a ticket or other notice cannot, in itself, evidence *volenti* consent. And given the generally non-hazardous nature of golf, it is difficult to see how *volenti* can arise as regards spectators because the negligent act complained of would probably be the lack of appropriate crowd segregation from participants or crowd control, and a spectator's consent would, truly, only be consent to the risk of a mis-hit golf shot where the injured spectator was not in fact negligently placed in the line of fire. So the consent would be, as explained in *Condon v Basi*,[63] consent to the normal risks of the game—the consent of a spectator who was properly segregated, being hit by a particularly bad shot against which there was no obligation to take precautions.

---

[61] 1964 SLT 121.

[62] 1993 SLT (Sh Ct) 43.

[63] [1985] 2 All ER 453.

10-35   Circumstances might arise, however, as between participants which could give rise to a plea of *volenti*. Suppose A and B regularly play together. A is aware of B's abysmal golfing prowess and of his lack of appreciation of his ineptitude, which leads him on occasion to gross over-ambitiousness. B is in rough; A is nearby. Between B and the green is a "coppiced hazel", the kind of obstruction which caused all the problems in *Pearson v Lightning*.[64] B decides to go for the green. A knows he is going to do so and stands fairly close by. It is a shot which, in B's hands, has a ready potential for going badly wrong. It is the sort of shot which, with other players in the vicinity, really ought not to be played because it could go anywhere. If someone is in the "danger area" it would be prudent to await their departure before attempting it. But A, as B's playing partner, is standing close by behind B as would be not unusual. B's ball crashes into the tree, rebounds and blinds A. It is suggested that, on these facts, a *volenti* defence by B could succeed, A having impliedly consented, knowing of B's golfing prowess, to his hitting a potentially bad shot when he did with A in the position in which he was standing. Compare *Crawford v Bonney*[65] where the argument (which failed on the facts) was that the positioning of the plaintiff negatived, in the circumstances, any duty being owed by the defendant to him. So a *volenti* defence may not be wholly dead.

PRACTISING AND TUITION

10-36   The foregoing consideration of the circumstances in which playing or watching the playing of golf may involve the acquisition of rights and obligations, is principally concerned with the actual playing of the game on the golf course itself. But similar considerations attend practice, instruction and the use of driving ranges.

Many courses have cramped and inadequate practice facilities. Some are situated adjacent to parts of the course where normal play takes place; others are adjacent to neighbouring subjects. Many golfers, when practising, can be less than assiduous about the destination of their shots; some may be experimenting with their swing or grip. A practiser, using a bucket of balls from the pro shop, may not much care where the balls end up. These may all be factors in the negligent equation should injury occur; and will almost inevitably feature in neighbours' claims for reparation if their property is damaged by wayward shots struck by practisers or, worse, applications for interdict against continuing use of the practice facilities.

10-37   Driving ranges, with only the man in the middle distance in the bullet-proof ball-collecting tractor machine, ought, because of their design and the physical separation of the participants (however inept) from each other, to ensure safety or at least negate foreseeable real risk of injury. One reported case involving injury in golf instruction comes from the Isle of Man: *Tweedy v Department of Education & Avery*.[66] The plaintiff was engaged in a

---

[64] [1998] 20 LS Gaz 33.

[65] Tasmanian Supreme Court, 6 December 1994 (Judgment B1/1995).

[66] 1993–95 MLR 68. [But see now a decision on relevancy where the case failed: *Cuthbertson v Merchiston Castle School* 2000 GWD 15-628.]

physical education lesson which involved a number of pupils undertaking practice swings with golf clubs. All had been told to take care to stand apart from other pupils when doing so. But the plaintiff was hit in the face by a carelessly swung club, wielded by a fellow-pupil. The education authority was found liable, vicariously, for the negligence of the teacher, for want of supervision of the pupils. Consideration was given to the expert evidence of a teaching professional and, significantly, to guideline instructions for group golf teaching issued by the PGA. The finding of negligence essentially arose because of the teacher's failure to provide close personal supervision of what was being done by the pupils, and the giving of general safety instructions was held not to be sufficient in circumstances where a number of pupils were able to swing clubs without being closely monitored. The case has no particular specialty from the golf perspective and turns on its own facts. On these facts, the result was inevitable and unsurprising.

CONCLUSIONS

Though the incidence of golf-related damages claims may be on the **10-38** increase, the principles which the courts apply to them, whether they relate to injury to participants themselves or to other parties, do not appear to have materially altered since the early cases of *Castle*[67] and *Cleghorn*.[68] In particular, liability will arise in the case of participants—and probably spectators, too—only as a result of the application of well-understood negligence principles like foreseeability of real risk (as opposed to theoretical possibility of risk) and the reasonableness and practicability of precautions. Neighbour liability may be capable of extension by application of modern nuisance-fault principles—but, as it appears, only if being injured or sustaining property damage by a golf ball hit arises from a "special" risk, and the damage is "abnormal".[69]

---

[67] (1922) 38 TLR 615.

[68] *Cleghorn v Oldham* (1927) 43 TLR 465.

[69] *Kennedy v Glenbelle Ltd* 1996 SC 95 at 100.

11

SKIING

William J Stewart

Specialities of the sport

This chapter deals only with recreational downhill skiing.[1] An attempt is **11-1** made to state the legal obligations of the main actors in the sport in Scots law. It does not deal with cross-country skiing or skiracing. It omits the now popular snow-boarding which raises some different issues. One of the reasons why this sport is treated in this book, aside from its enormous popularity, is that it is a major part of the economy of the Highlands. It is a multi-million-pound industry.[2] There are now a number of commercial downhill snow skiing centres in Scotland, unlike the rest of the United Kingdom where there are none.[3] In addition, there are a number of dry ski slopes around the country.[4]

Another reason for the treatment of this sport is that it has been the subject of special legislation in other countries—most notably France and the United States: one a civil law jurisdiction, the other a common law jurisdiction—yet there is no legislation here. There is a body of skiing caselaw from all over Europe, again notably in France and in the common law jurisdictions that have substantial ski industries—in particular many of the states of the United States and Canada. Accordingly, the application of the law to skiing raises some interesting jurisprudential problems.

Skiing, unlike some of the other sports considered in this book, is essentially an individual sport and not a team game. Yet because of the proximity of parties actions arise not only between the injured skier and the operator but also between skiers themselves.

---

[1] This chapter retains some of the core material which can be found in WJ Stewart, *Skiing and the Law* (W Green, 1987). There have been many important developments since then, most of which are charted here.

[2] Skiing in the Spey Valley alone was said to be worth £10 million to the local economy according to a study by MacKay Consultants, cited in *Ski-ing UK*, Jan/Feb 1987, p 4. The study is now out of date but it would be hoped that with the new Nevis Range and a mountain railway being built at Cairngorm the economics are stronger.

[3] They are Cairngorm, Aviemore, Glenshee, Glencoe, the Lecht and Nevis Range. For descriptions of these areas then current, see H Parke, *Scottish Skiing Handbook* (Luath Press, 1989) (hereinafter "*SSH*").

[4] *SSH*, pp 37–38.

An interesting legal question arises (again common to some other sports) where participants, albeit they are enjoying their sport within a particular legal system, consider themselves to be taking part in a global activity. Indeed it is now not uncommon for people to ski in at least two countries in the one day.[5] Both the skiers and those providing the skiing are essentially seeking to find and offer the same kind of experience and these expectations of the only two interested parties pose a test for legal systems.[6]

Liability of participants

11-2 In this chapter the participant is the skier. The core example is that of colliding skiers.[7]

In France and other continental countries the police have a jurisdiction and a presence on the slopes and criminal proceedings are encountered. Criminal liability is not considered in this chapter. So far as civil assault is concerned, it is worth noting that in Scotland injury sustained during horseplay, not uncommon on the ski slopes, is not exempted from civil liability.[8] Most likely a case would be taken based on negligence[9] where through lack of care one skier collides with another. Strictly speaking all the court has to do is examine the facts and circumstances and come to a view based on the general principles. That is not sufficient for legal advisers: it is essential in a case where the reasonable man is being asked about an unusual pastime that the facts and circumstances relating to that pastime are explained to the court. This necessitates the calling of a skilled witness—even where the judge may in fact be a skilled skier.

11-3   It is submitted that, in the first instance, many practical problems can be resolved by reference to the Skiers Code of Conduct.[10] In the same way as

---

[5] "From then on it's a matter of 'where shall we go today?', planning your route on the link map, then it's off with your Portes du Soleil pass (no passport needed), French and Swiss francs zipped into your latest outfit. Shall it be lunch at Cocoquoz or a snack at Les Prodains or a picnic high on the Morclan with its glorious views through to Mont Blanc?": S Nesbitt, and Lord Hunt, "Border Crossing: Portes du Soleil" in Martyn-Hemphill (ed), *Debrett's Ski Resorts of Europe* (Sterling Publications, 1987), p 66.

[6] See Charpentier and Peiser, "Vers une réglementation Européenne de la pratique du ski" Dalloz-Sirez, 1966 – Chron 179. Rabinovitch had essayed a code in the first edition of his *Les Sports de Montagne et le Droit* (1959).

[7] It can be said with some justification that this problem is not new. Simpson recounts that: "the fields at Abergeldy soon became so congested that a letter appeared in the press from a beginner who said he had been terrified by the 'downhill boys' tearing through the middle of the field, and asked if it was possible for the police to institute some form of control over the slopes": M Simpson, *Skisters: the story of Scottish Skiing* (Carrbridge, The Landmark Press, 1982) at p 125.

[8] See, *eg, Reid v Mitchell* (1885) 12 R 1129.

[9] See Chapter 1 for a layman's description of negligence.

[10] There is still a problem in that this code is not entirely the same as the international FIS code. For the text of the FIS code, see Maxlow-Tomlinson, "Skiing and the Law" (1995) 3 (3) SLJ 19 at 24—a more up-to-date version than that appearing in Stewart, App 2. The code was developed from 1965 onwards by the Juridical Committee of the International Ski Federation (FIS) and the first version was adopted at Beyrouth in May 1967. In the past in Scotland there had been some very serious difficulty in that there existed rather idiosyncratic, yet still useful, codes, which may well have operated satisfactorily had everyone followed them but which caused difficulty and conflict with other codes. See Stewart, *Skiing and the Law* (1987), p 20; Stewart, "Skiing and the Law: Codes", 1989 SLT (News) 38.

the Highway Code tells us what good drivers do,[11] a Ski Code can provide the same guidance, although obviously it is a matter for the court in the facts of a particular case. It is submitted that the code would be found helpful in a Scottish case. *McEvoy v Biggs*,[12] although an English court decision, is persuasive. The collision took place in Isola, France but it was agreed that the case should be decided according to English law. At this stage it should simply be noted that at the end of the judge's examination of the matter of liability he said:

> "The defendant was in breach of rule 3 of the FIS Code. This says: 'Choice of route. A skier coming from behind must choose his route in such a way that he does not endanger skiers ahead.' Although Christopher Briggs had not seen the rules, rule 3 amounts to no more than common sense. It is a useful guidance as to what a reasonable skier would or would not do. It would be a valid criticism of the defendant which would be equally valid if his age was immaterial ... The plaintiff succeeds in liability."[13]

The following US case may also be of assistance. In *Ninnio v Hight*[14] the defender, an experienced skier, collided with three ski school members, including the plaintiff. The plaintiff cited the National Skiers' Courtesy Code, a code promulgated by the US Ski Areas Association, the National Ski Patrol System Inc, the National Ski Areas Association and the Professional Ski Instructors of America. It was said: "[the Code] may well set forth the standards of care and prescribe the acceptable methods of conduct on the ski slope. The skier who violates a rule may be considered to have acted in such a way as to make him negligent and consequently liable for the injuries he has caused by such violation." The particular rule considered in *Ninnio* was the one which stated that "when skiing downhill and overtaking another skier, the overtaking skier shall avoid the skier below him".[15] While these rules are very helpful, application is not always clear and in one US case a statutory rule putting the onus of care on the "uphill" skier proved to be difficult to apply as it was not clear which skier was the "uphill" skier.[16]

Turning now to the civilian jurisdictions, Maxlow-Tomlinson recounts **11-4** one of the cases in which he was able to recover damages in a Belgian court

[11] The Highway Code states what is generally thought to be reasonable care: *Hoaxley v Dartford District Council* [1979] RTR 359. However, adherence to the code does not always exculpate: *White v Broadbent and British Road Services* [1958] Crim L R 129; and a breach of the code does not create a presumption of negligence: *Powell v Phillips* [1972] 3 All ER 864. See also: *Bell v Glasgow Corporation* 1965 SLT 57 at 61; *Cavin v Kinnaird* 1994 SLT 111. The most important feature to be remembered is that in skiing cases the problem arises along three dimensions whereas in relation to road traffic often the problems are two dimensional.

[12] Mayors & City of London County Court, Judge Simpson, 29 November 1993 (case no 9380189), unreported.

[13] Transcript at 36.

[14] (1967) 385 F2d 350.

[15] R Kennedy (1986) 45 Denver Law Journal 775.

[16] *Ulissey v Shvartsman*, US Court of Appeals, 10th Circuit, 8/1/95, internet edition.

by relying on an earlier criminal decision in Switzerland.[17] In that case, *Haines v Dumont*,[18] the criminal judgment commented:

> "These rules [FIS Skiing code] have been drawn up by an experienced set of lawyers in the Countries of the Alps, supplemented on a few points and set into an easily understandable form. The Court has recognised that these FIS Rules are not legal standards but behaviour recommendations for skiers. As they are released by an International Concern there is nothing to prevent them from being used as guidelines for the standard that skiers should accept."[19]

In French law the code can be considered to be a coherent body of rules permitting a practical approach to each litigation.[20]

In the absence of a particular point in the code, general principle applies; and there is, of course, some general controversy in sports cases as to whether participants *inter se* are governed by a general test or whether the test of reckless disregard (if indeed that is a different test) applies. In *Fink v Greenius*[21] the plaintiff was skiing at a slow to medium speed when she was struck by the defendant, who was flying in the air having come off a plateau some 10 to 15 feet above her. It was held that the defendant was liable on the reckless disregard test.[22] It was said:

> "I do hold that his conduct in proceeding down an established run at a ski club at an hour of the day when skiers might be expected to be tired and slow to react, and in proceeding directly down the short turns so that he reached a high speed at the edge of the plateau; that he permitted himself to become airborne at a point where even if he did not know there was a blind spot he should have known, by reason of his length of time on that run, there was a blind spot, together with his lack of ability to avoid a skier hidden in the blind spot constituted negligence in the circumstances and his conduct sufficient to satisfy the test."[23]

In *McEvoy v Briggs*,[24] the defendant was aged 13 at the time he collided with the pursuer. Both the pursuer and the defender were members of the same ski class.

---

[17] Maxlow-Tomlinson, "Skiing and the Law" (1995) 3 (3) SLJ 19.

[18] Visp Dist 15 June 1988, unreported: cited in Maxlow-Tomlinson, "Skiing and the Law" (1995) 3 (1) SLJ 19.

[19] Quoted in Maxlow-Tomlinson, above.

[20] W Rabinovitch, *Les Sports de Montagne et le Droit* (Litec, 1980), para 207.

[21] (1973) 20 R (2d) 541.

[22] Indeed, under reference to the well-known English case of *Wooldridge v Sumner* [1963] 2 QB 43.

[23] (1973) 20 R (2d) 540 at 550–551.

[24] See n 12 above.

The next test considered in *McEvoy* was that of "reckless disregard".[25] **11-5** Support for this test was found by citation of *Fink*, the Canadian case just discussed. However, *Fink* was not followed because his lordship considered that spectator cases were different from participant cases. He next considered the well-known football case, *Condon v Basi*.[26] He held the defendant liable on the basis of a general test of reasonable care in the circumstances and, as noted above, taking into account the FIS code.

One other argument of some general interest in *McEvoy* was that the *Nettleship v Weston*[27] rule ought to be applied and the boy held to the standard of a competent amateur skier. Perhaps surprisingly, the judge held that the age of the child could be taken into account.[28] The main and best justification for the decision on this point is that the parties were both in a ski class and could be said not to be involved in "a dangerous adult activity".[29]

The operator's liability

The mechanical uplift

Originally skiers walked up a hill themselves to ski down it and at that **11-6** time, as the operator did not claim to have done anything to make the hill suitable for skiing, he did not provide any uplift. It could easily be said that there was no liability on the owner of the hill on the basic principle that there is no liability simply from ownership of land. The position begins to change when people are invited to use equipment to take them up a hill.[30] The commercial development of skiing begins when people are charged to use the uplift.[31]

The forms of uplift come in various guises including rope tows, poma or button-tows, t-bars[32] and the more familiar chairlift; and indeed, in

---

[25] A departure from the standards which might reasonably be expected in anyone pursuing the competition or game. *Wooldridge v Sumner* [1963] 2 QB 43.

[26] [1985] 1 WLR 866.

[27] [1971] 2 QB 43.

[28] Transcript at 13 *et seq*.

[29] Transcript at 21.

[30] Again, in the early days this was a matter of membership of a club—persons using their own uplift—and it is not intended to discuss this issue here. See Simpson, *Skisters* at Chapter 5.

[31] In France criminal penalties against the operator are available. In the US criminal charges are certainly possible, although in one recent case in Colorado the resort was acquitted of charges of reckless manslaughter and criminally negligent homicide: *Denver Rocky Mountain News*, 22 Jan 1999, Internet edition. There are sufficient marks or notes in the Scots cases relating to stadiums to suggest that criminal charges could be brought against operators on the basis of criminally culpable carelessness. See R Shiels, "The Ibrox Disaster of 1902" (1997) JR 230.

[32] "The T-bar consists of a number of bar supports in the form of inverted Ts which are suspended from a loop of cable ... each T-bar supports two skiers who rest their lower backs or upper thighs against the bar and brace their skis on the snow-covered track below the tow" (*Garven v White Corries* transcript, 21 June 1989, Fort William).

Scotland since the opening of Nevis Range, the cable car.[33] Legally some of these forms of uplift could be analysed as carriage. Contractually the pursuer will be entitled to the benefit of the exercise of reasonable care in the operation and maintenance of the apparatus. In some jurisdictions common carriers of passengers are strictly liable, so there are many cases on whether or not a particular form of uplift constitutes carriage as opposed to assistance, but that does not appear to be an issue in Scots law.[34] Contractual analysis is now unlikely as a general duty was created by the Occupiers' Liability (Scotland) Act 1960, s 2(1), which requires reasonable care for a person entering on the premises and which also applies to any fixed or moveable structure including any vessel, vehicle or aircraft and to persons entering thereon.[35] On the other hand, it might be expected that an argument could be taken that the possession and control of the mountain is not sufficient to allow the Act to apply. It is submitted that that is a proof before answer point and at least in relation to cases where the operator requires the skier to buy a ticket to use the lift, reserves the right to withdraw access and grooms a skiable area where the accident occurs, the Act should be held to apply.

11-7 While it is of course the case that liability depends upon the law in each different jurisdiction, the similarity of the activity suggests that precautions available and found to be reasonable precautions in one jurisdiction are available and reasonable in other jurisdictions. The FIS has laid down rules for the operation of ski centres and they ought to have the "highway code" effect of setting out what reasonable operators do.[36]

In the US liability was always tempered by respect for the fact that there were inherent risks in the activity. In general liability exists, as it is submitted ought to be the position in Scotland and England, where avoidable foreseeable risks are presented to pursuers. In *Arapahoe Basin v Fisher*[37] the plaintiff was sitting in a double chairlift. She sat forward ready to ski down the offramp; when she did so, her left arm was caught in the chair and, being unable to get off, her body collided with a nearby snow fence. The operator was held liable. In *Allen v State of New Hampshire*[38] it was accepted that instruction and advice might have to be given to lift users in cases of apparent necessity. Liability could arise where a skier actually asks for help. In *Bayer v Crested Butte*[39] it was held by the Supreme Court of Canada that a chairlift operator owed the highest standard of care to the user based on

---

[33] Cairngorm may one day be allowed to build an underground railway up the mountain.

[34] See Walker, *Civil Remedies*, p 724. See, *eg*, *McDaniel v Dowell* (1962) 26 Cal Rptr 140 at 143, where it was said that the operator of a rope tow could not be classified as a common carrier because the tow "did not physically carry the plaintiff to ease the burden of moving her body up the hill.... There is not sound reason for differentiating the duty owed to her while she was ascending from that applicable while she was skiing down the slope in a designated trail."

[35] s 13 of the Act.

[36] See the appendix to Maxlow-Tomlinson, "Skiing and the Law" (1995) 3 (3) SLJ 19.

[37] (1970) Colo App 4; 75P2d 631.

[38] 1969 (260)A2d.

[39] 18 May 1998. Source: Jim Chalats, Internet *Ski Safety News*, http://www.chalat-justino.com.

the circumstances of the surrender of the person and not on any doctrine of common carrier liability; and it did this despite legislation imposing *prima facie* responsibility for skier injury on the skier. This is consonant with the Scottish approach to *culpa*, which is variable in the circumstances and which can, where there is obvious danger, come close to strict liability.

In the Scottish case *Garven v White Corries* the pursuer was injured when **11-8** her ski hit a rock on the tow path and the bindings released. She came off the t-bar, collided with another passenger and fell straight down the tow path, eventually colliding with an unprotected pylon, sustaining severe injuries. Not being entitled to legal aid, the pursuer's case had to be run as best it could in the circumstances. Elsewhere the writer has commented on the likely outcome had the case been decided in France.[40] It is also apparent that had the same facts been before the courts of many of the states in the United States the pursuer would have won.[41] The principal occupier's liability ground was that there was a rock on the tow path. This case failed because it was accepted that "while the tow was in operation the ski patrol regularly inspected it and shovelled more snow when this was necessary".[42] The second ground argued in *Garven* was equally strong—that the premises were dangerous because of the unpadded pylons on the fall line. This would not be acceptable in France nor would it be acceptable in many of the states in the United States.[43]

Running a ski lift when wind conditions are too severe, causing a t-bar cable to derail and cause injury, has been held actionable in Canada.[44]

A Scottish law firm successfully sued on behalf of a UK citizen injured in Alpe d'Huez in Grenoble Regional Court.[45] As a beginner, the plaintiff had found it difficult to release the t-bar and was still holding on to it as it came to the machinery at the top. The plaintiff had the advantage of orders and ministerial circulars which made special provision for the equipment.[46] These provided that there ought to be functioning safety devices which switch off the t-bar should it go beyond the disembarkation point. The operators were held to be 100 per cent liable.

---

[40] WJ Stewart, "Sking and the Law: the first case" 1990 (35) JLSS 27.

[41] See, *eg*, New York Legislation 1978–1989: "Ski area operators shall ensure that lift towers located within the boundaries of any ski slope or trail are padded or otherwise protected ... unless ... covered with such devices as, but not limited to, the following: 1. commercially available tower padding; or 2. air or foam filled bags; or 3. hay bales encased in a waterproof cover; or 4. soft rope nets properly spaced from the tower."

[42] *Garven v White Corries*—transcript.

[43] It is clear from a US case, *Leopold v Okemo Mountain Inc*, District Court, Vermont, 420 F Supp 781 (1971), decided in different circumstances, that protective foam padding for chairlift towers had been commercially available prior to 1971 and had been in use in some resorts before then. In that case and at that time it was accepted that such protection was effective by both sets of experts but the defendants denied that it would prevent a fatal collision at speed. In a case today it would be necessary to see what material is currently available (some 25 years later).

[44] *Lyster v Fortress Mountain Resorts Ltd* (1978) 6 Alta LR (2d) 338 (SC).

[45] *Woodness v SATA and Others*, Grenoble, 16 October 1997.

[46] 28 June 1979. See, generally, W Rabinovitch, *Les Sports de Montagne et le Droit*, paras 116–163.

The condition of the slopes[47]

11-9 In the early days there would be no liability on the operator at all. There were no pistes. Skiers just launched off down the mighty mountains. However, for a very long time paths, pistes or trails have been set out down the mountain. For a long time it has been these pistes which have attracted recreational downhill skiers and it is the selling of that attraction which has attracted the operators. As a result, the law has responded by imposing liability for lack of care on the operator of the uplift. In France this is again a matter of extensive regulation, the skier being protected sometimes by ordinary principles, sometimes by regulations, sometimes by police regulation and, in cases where the state runs the resort, by administrative law.[48] French cases are accordingly complicated by these jurisprudential issues but it remains the case that the fact that there is legal recognition of certain dangers and precautions in place can be argued to be part of the factual matrix of which a responsible commercial ski area operator should be aware.

In the United States, contrary to popular belief, plaintiffs normally had a difficult time in the courts—this was *and is* because skiing is a dominant economic interest in many states. This protection of the ski resorts was usually as a result of the application of *volenti* or of an over-application of the concept of inherent risks. So in *Wright v Mt Mansfield Lift Inc*[49] the plaintiff lost—she was "not seeking a retreat for meditation" and the timorous, it was said, could stay at home. However, the common law, in the United States, took a different course, which it has essentially retained in *Sunday v Stratton Corporation.*[50] In this case the plaintiff was injured when he caught his ski on a bush stump hidden beneath the surface of the piste. The defendants were held liable. The circumstances are important: the trail in question was for beginners and the defender's own evidence was along the lines that such a stump could not exist, so good was their attention to cutting vegetation, even eliminating shoots. The broader point made by the Vermont Supreme Court, more than 25 years after the robust decision in *Wright*, was that "the timorous no longer need stay at home. There is a concerted effort to attract their patronage and to provide novice tracks suitable for their use."[51] Thus the social and economic conditions are right for liability to be acceptable in Scotland.

11-10 The industry responded by promoting legislation to exempt them from liability or to define (usually in their favour) the inherent risks of skiing.[52]

---

[47] The word "slope" for the purposes of ski area operators' common law and statutory duty (in the US) to the skier when he or she is on "slope within the area" includes the entire area served by a single chairlift and includes the area between runs in which the skier's accident occurred: see *Codd v Stevens Pass Inc* 725 P2d 1008 Wash App 1986.

[48] See, generally, W Rabinovitch, *Les Sports de Montagne et le Droit*, paras 164–199.

[49] (1951) 96 F Supp 786. Applied, *eg, Kaufman v State of New York* (1958) 172 NYS 2d 276.

[50] (1978) 390 A3d 390. Liability had already been established in Canada—see below.

[51] at 402.

[52] See discussion and examples below. Colorado in fact had to amend its Act in 1990 to "clarify" inherent dangers.

Nonetheless, the fact that this has and is being done rather suggests that *Sunday* properly reflects the underlying common law position.[53] Decisions since *Sunday* show a respect for that decision and an approach to the legislation as taking away rights that the plaintiff would otherwise have. A ski area operator was held liable in *Bergin v USA*[54] for failure to groom a beginners trail despite citation of *Wright*. Moguls—snow bumps appearing on the piste because of the passage of skiers—are generally considered part of the fun and have regularly been held by the courts to be inherent risks in skiing, although it took statutory protection to assist a resort where the complaint was that the mogul field was allowed to exist unseen just over a ridge.[55] In *Graven v Vail Associates, Inc*[56] the Colorado Supreme Court narrowly interpreted the protection for the resorts legislation to allow an action to proceed to trial where the risk was not integral to the sport—namely allowing a ravine right beside a run to remain unmarked. In *Dovey v Breckinridge*[57] the court allowed a case to proceed to trial despite the legislation where a boy died when he collided with a warning post.[58]

Resorts will be liable where there are unusual or obvious risks which are **11-11** known or which ought to have been known and such hazards are not among the inherent risks of skiing. In the Canadian case *Wilson v Blue Mountain Resorts Ltd*,[59] the plaintiff, formerly a member of the Canadian Olympic ski team, was injured when he skied into an unmarked gully, the existence of which was known to the resort. He was successful in his claim.[60]

In every jurisdiction it seems that the ski patrol have a role to play. Such patrols seem to have been common in Scotland, probably under influence of conditions on the continent. There is no doubt that an efficient and regular ski patrol is part of the safety measures which an operator normally provides—partly at least for taking care of users by checking the nature of the piste and partly for controlling the behaviour of others. As a result it can

---

[53] This reaction continues. The British Columbia Law Reform Commission discussion paper (1993), hereafter BCDP, although bearing to be about recreational activity generally, was partly brought about by the efforts of the Canada West Ski Areas Association to have a Ski Area Safety Act enacted: BCDP at paras 5–6.

[54] Lexis, Slip opinion, US District Court for Southern District of New York, 7 June 1985.

[55] *Swenson v Sunday River Skiway Corporation*, Court of Appeals, First Circuit, 19 March 1996, Internet edition. It was held, it is submitted rightly, that the break itself provided the natural warning to slow down or stop. See also *Knight v Jewett* (1992) 11 Cal Rptr 2d 2; *O'Donoghue v Bear Mountain Ski Resort* (1994) 35 Cal Rptr 2d 467.

[56] P 2d 94 SC 416, 1995 WL 748057 (Colo Sup Ct, 18 December 1995). Source : Jim Chalats, Internet *Ski Safety News*, http://www.chalat-justino.com.

[57] District Court, City and County of Denver, 3 January 1996. Source: Jim Chalats, Internet *Ski Safety News*, http://www.chalat-justino.com.

[58] The matter is one for a jury in the absence of the legislative bar. It might be interesting to note that the legislation provides for padding only where an obstruction is closer than 100 feet.

[59] (1974) 49 DLR (3rd) 161.

[60] See also *Simms v Whistler Mountain Corporation Ltd* [1990] BCD Civ 3124-01 (CA).

be argued that the operator is obliged to provide patrollers. Some of the US legislation requires a ski patrol and it is not thought that this will normally be too onerous a burden for an operator.[61] In Quebec, under the Civil Code, a ski area was found 50 per cent liable for leaving a run unmonitored for more than an hour, during which time the slope had been used six or seven times by a reckless downhiller.[62]

Overcrowding

11-12 It has long been established in Scotland that those organising recreational activities may be liable for the acts of others not under their control, such as football supporters or crowds of onlookers.[63] Ski lift operators know that when the number of skiers on a given slope increases beyond a certain level, the likelihood of collisions also increases. Access is normally by lift tickets sold, so the operator has the knowledge or means of knowledge of the numbers going on to the slope (but not always the numbers coming off). The ski patrol and operatives will have a good idea of density through observation and the size of lift queues. Such a factual matrix could establish liability.

Miscellaneous

Ski instruction

11-13 As with other sports, questions arise in relation to instruction; it must simply be assumed that cases in other areas of instruction relate to skiing also.[64] In this regard, in making a case it is important to study what a competent instructor should know. A useful first step is to obtain any training handbooks used by instructors. There are plenty of former expert ski instructors available who can be expert witnesses. The matters which arise are familiar ones such as evaluating the student for the course; taking care as soon as possible to make sure that the student is in the right class; and thereafter to ensure that the instruction is conducted at the proper level and on the proper type of slope in the proper weather for the grade of pupil.

Ski boots and bindings

11-14 Equipment is of importance, as in any other area of activity. Skiing does raise one special question and that is that the modern ski binding is

---

[61] See BCDP, pp 99–103.

[62] L'Ecuyer v Quail (1991) 38 QAC 90.

[63] *Hosie v Arbroath Football Club* 1978 SLT 122 and *Scott's Trs v Moss* (1899) 17 R 32.

[64] The record was closed in an instructor case but, aside from the fact that formally the first defenders were let out by minute of abandonment, no formal record exists of the outcome: *Murton v D'Ecosse Ski & Sport Ltd and Others* (23 September 1987, Lord Cullen's interlocutor). For a case which failed, see *Jaegli Enterprises v Ankeman et al* (1981) 124 DLR (3d) 415. For a very helpful case on the liability of those employing guides or instructors for outdoor sports see the Inner House decision in *Reitze and Others v Strathclyde Regional Council* (unreported, 4 May 1999) in which proof before answer was approved in a white-water rafting case.

paradox. In the early days the skier was strapped into his boots and then the boots were strapped on to the ski. This provided an excellent contact and thus excellent control; the problem was that it produced the broken leg beloved of the cartoonist! The modern binding is actually a mechanical device bolted on to the ski. Special boots fit into the binding. There is thus a boot/binding/ski unit. The binding has to be adjusted in various ways to hold the skier onto the ski and to allow him to control it but at the same time to allow for early release. Aside from simple malfunction, the issue of adjustment arises. The basic legal concepts appropriate here will usually be those in the Sale of Goods Act 1979, as amended. The skier should obtain kit which is of satisfactory quality. One of the specific aspects of satisfactory quality is that of safety and safety for a skier will be a matter of fact but it is submitted that so far as the supply of a ski is concerned safety involves adequate and proper instruction in relation to adjustment.[65] Another feature of the revised Act is that goods should be reasonably durable. This concept is not an easy one.[66] It is submitted that the bindings vendors ought to suggest fixed times of reasonable durability; otherwise the ordinary skier is likely to think that they should last a lifetime.[67]

In *Salk v Alpine Ski Shop and Cube Co Incorporated*,[68] the plantiff broke his leg when he fell because his skis did not release. He sued on the basis of an express warranty that, "the bindings would release in such a manner as to guarantee freedom from injury". He was unsuccessful in justifying the rather high warranty he sought. The manufacturers really only promised that it "had a multi direction of release which could be adjusted to operate a variety of tensions and once adjusted would release whether the selected tension was implied". He failed on the causation point.[69] In the US and Canada signed disclaimers are sought but in view of the Unfair Contract Terms Act 1977 such a course is not likely to be helpful in the UK. Much more helpful to the lessor would be the practice of keeping a note of the fact that the skier's height and weight have been recorded and that he has signed a declaration as to his skiing ability.

The use of experts

An expert wanders from the piste of technical evidence at his peril: **11-15**

> "[The expert] spent some time commenting on matters in the Statement of Claim. He said that the accident was not caused as the result

---

[65] Indeed, the view taken by one ski equipment manufacturer for whom the present writer was asked to testify by affidavit in a High Court action in England, was that simple written instructions were not sufficient and trained operatives were in fact required. This was a competition case taken with a view to preventing skis being sold off the shelf at a lower cost; the attempt was to justify a resale price maintenance.

[66] See WJ Stewart, "Sale and Exchange" in *Stair Memorial Encyclopaedia*, Vol 20, para 827.

[67] Certainly, in the writer's experience it has not been uncommon for people to transfer bindings on to new skis or give them to others.

[68] (1975) 342 A2d 622.

[69] See also *Tarlow v Metropolitan Ski Slopes Inc* (1971) 271 NE 2d 515. A very full examination of bindings and the obligations of the lessor can be found in *Bergin v USA* Lexis, Slip opinion, US District Court for Southern District of New York, 7 June 1985.

of the defendant's negligence. He also added that the Particulars of Negligence pleaded in the statement of claim are unfounded. That is the very point I have to decide. I need hardly say that no expert should ever behave in this manner. He has trespassed on my province and I am not impressed by that. An expert should not do that."[70]

Yet experts are essential in almost every case.[71] A first step in locating an expert might be to contact Snowsport Scotland which promotes the "Be aware ski with care" project and states that it maintains links with both the ski area operators and safety organisations in North America. It is worth consulting the English Law Society register of experts.

Ski holidays

11-16 It is worth reminding the general practitioner that injuries sustained on a ski holiday may well be governed by special provisions beneficial to the pursuer.[72] While Thomas Cook may well have been present at the birth of package travel, Sir Arnold Lunn's ski holidays contributed to the early growth of the arranged holiday.[73] A Scot injured on a ski holiday may be able to sue those who arranged his holiday as well as those actually responsible for it. The practical benefit is that the action can be brought in the United Kingdom. The EC Package Travel Directive[74] was brought into force in the United Kingdom by the Package Travel, Package Holidays and Package Tours Regulations 1992. Discussion of these is outwith the scope of this book but regulation 15 places upon the operator the liability for the proper performance of the holiday and makes the operator liable notwithstanding that the fault may be that of a service provider. There is not strict liability but if the skier proves that there has been loss due to a failure to perform by the operator or those it has arranged to provide services, the onus then falls on the operator to exculpate.

The defence of *volenti non fit injuria*

11-17 This is a general defence to liability—that the pursuer willingly accepted the risk of injury. It has often appeared in skiing cases, perhaps because of the history of skiing as a dangerous pastime for dare devils.[75] *Volenti* is not

---

[70] Transcript at 33–34.

[71] See, *eg,* the successful party in *McEvoy v Briggs; Tarlowe v Metropolitan Ski Slopes Inc* (1971) 271 NE 2d 515.

[72] As opposed to the common law: see the famous *Jarvis v Swan Tours* [1973] 1 All ER 71 in which the solicitor who was provided with very dull après-ski was compensated for the lack of pleasure in contract.

[73] His so-called *Public Schools Ski Club Annual* was no more than a disguised holiday brochure.

[74] Directive 90/314/EEC.

[75] While it is dangerous for some small number of daredevils, that is no longer a description of recreational downhill skiing and it has not been for some time. A study for the Ministry of Tourism in Canada found that the average skier in British Columbia was a married professional, manager or proprietor aged between 25 and 44 with some post-secondary education: *BCDP,* p 102, n 21. Most skiers ski very slowly—less than 25 mph—and half ski for better recreational use of free time: M Heller, and D Godlington, *The Complete Ski-ing Handbook* (Martin Dunitz Ltd, 1979) (trans Dunitz Munich, 1977).

a clearly understood doctrine and there is often confusion with the basic question of the existence of a duty.[76] In *McEvoy v Biggs*,[77] it was expressly held that while the plaintiff accepted the risk of falling and hurting herself and that others would fall, she did not accept that others would collide with her. In *Garven v White Corries* the Sheriff said (*obiter*): "The sport of skiing will always involve some degree of danger which presumably participants are prepared to accept." It is the case that some risks are accepted. In the circumstances of *Garven*, it is possible that at that time at that resort in Scotland persons who knew of the level of safety provided might have accepted the risk of the rock on the tow. Most people who have skied elsewhere would not even contemplate that there would be rocks on the uplift tow. Nor is it the case that skiers would accept that if they fall off they become a human sledge aimed at metal pillars. Where pillars are essentially straight down the fall line they need to be padded or at the very least the skiing public ought to be specifically warned that the tow is essentially dangerous rather than presumably safe. It remains the case that on the limited skilled evidence before the court the sheriff was entitled to make his finding.

The key concept in a skiing case is not, it is submitted, *volenti*, but that of inherent risks.[78] The skier does accept that there are inherent risks in each and every aspect of recreational downhill skiing but does not usually exempt the wrongdoer from liability to take reasonable care. That this is the correct analysis is, it is submitted, vouched for, not only by *McEvoy v Biggs*,[79] but by the experience in the United States of legislating for defences. The various models there have produced the focus on inherent risks. An example of a true *volenti* case is *Abbott v Silver Star Ports Ltd*[80] in which the plaintiff deliberately skied into a junction at speed in a tuck position.

In the United States and Canada there is an appreciation that *volenti non* **11-18** *fit injuria* actually describes two jurisprudential concepts which are sometimes called the primary and secondary assumption of risk. Primary assumption is the acceptance that the skier might catch an edge and break a leg; secondary assumption is where the skier sees the fence and decides to take a chance by skiing through it. This perhaps helps explain the confusion in many Scots writings and judgments. Taking note of *dicta* in the cases it could crudely be put that one type of *volenti* case is a "no duty" case and the other is a waiver case. These ideas are not, as is sometimes thought, exclusive alternative views of *volenti* but are two different ideas which are inconveniently encompassed within one legal tag.

Skiing legislation

It will be recalled that sports law is both the application of the ordinary law **11-19**

---

[76] Stewart, *Skiing and the Law* (1987), p 23; *Stair Memorial Encyclopaedia*, Vol 19, para 1242; Stewart, *Delict*, para 11.19.

[77] Note 12 above.

[78] See BCDP at pp 27–28, 54–56.

[79] Note 12 above.

[80] (1986) 6 BCLR (2d) 83 (SC).

to sport and specific laws directed to sport. In Scotland there is no special legislation relating to skiing but it must be noted that in very many other states and systems which have skiing industries there is legislation. France, Germany and Switzerland have specific rules and regulations. In the United States there are at least 25 states which have adopted legislation with a view to protecting their ski industry from litigation.[81] In British Columbia the issue was investigated at length in a very interesting paper by the Law Commission.[82] The experience of such legislation is that it is not the end of the debate—there is the need to interpret concepts like inherent dangers.[83] The actual form may vary but it will often be wondered whether the statute books need to be filled with definitions of obvious aspects of skiing which can be supplied by joint minute or expert evidence.[84]

Some practical points

11-20 The evidence of an accident is hard to obtain even from the dazed victim. The location should, if at all possible, be noted as soon as possible. A locus inspection to obtain data while the incident is still fresh is probably much more important in this kind of case than many others. Obviously this is important for the pursuer, but defenders with a good defence to make can easily be prejudiced by a failure to ably demonstrate that at the actual locus they had taken care. Patrollers probably do note the location of accidents in some way and these records may be recoverable and should be recovered. Account must be taken of the fact that conditions at the time of an accident can completely change the appearance and safety of a location. Surprisingly, not all ski resorts in Scotland keep a "street-plan" type map of their pistes—they may simply rely upon the schematic piste map such as that supplied to skiers. Another phenomenon is that in Scotland each run may not even have a name, simply being referred to by reference to the nearest uplift machinery. This is in contrast to the numeric references found on the continent: *eg* "7b" or the more dramatic US appellations such

---

[81] J Chalat, "Survey of Ski Law in the United States" Winter 1993–94, Vol IV, issue 2 (Internet edition).

[82] Law Reform Commission of British Columbia, Consultation Paper on Recreational Injuries (1993).

[83] Faber, "Utah's Inherent Risks of Skiing Act: Avalanche from Capitol Hill", 1980 Utah LRev 355; Frakt & Rankin, "Surveying the Slippery Slope: The questionable value of legislation to limit ski area liability" (1991–1992) 28 Idaho LRev 227; AH Harkins, "A Guide for the Judicial Interpretation of Maine's Ski Liability Statute", 6 Maine BJ 344 (Nov 1991); Biglow, "Ski Resort Liability for Negligence Under Utah's Inherent Risks of Skiing Statute", 1992 Utah LRev 311–320; Manby, "Assumption of Risk after Unday v. Stratton Corporation: The Vermont Sports Injury Liability Statute and Injured Skiers"(1978) 3 Vermont LRev 129. See cases, *eg Lewis v Canaan Valley Resorts Inc* 408 SE 2d 634 (Wva 1991).

[84] *eg* " 'Lift ticket' means any item issued by a ski area operator to any skier which is intended to be affixed to the outwear of the skier, or otherwise displayed by a skier, to signify lawful entry upon and use of the passenger tramways, etc; 'Peel off backing' means any material present upon any lift ticket at the time of original issue by a ski area operator which must be removed by a skier before such ticket may be affixed to the outerwear, etc." (From the New York Statute, Jan 1979.)

as "White Hell" or "Timid Trail". An averment that "the Scottish skiing fraternity" took a particular view of danger has been seen but was deleted. It may well be that skiing in Scotland is more dangerous but the resorts must pin their colours to the mast—is it more dangerous or even (just?) fundamentally different (*eg* semi-arctic gully skiing), in which case that should be stated clearly and differentiated in the brochures (not always produced by the operators themselves) which portray a generally alpine type of skiing; or is it like the rest of the recreational skiing world where the mountains have been tamed and any ordinary recreational piste skier can now expect at least a general European standard of safety such as was canvassed more than 30 years ago?[85]

---

[85] See n 6.

INDEX

Index entries refer to paragraph numbers.